PHILOSOPHY
OF
PLATO AND ARISTOTLE

PHILOSOPHY
OF
PLATO AND ARISTOTLE

Advisory Editor
GREGORY VLASTOS
Princeton University

SCHLEIERMACHER'S

INTRODUCTIONS

TO THE

DIALOGUES OF PLATO

[Friedrich Ernst Daniel] Schleiermacher

TRANSLATED FROM THE GERMAN

BY WILLIAM DOBSON

ARNO PRESS
A New York Times Company
New York / 1973

Reprint Edition 1973 by Arno Press Inc.

Reprinted from a copy in
The Harvard College Library

PHILOSOPHY OF PLATO AND ARISTOTLE
ISBN for complete set: 0-405-04830-0
See last pages of this volume for titles.

Manufactured in the United States of America

卍卍卍

Library of Congress Cataloging in Publication Data

Schleiermacher, Friedrich Ernst Daniel, 1768-1834.
   Introductions to the Dialogues of Plato.

   (Philosophy of Plato and Aristotle)
   Reprint of the 1836 ed.
   1. , Plato. Dialogues. I. Title.
B395.S3 1973   184   72-8996
ISBN 0-405-04868-8

INTRODUCTIONS

TO THE

DIALOGUES OF PLATO.

SCHLEIERMACHER'S

INTRODUCTIONS

TO THE

DIALOGUES OF PLATO.

TRANSLATED FROM THE GERMAN

By WILLIAM DOBSON, M.A.

FELLOW OF TRINITY COLLEGE.

CAMBRIDGE:

PRINTED AT THE PITT PRESS, BY JOHN SMITH,
PRINTER TO THE UNIVERSITY.

FOR J. & J. J. DEIGHTON, TRINITY STREET.

LONDON:

JOHN WILLIAM PARKER, WEST STRAND.

M.DCCC.XXXVI.

ADVERTISEMENT.

THE apparently unfinished state in which the present work comes before the public requires some explanation. The Author of the following Introductions died in the year 1834, having then completed the translation, into German, of all the Dialogues the Introductions to which are here given. It was his intention to have published the whole of the works of Plato upon this plan; and we have thus to regret the loss of Introductions to the Timæus, the Critias, the Laws, and all those smaller and spurious pieces not found in the Appendices to the first and second of the three parts into which Schleiermacher divided the Platonic works. The German translation, moreover, is furnished with various notes, critical and explanatory; a circumstance which I consider it necessary to mention, as the reader of these introductions will find in them occasional allusions to those notes. Such as referred immediately to passages in the Introductions themselves will be found at the end of the volume.

CONTENTS.

		PAGE
GENERAL INTRODUCTION		1
INTRODUCTION TO THE	PHÆDRUS	48
	LYSIS	74
	PROTAGORAS	81
	LÁCHES.	97
	CHARMIDES	104
	EUTHYPHRO	109
	PARMENIDES	112
	APOLOGY OF SOCRATES	134
	CRITO	141
	ION	145
	LESSER HIPPIAS	152
	HIPPARCHUS	157
	MINOS	163
	ALCIBIADES II.	165
	GORGIAS.	169
	THEÆTETUS.	189
	MENO	204
	EUTHYDEMUS	219
	CRATYLUS.	228
	SOPHIST	246
	STATESMAN	264
	BANQUET	277
	PHÆDON.	291
	PHILEBUS	309
	THEAGES.	321
	ERASTÆ.	325
	ALCIBIADES I.	328
	MENEXENUS.	337
	LARGER HIPPIAS	341
	CLITOPHON	347
	REPUBLIC	350
NOTES		417

ERRATUM.

Page 82, last line, for *her* read *his*.

INTRODUCTIONS,

&c.

GENERAL INTRODUCTION.

THE Greek Editions of the works of Plato generally prefix to them the biography of the Author from the well-known collection of Diogenes. But only the most indiscriminating attachment to an old custom could honour so crude a compilation, put together as it is without any judgment, with a translation. And Tennemann, in the life of Plato prefixed to his system of the Platonic philosophy, has already subjected to a sifting process this and the other old biographies of Plato, compared with what is found scantily dispersed in other sources. As, then, since that time neither materially deeper investigations have been published, nor new facts discovered, affording any well-grounded hope of leaving far behind them, in their application, the labour already bestowed upon this subject, it is best to refer such readers as wish to be instructed upon that point, to what they will there find. And there is the less need for anything further, as no one who would be a worthy reader of Plato can entertain the notion of wishing to strike out a light upon the sentiments of the philosopher, which might illuminate his works, from multifariously

A

told and deformed trifles, or epigrammatic answers, even were they of undoubted authenticity—especially as, in the case of such an Author, the intelligent reader undertakes to learn the sentiments from the works themselves. And as regards the more important circumstances of his life, those more accurate relations, from a knowledge of which, probably, a more thorough understanding of many details in his writings might be developed, seem to be for ever so far withdrawn without the range of modern investigation, that any supposition which one might feel inclined to contribute upon these subjects, would be made at a venture; and very often in his writings we can point out, in the most decisive manner, where an allusion exists to some personal relation, without however being able to guess what it is. Nay, even with regard to the more well-known circumstances of his life, his remarkable travels for instance, so little that is definite can be with certainty made out, that no particular use can be made of them for the chronology and arrangement of his writings, and the most we can do is, here and there to guess, with a degree of probability, at the place where the former interrupt the series of the latter. Such particular conjectures, therefore, will be brought forward to more advantage in those places immediately in which they may perhaps spread some light around them.

It would certainly be more to the purpose, provided it were possible within the prescribed limits, to adduce something relative to the scientific condition of the Hellenes at the time when Plato entered upon his career, to the advances of language in reference to the expression of philosophical thoughts, to the works of this class at that time in existence, and the probable extent of their circulation. For upon these points there is not only

much to explain more accurately than has been hitherto
done, and some quite new matter to investigate, but there
may perhaps still be questions to throw out, which, though
to the professor in these subjects they must be anything
but indifferent, have, however, up to the present time,
been as good as not thought of at all. But to pursue in
connexion what is new and ambiguous in such investigations, would not be adapted to this place; and some
particulars even in this province, whether in the way
of illustration, or of suspicion tending to confute what
has been hitherto assumed, are better by all means to
remain reserved for the particular places to which they
refer. And what is common and well known is, moreover,
pertinently set forth in the works of German writers
illustrative of the history of that period of philosophy,
as far as is absolutely necessary to prepare the way for
the reading of the Platonic writings, so as not to grope
about in the dark, and thus completely to miss, from
first to last, the right point of view for the understanding
and estimation of them. For these writings are throughout full of clear and covert references to almost every
thing, both earlier and cotemporary. And in like manner, also, whoever does not possess a competent knowledge of the deficient state of the language for philosophical purposes, to feel where and how Plato is cramped
by it, and where he himself laboriously extends its grasp,
must necessarily misunderstand his author, and that, for
the most part, in the most remarkable passages.

Of the Philosophy itself we are here purposely to
avoid giving any preliminary account, even were it ever
so easy to do so, or possible to dispatch it in ever so
small a space, inasmuch as the whole object of this new
exposition of his works is to put it within the power

of every one to have, through an immediate and more accurate knowledge of them alone, a view of his own of the genius and doctrines of the philosopher, quite new it may be, or at all events more perfect. And nothing certainly could work more effectually towards preventing the accomplishment of this object than an endeavour, just at the outset, to instil into the mind of the reader any preconception whatever. Whoever, therefore, has not yet been hitherto acquainted immediately with these works, let him leave all that external reports have taught him respecting their contents, and the consequences to be drawn from them, to rest meanwhile upon its own merits, and endeavour to forget it; but whoever from his own knowledge of them has already formed an opinion for himself, will soon feel how far, by means of the classification in which he here finds these writings arranged, even his own views experience an alteration, or at least combine themselves better, and gain a greater comprehensiveness and unity, from his learning to know Plato more strictly as a Philosophical Artist, than, certainly, has been hitherto the case. For of all philosophers who have ever lived, none have had so good a right as Plato, in many respects, to set up the only too general complaint of being misunderstood, or even not understood at all. The grossest indeed of these misunderstandings have been for the most part severally removed by modern exertions deserving all our gratitude; meanwhile, whoever observes how superficially, or with a feeling of uncertainty which they try in vain to conceal, even the best interpreters speak of the objects of particular works of Plato, or how slightly and loosely they treat of the connexion of the subject with the form in detail, as well as in

general, will find traces enough to shew him that the
authors of these views, however superior, have not yet
generally gone upon a perfect understanding of the
matter in hand, and that this is not yet brought to the
point to which we might ourselves bring it even with
the insufficient means we possess. And thus that feeling
of satisfaction seems to be somewhat premature, which
maintains that we might now be able to understand
Plato better than he understood himself; and it may
excite a smile to observe how unplatonically one who
entertains such a feeling comes to the investigation of
Plato, who puts so high a value upon the consciousness
of ignorance. He deceives himself by at least one half—
by all that, I mean, in the philosophy of Plato which
can only be understood by an ability duly to estimate
the pervading presence of a *purpose* in the connexion
of his writings, and, as far as possible, to divine it
when not obvious at first sight. And in this view,
especially, an attempt like the present is a supplement,
not very easily to be dispensed with, to what others
have done in other ways, and must, in proportion as
it succeeds, contribute to advance the right understanding
of Plato. This must certainly be self-evident to every
one; for it cannot be denied, that besides the ordinary
difficulties in the province of Philosophy of thoroughly
understanding any one except a sympathetic thinker,
a peculiar and additional cause exists as regards Plato,
in his utter deviation from the ordinary forms of philosophical communication. For of these forms there
are two in particular, the most choice vehicles of the
great bulk of what generally goes by the name of Philosophy. First, that which is called the systematic form,
because it divides the whole field into several particular

compartments of sciences, and to every one of the separate
parts of the whole devotes its particular work or section,
in which it is regularly built up, according to plan,
with rooms and stories, so that any one whose memory
and fingers do not refuse to work, may measure and
point out, if not without trouble, at all events without
error, every particular detail; whence an opinion easily
arises, that there is something in the system, and that
the student has followed and understood it. For, however
weak the foundations of these structures often are, and
their compartments taken at random, they have still an
attractive look of firmness and arrangement, and it is considered easy to understand not only the details in themselves, but also in connexion with the other parts of the
edifice; and the Author himself must afford a clear guide
to this by references not to be overlooked. The second
form, neither more rarely used nor less favoured, is the
fragmentary, which has only to deal with particular
investigations, and which, from disconnected pieces, with
regard to which it is difficult to be sure whether or no
they are real members, or only masses capriciously and
unnaturally separated from the whole body, professes,
notwithstanding, to make Philosophy comprehensible.
Although, then, in this case superficiality and ignorance
are perfectly natural, because the authors have not even
come to an understanding with themselves as to the
centre point and ground upon which they stand, yet
does this method assume an appearance of ease and
certainty, for the reason that it defines and names at
starting the object in view, and makes at once straight
for it. In this sense even the dialogistic treatment has
been often applied; and many a writer has crept into
a reputation of being a happy imitator of Plato, per-

haps still more Socratic and clear than he, who yet could make nothing of Plato's form of art but a loose dress for this loose method of discussion. Whoever then is spoiled by use of the expedients which these methods seem to afford, will necessarily find everything in Plato strange, and either devoid of meaning or mysterious. For although the division of Philosophy into different compartments of science was so far from being unknown to him, that he may be looked upon much rather as the first originator of it to a certain degree, still hardly any of his writings are confined to any one of these compartments in particular. But since he considered their essential unity and their common law as of the greater importance, and made it pre-eminently the object of his aim, the various problems are in consequence every where multifariously involved one with another. But whoever, on the other hand, would on this account degrade these works to the denomination of fragmentary, will yet find himself constantly embarrassed as to the real subject-matter, which is seldom verbally enunciated, and and he will be compelled secretly to confess that the Philosopher does not appear to have had the modest intention of treating only of particular subjects, but that he either was completely devoid of this, or had one much more comprehensive.

Hence, then, the twofold incorrect opinions upon Plato and his writings which have been given almost from the earliest times. The one, that it is in vain to search in his writings for any thing entire, nay, even for the very first principles of a consistent and pervading philosophical turn of thought or doctrine; on the contrary, that every thing in them vacillates and wavers, and that scarce any thing whatever stands in regular relation to the rest; nay, that frequently one part contradicts another, because he is more of a dialectician than a logical Philosopher, more desirous of contradicting others, than capable of, or caring to produce, a well-founded structure of his own; and that when he has to deal with the plausibility of his own propositions, he first seeks up his elements sometimes from this, sometimes from that, elsewhere perhaps disputed doctrine, according as his object may be on each occasion. Now such an opinion is nothing else but a disguised confession of a total absence of any understanding of the Platonic works, and that especially on account of their form, when it is only the ground of the sentiment that is misapprehended, and instead of being looked for in the judge, it is transferred to the thing judged. But it is not necessary to honour this depreciating view with a lengthened discussion, as it yields in itself a sufficient testimony against itself. For while it adduces accusations about contradiction and want of connexion, it does not, however, prove that it has rightly understood the details; otherwise whence those strange inquiries, in what persons' mouths Plato has brought forward his own opinion at least upon this or that subject; a question which, as it supposes that his dialogistic form is only a somewhat useless and more confusing than illustrative embellishment of the perfectly common method of expressing thoughts, can only be thrown out by one who does not understand Plato at all. This view, therefore, is founded upon nothing, and explains nothing, but leaves the whole problem as it was before, and may, without going further, be contradicted by fact, if a successful attempt is made to bring our Platonic works into a connexion by means of which every detail with the doctrines therein contained becomes intelligible. And the demand for such an attempt is in this point of view so much the more pressing, as the majority of those who pass so mean an opinion upon the writings of Plato still cannot resist a certain feeling of admiration for the Philosopher. Now as we have no other tangible proof of his greatness and preeminence except these writings, the two will not agree together, that opinion, I mean, and this admiration, and the latter will scarcely have any other object except those beauties of language and composition lavished on matter of no importance, or particular fine passages as they are called, or moral sentiments and principles, all pointing to very subordinate if not very dubious merit, so that if these men would advance uninterruptedly in their admiration, they must themselves wish to find something more in him than they have hitherto found. Hence, therefore, others, with quite as little of a correct insight but with more good will, induced partly by particular expressions of Plato himself, partly also by a far-spread tradition preserved from ancient times, of an esoteric and exoteric in his Philosophy, have adopted the opinion that in the writings of Plato his own peculiar wisdom is either not contained at all, or only in secret allusions, and those very difficult to discover. This notion, in itself utterly vague, has shaped itself into the most multifarious forms, and the writings of Plato have been robbed of sometimes more and sometimes less of their subject-matter, and his genuine wisdom, on the contrary, sought for in secret doctrines which he as good as not at all confided to these writings; nay, extensive investigations have been entered upon in order to determine what writings of Plato were exoteric and what esoteric, and so to discover where most a trace might be sought out of his genuine and secret widom. Setting aside therefore the truth contained in this proposition, in so far as what is secret and difficult to find out is so only in a relative point of view, and there may always be something obscure and hard to find for some person or other; the whole is only a tissue of mis-apprehensions and confused conceptions which must first of all be unravelled and exposed.

For these conceptions of an exoteric and esoteric philosophy demand a critical sifting, inasmuch as they appear at different times with quite different meanings. For among the earliest Pythagoreans this distinction referred so immediately to the matter, that subjects were denoted as esoteric concerning which they would not commit themselves without the limits of their most intimate circle of connections; and it is to be supposed that their political system occupied the place of the esoteric far more than their metaphysical speculations, which were as imperfect as unsuspicious. But at that time even Philosophy was bound up with political views, and the schools were connected by a practical fraternization which did not afterwards exist among the Hellenes. In later times, on the contrary, that was chiefly called esoteric which could not be communicated in the popular method of instruction, to which, after the admixture of the Sophists with the Socratic Philosophers, certain teachers condescended, and the distinction therefore referred immediately to the mode of delivery; and only mediately, and on account of the other first, to the subject-matter. Plato now stands in the intermediate period between these two; but in whichever of the two senses it should be attempted to apply these notions to the Platonic writings and Philosophy, in order thereby to divide the two into two parts, hesitation and doubt generally must

ensue. For the last signification could hardly be embraced by those, who would make such an application
of it, as they start with asserting that the works *collectively* are hardly intelligible, and consequently must
allow that Plato might as easily have committed to them
what was most difficult and mysterious in his wisdom,
as what was otherwise. And as regards the first signification, of doctrines of his Philosophy, concerning which
he purposely delivered himself, without the interior circle
of his confidential friends, either not at all, or in mysterious hints, it must be either regularly maintained and
demonstrated that such was the case by a connected exposition of such doctrines, and the indications referring
to them, however slight, or at least shown in a less degree, by some kind of historical traces. Therefore, of
all the advocates of this opinion, the so-called modern
Platonists are deserving of most praise, inasmuch as
they have actually attempted to accomplish the first.
But the other parties would not have anything to show
in support of their view of the subject. For apart from
theosophistic matter, and unless they would ascribe to
Plato some sort of physical sciences which he could not
possess, and which his own writings moreover would at
once disavow, they would be at a loss to discover anything in the whole region of philosophy upon which
some opinion, either directly and distinctly, or at least
as far as a notice of the principles goes, is not to be met
with in these writings. And those indeed who reduce
the distinction of what is esoteric, merely to the war
against Polytheism and the vulgar religion, do, in fact,
completely cancel the same, and reduce it to a piece of
political caution, which would be unsatisfactory in the
extreme, as Plato's principles upon these points may be

read distinctly enough in his writings, so that one can scarcely believe that his scholars needed still further instructions about them, from the publication of which he shrank, or to a puerile contrivance which indulged itself in delivering in a loud voice with closed doors, what might indeed have been as well said with open ones in a lower. And quite as little would really genuine historical traces be discoverable, supporting the opinion of a distinction between the esoteric and the exoteric in Plato. For if it refers merely to the subject-matter, and we are to suppose the secret doctrines to have been contained in the esoteric writings in the same manner in which the commoner are in the exoteric; the first and most indispensable point must then be to make it probable, somehow, that those writings were made public in some way different from these, since otherwise the whole endeavour would have been useless; but of doing this no one seems seriously to have thought. And, further, how should it happen that Aristotle, who indisputably was concerned with a true understanding of the true Philosophy of Plato, and from whom, as many years an intimate scholar of that philosopher, nothing could easily remain concealed, does never, notwithstanding, either appeal to other sources, or appear to found his own writings upon a secret understanding of these. On the contrary, he appeals in every instance in the most unconstrained and simple manner to the works open to ourselves, and even when, as is now and then the case, other lost writings or perhaps oral lectures are quoted, these quotations do in no way contain any thing unheard of in the writings we possess, or completely different from them. If therefore these either did not contain at all the true doctrines of

Plato, or only conformably to a secret interpretation, how could Aristotle, especially considering the manner in which he attacks his master, have been able to escape the most severe censures from the genuine followers of that Philosopher, if, contrary to his better knowledge, he had then fought only against a shadow?

Now in order to make these misapprehensions and their causes perfectly manifest, and to bring even those who are involved in them to a confession and consciousness of the same, it is certainly a praiseworthy undertaking to work out analytically the philosophical subject-matter from the Platonic works, and thus to expose the Philosopher to view, dissected and in detail, divested of his superfluities and combinations, and with as little as may be of his own peculiar *form*. For if they could thus survey the pure treasure, and convince themselves on authentic grounds that it is actually taken from those writings, they must be fain to confess that it was the fault of themselves alone not to discern it, and that it is useless to lament over, or to dream of, other lost riches of Platonic wisdom. Thus much therefore may be attained by this method, that the ungrounded suspicion against the works of Plato vanishes, and the fact of his not being understood is brought more to light. And it is even certain that he who is thus to expose this truth thoroughly and completely must have himself understood Plato in the same degree: and quite as certain also is it, that the understanding of Plato as concerns others is neither facilitated nor advanced thereby: but that, on the contrary, whoever should stick exclusively to even the best exposition of this kind might easily attain to an imaginary knowledge only, and on that very account remove himself still further

from the true. For though he must be accurately acquainted with the whole nature of a body who is to
separate the particular vessels or bones in it for the
purpose of comparison with corresponding parts of another similarly dissected, which would be the fullest
use to which that philosophical process could be put;
still the mere passive spectator of the exhibition and
comparison of these parts will not attain, by those
means alone, to a knowledge of the proper natures of
the whole. So also will those spectators of the analysis
fail altogether to attain to a knowledge of the Philosophy of Plato, for in that, if in any thing, form and
subject are inseparable, and no proposition is to be rightly
understood, except in its own place, and with the combinations and limitations which Plato has asssigned to
it. And still less will they comprehend the Philosopher
himself; and least of all, will his purpose have succeeded
in their case, tending as it did not only to exhibit vividly
his own thought to others, but by that very means vividly
to excite and awaken theirs. Hence, therefore, to that
analytical exposition which we have now been in possession of for a short time, in a perfection far exceeding
former attempts, it is a necessary supplementary process
to restore to their natural connection those limbs, which
without dissection, usually appear so very deplorably
involved one with another, I mean, not the particular
opinions but the particular works—to restore them to
the connection in which, as expositions continuously more
complete as they advance, they gradually developed the
ideas of the writer, so that while every dialogue is
taken not only as a whole in itself, but also in its
connection with the rest, he may himself be at last understood as a Philosopher and a perfect Artist.

Now whether there is any such connection, and such an undertaking is not, perhaps, unsuitable to the subject and far too great ever to succeed, will best appear from the first conception which Plato himself suggests to us with regard to his writings and their objects, and which we shall shortly hear him propound in the Phædrus. Treating the subject in a somewhat trifling manner, he complains of the uncertainty which always attaches to written communication of thoughts, as to whether the mind also of the reader has spontaneously conformed to such communication, and in reality appropriated it to itself, or whether, with the mere ocular apprehension of the words and letters a vain conceit is excited in the mind that it understands what it does not understand. Hence, that it is folly to build too much upon this, and that true reliance can be placed only upon oral and living instruction. But, he continues to argue, writing must be hazarded at a venture, and more for what it is as regards the writer and those who already share in his knowledge, than for what it can do for those who as yet know nothing. Whoever then will consider what that so exalted preference for oral instruction means and upon what it rests, will find no other ground but this, that in this case the teacher, standing as he does in the presence of the learner, and in living communication with him, can tell every moment what he understands and what not, and thus assist the activity of his understanding when it fails; but the actual attainment of this advantage rests, as any one must see, upon the form of the dialogue, which, accordingly, truly living instruction must necessarily have. To this also is to be referred what Plato says, that a sentence orally delivered may always be supported by its Father and receive his protection, and that not only against the objections of one who thinks otherwise, but also against the intellectual stubbornness of one as yet ignorant, while the written sentence has no answer to make to any further inquiries. Whence it is at once clear, in passing, to what a degree that man has forfeited all right to utter even a single word about Plato who could take up with a notion that that Philosopher, in his esoteric and oral instruction could have availed himself of the Sophistical method of long and continuous discourses, when, even by his own declaration, such a method appears to Plato farthest removed from that preeminence which he gives to its opposite. But in every way, not accidentally only, or from practice and tradition, but necessarily and naturally Plato's was a Socratic method, and indeed, as regards the uninterrupted and progressive reciprocation, and the deeper impression made upon the mind of the hearer, to be certainly as much preferred to that of his master, as the scholar excelled him as well in constructive Dialectics, as in richness and compass of subjective intuition. As then, notwithstanding this complaint, Plato wrote so much from the period of his early manhood to that of his most advanced age, it is clear that he must have endeavoured to make written instruction as like as possible to that better kind, and he must also have succeeded in that attempt. For even if we look only to the immediate purpose, that writing, as regarded himself and his followers was only to be a remembrance of thoughts already current among them ; Plato considers all thought so much as spontaneous activity, that, with him, a remembrance of this kind of what has been already acquired, must necessarily be so of the first and original mode of acquisition. Hence on that account alone the dialogistic form, necessary as an imitation of that original and reciprocal communication, would be as indispensable and natural to his writings as to his oral instruction. Meanwhile this form does by no means exhaust the whole of his method, as it has been often applied both contemporaneously and at a later period to philosophical objects, without a trace of the spirit of Plato, or of his great adroitness in the management of it. But even in his oral instruction, and still more in the written imitation of it, when we consider further, that Plato's object was to bring the still ignorant reader nearer to a state of knowledge, or that he at least felt the necessity of being cautious with regard to him not to give rise to an empty and conceited notion of his own knowledge in his mind, on both accounts it must have been the Philosopher's chief object to conduct every investigation in such a manner from the beginning on-wards, as that he might reckon upon the reader's either being driven to an inward and self-originated creation of the thought in view, or submitting to surrender himself most decisively to the feeling of not having discovered or understood anything. To this end, then, it is re-quisite that the final object of the investigation be not directly enunciated and laid down in words, a process which might very easily serve to entangle many persons who are glad to rest content, provided only they are in possession of the final result, but that the mind be re-duced to the necessity of seeking, and put into the way by which it may find it. The first is done by the mind's being brought to so distinct a consciousness of its own state of ignorance, that it is impossible it should willingly con-tinue therein. The other is effected either by an enigma being woven out of contradictions, to which the only possible solution is to be found in the thought in view, and often several hints thrown out in a way apparently utterly foreign and accidental which can only be found and understood by one who does really investigate with an activity of his own. Or the real investigation is over-drawn with another, not like a veil, but, as it were, an adhesive skin, which conceals from the inattentive reader, and from him alone, the matter which is to be properly considered or discovered, while it only sharpens and clears the mind of an attentive one to perceive the inward con-nection. Or when the exposition of a whole is the ob-ject in view, this is only sketched by a few unconnected strokes, which, however, he who has the figure already before him in his own mind, can easily fill up and com-bine. These are something like the arts by which Plato succeeds with almost every one in either attaining to what he wishes, or, at least, avoiding what he fears. And thus this would be the only signification in which one could here speak of an esoteric and exoteric, I mean, as in-dicating only a state of the reader's mind, according as he elevates himself or not to the condition of one truly sensible of the inward spirit; or if it is still to be referred to Plato himself, it can only be said that immediate in-struction was his only esoteric process, while writing was only his exoteric. For in that certainly, after he was first sufficiently assured that his hearers had followed him as he desired, he could express his thoughts purely and perfectly, and perhaps even regularly work out in com-mon with those hearers, and according to outlines framed in common with them, the particular philosophical sciences, after having first grasped in his mind their higher ground and connection. Meanwhile, since in the writings of Plato

the exposition of Philosophy is in the same sense progressive from the very first excitement of the original
and leading ideas, up to an all but perfected exposition
of particular sciences, it follows, what has been above
said being presumed, it follows, I say, that there must
be a natural sequence and a necessary relation in these
dialogues to one another. For he cannot advance further
in another dialogue unless he supposes the effect proposed in an earlier one to have been produced, so that
the same subject which is completed in the termination
of the one, must be supposed as the beginning and foundation of another. Now if Plato ended with separate
expositions of the several philosophical sciences, it might
then be supposed that he had also advanced each for
itself in gradual progression, and we should be compelled
to look for two separate classes of dialogues, an ethical
and a physical series. But as he represents them as a
connected whole, and it is ever his peculiar theory to
conceive of them generally as essentially connected and
inseparable, so also are the preparations for them united
in like manner, and made by considering their common
principles and laws, and there are therefore not several
unconnected and collaterally progressing series of Platonic Dialogues, but only one single one, comprehending
every thing in it.

The restoration then of this natural order is, as
every one sees, an object very far distinct from all attempts hitherto made at an arrangement of the works
of Plato, inasmuch as these attempts in part terminate
in nothing but vain and extravagant trifling, and in
part proceed upon a systematic separation and combination according to the established divisions of Philosophy, in part also, only take particular points into

consideration here and there, without having anything like a whole in view. The classification into tetralogies, which Diogenes has preserved for us after Thrasyllus, manifestly rests merely upon the almost dramatic form of these dialogues, which gave occasion to arrange them in the same manner as the works of the Tragic Poets spontaneously arranged themselves according to the regulations of the Athenian festival, and even on this poor chance-work the classification was ill kept and so ignorantly executed, that for the most part, no reason whatever can be discovered why, in particular instances, the results of it are at all as we find them. Not even is the resemblance carried on so far as that, as every dramatic tetralogy ended with a satirical piece, so also in this case the dialogues in which irony and epideictic polemics are most strongly preeminent, were assigned to the concluding portions; on the contrary, they are all heaped together in two tetralogies. Quite as little regard was had to an old tradition, and one, in itself, at first sight extremely probable, that Plato, when actually a pupil of Socrates, made some of his dialogues public; for how otherwise could those which refer to the condemnation and death of Socrates be the first, and the Lysis and Phædrus, which the ancients regard as works of so early a date, be thrown far into the middle of all? The only trace of an intelligent notion might perhaps be found in the fact that the Clitophon is placed before the Republic, as a justifying transition from the so-called investigative dialogues, and in appearance sceptical, to those that are immediately instructive and exponential, and in this case it is almost ridiculous that so suspicious a dialogue can boast of having suggested this solitary idea. The Trilogies of Aristophanes, although they proceed upon the same comparison, are more intelligible, at least in so far as that he is not for subjecting the whole mass of writings to this frolic of fancy, and constructs a trilogy only in cases in which Plato has himself, with sufficient clearness, projected a combination; or when such is implied by some external circumstance, leaving all the rest subordinate to that arrangement. Meanwhile both attempts may only serve to show how soon the true arrangement of the Platonic works was lost, excepting very few traces of it, and how ill suited that kind of criticism which the Alexandrian Philologists knew how to apply, was to discover the principles of a correct arrangement of Philosophical works. Less *external*, indeed, but otherwise not much better are the well known dialectic divisions of the dialogues which Diogenes likewise has prepared for us without indicating the author of them, and according to which moreover the editions usually mark every dialogue in the title. At first sight, indeed, this attempt does not seem deserving of any notice in this place, as its tendency is more to separate than connect, and it relates to matters which do not profess to indicate the exponent of the natural order. But the great division into the investigative and instructive might certainly, if properly understood, be a guide for marking the progress of the Platonic dialogues, at least in the main, since the former can only be preparatory to the latter as explanatory of positive theories. Provided only that the further subdivision were not made in the most utterly illogical manner, in the one according to the form alone of the investigation, in the other according to the subject, while the latter of the two methods again quite unplatonically arranges the works according to the different Philosophical sciences, so that even what Plato had himself expressly combined is split asunder, as the Sophist and the Politicus, the Timæus and the Critias, not to mention other most strange exhibitions of criticism in the details. The same unplatonic principle is followed also in the Syzygies of Serranus, which are therefore perfectly useless for the arrangement of Plato, and at the most can only serve as a register to any one wishing to inform himself of the opinion of Plato upon particular subjects, where he has to look for the decisive passages, although even this, considering the character of the Platonic writings, is ever very uncertain, and can only be productive of very deficient results. Besides these attempts at arrangement there is scarcely any other to mention, unless it be that of Jacob Geddes the Scotchman, and our own countryman Eberhard, in his treatise upon the Myths of Plato and the object of his Philosophy. The first would not indeed deserve to be mentioned, had not great merit been attributed to him in a variety of places, and even demands made that any future translator should arrange the works of Plato according to his plan. It is however impossible that these should be complied with, supposing even the best disposition to do so. For the man's whole discovery amounts but to this, that certain dialogues of Plato reciprocally illustrate each other, and upon this principle he takes occasion to write a few at the most very meagre lines about each of them, shewing nothing so clearly as that there is scarce a single instance in which he has traced out Plato's object with any thing like ordinary understanding. But even supposing all this to be better than it is, and that the greatest proofs of ignorance, as well as misapprehension

of particular passages were not to be found, how can
an argument be undertaken upon a principle of reciprocal illustration? For which of the dialogues thus reciprocal is to be the first, and according to what law?
And as regards Eberhard's attempt, he sets himself to
prove a reference in all Plato's works to a common
object in his Philosophy, which, independent of the Philosophy itself, lies in the formation of the Athenian
youths of rank to be virtuous citizens. Now in this,
notwithstanding the very clear manner in which the position is enunciated, it is difficult to determine whether
this object was to have been at the same time the
basis for the discovery of all the higher speculations of
Plato, which, I suppose, it would be somewhat over-
hazardous to maintain, and even disregarding the circle
in which it is involved, as Philosophy must certainly
determine what is the virtue of a citizen, it is far too
subordinate a ground to rest the Philosophy itself upon.
But if the opinion is to mean, that Plato invented his
Philosophy independent of that particular object, and
that this, the Philosophy, must be supposed, while the
writings are to tend to that object of education, and
were worked out in the manner in which, under the circumstances of that time, such an object might demand,
this would be the strongest position ever taken up in
favour of their exoteric character. Meanwhile, according to that view, the philosophical writings of Plato
could only constitute a pædagogic, or rather a polemic
series, in which, from its reference to external circumstances and events, all must be accidental, and thus it
would be like enough to a string of pearls, only a capricious concatenation of productions, which, torn out of
their organic place, would be, considering further the

total failure in the object in view, a useless piece of ornamental finery. Equally worthless is the view maintained by others, that Plato published sometimes one part of his knowledge, sometimes another, either from mere vanity, or in opposition to that of other Philosophers. In all these endeavours, therefore, the restoration of the natural order of these writings, in reference to the progressive developement of the philosophy, is out of the question. Quite different, however, from all that has hitherto been done is the character of the attempt made in Tennemann's system of the Platonic Philosophy; the first, at all events, with any pretensions to completeness, to discover the chronological order of the Platonic dialogues from various historical traces impressed upon them; for this is certainly critical in its principle, and a work worthy in every way of an historical investigator like the author of that treatise. In this undertaking, indeed, his view is directed less to discover, by the method he adopts, the real and essential relation of the works of Plato to one another, than to discover in general the dates of their composition, in order to avoid confounding early and imperfect attempts with an exposition of the Philosophy of the mature and perfect Plato. And to that undertaking, generally, the present is a necessary counterpart; and thus, on the other hand, that method, resting as it does entirely upon outward signs, provided it could only be universally applied, and definitely assign to any Platonic dialogue its place between any two others, would be the natural test of our own method, which goes entirely upon what is internal. It may not indeed be necessary on that account that the results of the two should perfectly coincide, for the reason that the external production of a work is subjected to other external and accidental conditions than its internal development, which follows only such as are inward and necessary, whence slight variations might easily arise, so that what was internally in existence sooner than something else, does not yet appear externally until a later period. But with due regard to these effects of accident, which would hardly escape an attentive eye, if we had the two series complete, and they could be accurately compared, they could not fail by a pervading coincidence mutually to confirm, in the most decisive manner, their respective correctness. We discover, however, in proceeding upon this method, but few definite points; and for the great majority of the dialogues only somewhat indefinite limits between which they must fall, and often an extreme limit only on one side is given. For in strictness the historical traces should not extend beyond the life of Socrates, within which indeed all the dialogues come, with the exception of the Laws, and the few which Plato makes others narrate, and in which, consequently, he had a later date at command ; an advantage, however, which he has not always employed so as to leave a more accurate trace for us. Now the anachronisms which he occasionally allows himself, do indeed excite a hope of some little further historical evidence, so that one might wish that Plato had oftener been guilty of this fault; but even this slight advantage is made very ambiguous by the consideration that many of these facts may have been introduced on a subsequent recasting of the works in which Plato had naturally ceased to transport himself so vividly into the actual time of the dialogue, and might be more easily seduced to transgress its limits, unrestrained by fact. There might, perhaps, be yet another expedient hitherto unused with reference to this method. Thus the predominant rank given to Socrates, which, if the dialogues are placed in a certain order, gradually vanishes, might be regarded as a measure of the distance at any given point from the period of his life ; or even the choice of the other personages might be regarded as a sign of the liveliness of the interest which Plato took in Athens and in public life then, which was in like manner blunted and destroyed as time advanced. But all this is subject to so many limitations, that any confident use of it might be more delusive than beneficial, and no inference thence drawn can decide any thing, but only yield a slight increase of probability. So that by this method it might hardly be possible to attain more than what it has been applied to in that work with praiseworthy moderation, though, it may be, not always according to correct hypotheses. At all events, the results arising from the consideration upon internal grounds of the Platonic works, can certainly be neither criticised nor contradicted upon that of those historical notices, as that operation only determines an order of reference, but not one chronological point. It must, however, be as much as possible called in to assist, in order to gain certain points by means of which that order also may be brought into connection with the external circumstances. Now, if the natural order of the Platonic works is to be restored out of the disarrangement in which they at present are, it would seem necessary to determine first what pieces are really Plato's and what are not. For otherwise how can an attempt be made with any degree of certainty, or rather, in case of anything foreign being mixed up with the works of Plato, how can even what is genuine fail to appear quite in a false light, if violence be used to place what is ungenuine in connection with it? Or is it to be competent to take the problem given itself as a standard, and to declare, slashingly enough, that what will not adapt itself to that connection cannot belong to Plato? Scarcely any one, I suppose, would be found to favour this process, or not to see that this would be an extremely partial decision of a question to be answered upon quite different grounds, and that it is impossible that a notion arising from a consideration of the works assumed as Platonic, should pronounce at the same time upon the correctness of the assumption itself. Or more probably, the majority of readers will not expect to meet with the question about the Platonic writings perfectly entire, but regard it as one long since decided, with the exception of unimportant doubts touching only a few trifles, the adoption or rejection of which may be a matter of great indifference. Such, for instance, will be the opinion of all those who repose upon the long prescribed authority of editions. This authority does indeed coincide accurately enough with the list of Thrasyllus, in Diogenes, only that more modern criticism has withdrawn the Clitopho from our collection; and on the other hand, the explanations of words are wanting in that list; and these, therefore, would be the only dubious matters. Nay, we have still a better evidence in favour of this collection in that of the Grammarian Aristophanes, who has been already named, whose arranging catalogue Diogenes also had before him, and certainly would not have passed the matter over in silence if he had discovered anywhere a variation from it. But how, I would ask, can a searching criticism, even though it would pay no regard to the doubts which one's own feelings suggest, rest upon those authorties? For not only, with the

exception of a few poets, have spurious productions
insinuated themselves into all considerable collections of
works of particular authors preserved from antiquity, so
that it would be matter of wonder if those of Plato were
to make an exception, especially as philosophical literature
has in a less degree employed the industry of critics;
but in Plato's case, an additional circumstance comes in,
the importance of which does not seeem in this respect
to have been sufficiently considered, that those critics
have already rejected a considerable number of small
dialogues out of the collection which they found at hand,
as not belonging to Plato. For it is clearly manifest
from this fact that at the period when this was done,
these dialogues must have already maintained their place
among other works of Plato for a considerable time, since
otherwise no particular operation of criticism would have
been necessary again to deprive them of it. And this
usurpation, on the other hand, could not have taken
place if there had been evidence of the spuriousness of
these dialogues documentarily descended from the time
of the genuine academicians; for, generally, as long as
men were to be found, who preserved the genuine Platonic
tradition with zeal for the cause, it is not conceivable
that foreign work should have been commonly foisted
upon Plato. Upon what ground, therefore, did these
critics found their judgment when they adopted some
dialogues and rejected others? If it should be said
that they had, with regard to all not rejected, certain
and sufficiently old evidence of their recognition by those
who lived nearest after the time of their composition,
we might rejoin that the silence of contemporaries, who
do not take the case of a future confusion into consideration, and require an *occasion* for every quotation, is

neither collectively nor in detail a ground for rejection, and they might, therefore, very easily have judged wrong. In like manner, also, various grounds of suspicion might be raised against the sufficiency of the proofs applied, as several examples both in former and even in modern times have shown at how early a period of antiquity supposititious writings have been adopted even by philologists and learned men into the list of genuine works. Now, if they judged chiefly upon internal grounds, no prescription is valid as regards these at all events; but they must remain fairly subject to renewed trial at every period, however late. Hence then arises, especially as in the mind of every attentive reader many doubts will suggest themselves against much that he meets with, a question whether these men did not in their criticism start from too limited a point of view; or whether they may not have failed to push principles, though correct, to their full extent, and consequently have preserved much that might have been quite as appropriately rejected. There are two circumstances that give particular encouragement to this doubt. First, that the dialogues at that time rejected are not all of them separated by a decisive line from all recognised at the same period, but whether we look to the subject-matter, or to the composition and mode of treatment, some of the first class approximate pretty near to the second. Again, that from the same period at which these authorities were commonly recognised, among the well known suspicious circumstances attaching to the Erastæ and Hipparchus, a stock of doubts has lived, which perhaps only require to be planted in a better critical soil to spread perceptibly to a considerable extent, and strike out in many other places. But if our confidence in the authenticity of the collection is thus shaken, any one endowed with any, however little, talent for such investigations, will be fain to allow that, in strictness, each particular work must itself be its own voucher that it is Platonic. Now this, to continue, can be done in no other way except by coming back to evidences again; and, looking at what has been said above, it might be doubted whether for us, at the present time, there is any other valid evidence but Aristotle. Meanwhile even with him various grounds of suspicion come in, partly on account of the doubtfulness of many pieces which bear his name, as spurious works are mixed up even with this collection, partly by reason of the bad state of the text, which seems to be far more loaded with glosses than has been hitherto remarked; and in part, lastly, from his manner of quoting, as he often mentions the titles only of Platonic dialogues without the composer, or even the name of Socrates when we expect that of Plato. But the philological consciousness which should here confidently decide whether Aristotle had Plato in his mind or not, and whether or no he ascribed to him the dialogues named, must indeed have approved itself in possession of a high degree of practice, not only in general, but especially to avoid arguing in a circle in this case, and founding, it may be, the judgment passed upon the quotations of Aristotle on one previously formed upon the Platonic writings. Hence, any quotation in the works of Aristotle introduced only in a cursory manner, and, as is not seldom the case, almost superfluously and for mere ornament, need not necessarily be a proof of the genuineness of a Platonic dialogue. Now the only thing which rescues us from this state of uncertainty is a system of criticism upon Plato pervading the greatest part of the genuine writings of Aristotle, particular parts of which, any one with a little practice may learn easily to distinguish. When, therefore, we find this employed upon passages out of our Platonic writings, or even only on ideas distinctly contained in them, we may then conclude with certainty that Aristotle had these writings in view as Platonic, even though, as is sometimes the case, he should not give us the name of the dialogue, but only mention it, in general, as one of Plato or of Socrates. To explain this more accurately would carry us far beyond the limits of the present introduction, and is the less necessary as among those who are ignorant of both sets of works the doubts are not sufficiently strong to require such a proceeding, while those who know them will hardly make objections to the result, that by this method we can scarcely fail of sure proofs of the genuineness of the greatest of Plato's works, and of guides to the meaning of his philosophy in the most important of them. In these, then, lies that critical ground upon which every further investigation must build, and in fact no better is needed. For the Dialogues thus authenticated form a stock from which all the rest seem to be only offsets, so that a connection with them affords the best test whereby to judge of their origin. And for the next task likewise, that of arrangement, it follows from the nature of the case, that when we have that stock we are at once in possession of all the essential grounds of general connection. For it must have been natural for the first reviewer of the Platonic system to have especially taken a survey of all the most important developments of it without any exception, and thus we do actually find these in the instances of the works most accredited by Aristotle. As such, of a character which in both respects, as well

as regards their genuineness as their importance, entitles
them to constitute the first rank among the Platonic
works, we count the Phædrus, the Protagoras, the Parmenides, the Theætetus, the Sophist and Politicus,
Phædo, Philebus, and Republic, together with the
Timæus and Critias connected with it. In these, therefore, we have a firm footing-point from which to advance
further, both in the task of deciding the genuineness of
the rest, and investigating the place which belongs to each
of them ; and the second may be accomplished simultaneously with the first, and without the two by their
mutual relation contradicting one another, but either very
naturally supporting each other mutually in a variety of
ways, as, it is hoped, the following investigation will shew.

Now the first task, that of testing the remaining
dialogues in our collection, and thus investigating whether
or not they belong to Plato, is not without difficulty,
for the reason that the character to be drawn from those
that are proved genuine is made up of several traits and
distinguishing features, and it seems unfair to expect
that all should be united in an equal degree in all productions of Plato, and difficult to decide to which of
these distinguishing marks we ought especially to look
and what rank to assign to each. Now there are three
things which come particularly under consideration :
the peculiarity of the language, a certain common range
of subject, and the particular form into which Plato
usually moulds it. Now as regards the language, the
matter in question would be fortunately dealt by, if
any proof whatever could be drawn from that, regarding
the origin of these pieces. But if we look to the philosophical part of them, there are among the dialogues
whose claims to be considered as Plato's it will never-

theless be necessary to investigate, some which treat in general of no scientific subjects, nor of any in the spirit of speculation; while the rest take their subject-matter so immediately from the range of the undoubtedly genuine dialogues, and are so manifestly inspired by the same mode of thinking, that it is impossible to recognise in them a later or a strange hand, and yet they might, as far as depends upon this point, come only from a scholar or an imitator who faithfully followed the footsteps of his master. But as regards the properly dialogistic part of the dialogues, scarcely any one could presume to select first from the common property of the period that which was the work of the Socratic school in particular, and from this again to distinguish with certainty the peculiarities of Plato. Or, considering the great compass which the language of an author who has wielded the pen so long must acquire, and moreover the great loss of contemporaneous and similar works, and, finally, if the small and already long since rejected dialogues are to be accounted as forming part of the whole to be judged, considering the great difference in value and subject; all these circumstances considered, is there any one now-a-days who would venture to profess himself sufficiently skilled in Greek to pass sentence upon any expression whatever even in these small dialogues, and to decide that it is unplatonic with such certainty that he would undertake for that reason alone to reject the piece? Rather might we say that it is not so much the indication of the presence of what is strange or the absence of what is native, the want of choice and embellishing dialogistic formulæ, that may draw down the sentence of rejection upon those dialogues already accredited as far as the language is

concerned. Among those therefore which cannot be
accused of that deficiency there is much that need not
belong to Plato without its betraying itself in the language, so that this exclusively can scarcely decide anything. For when suspicions arise in our minds which
depend more upon a general impression than upon any
distinct grounds which we can bring forward in support of it, it may be assumed that these depend more
upon the composition in general than upon the language
alone. And such again might be the case when we
would judge of the genuineness of the remaining works
according to the subject-matter of those of the first
class. For this might be done in two ways. Either
it might be maintained that nothing can be Platonic
which stands in contradiction with the subject-matter
of these recognised dialogues. But Plato would thus
be deprived of a right enjoyed by every one else, that
of correcting or changing his opinions even after he
has publicly explained them; and it would be at once
supposed in his case, wonderful as such a supposition
on consideration of our modern philosophy must appear,
and so much so that it cannot be believed without the
strongest proof, that from the period of his entrance
upon his philosophical career, or still earlier, he always
thought the same as he did afterwards. Or, if less
regard be paid to the accurate coincidence of all the
particular thoughts than to the quality and importance
of the subject-matter generally, and a rule be laid down
that every work of Plato's must have the same importance and the same relation to the main idea of the
philosophy, it would in that case be forgotten that
external circumstances frequently occasion the production
of heterogeneous works of a somewhat limited size by

an author, who without the influence of such circumstances would never have produced them spontaneously.
In occasional pieces, properly speaking, like these, it
cannot be fairly demanded that those ideas of the
author which belong to a higher sphere should develope
themselves, and when traces of them are seen, their
appearance is accidental and supererogatory, and may not
even always be taken as an infallible proof of their
origin from him.   Equally manifest is it that every
great artist of every kind will work up studies out of
his own particular line, and though the adept will discover in them more or less of his style and spirit, yet
they neither belong to the class of works which peculiarly characterize their author, nor advance his great
views of art, or, what is more, he may in them, purposely perhaps, and for sake of some preparatory exercise, remove himself out of his accustomed circle of
subjects, and even the method natural to him.   There
are clearly in our Platonic collection several pieces which
can be ascribed to Plato only by regarding them in this
point of view, and to endeavour to decide with respect
to such from the trifling nature of the subject-matter,
or from particular deviations in the treatment of it,
might, according to this analogy, be a process very
liable to mistake.   These difficulties, then, clearly tend
to show, that we should judge neither from the subject
alone, nor from the language alone, but that we must
look to a third and more certain something in which
those two unite—the Form and Composition in general.
For even in the language, what affords most proof consists not in particulars but in the whole tenor and
peculiar colouring of it, which at once stands in the
closest relation to the composition.   In like manner

this will betray itself in its principal features even in those studies in which we miss the important matter of these works of a higher class. Moreover, and it is this which must contribute to give us a correct idea of this genuine Platonic form, we need not first abstract it, like those other two tests, out of the larger works as an analogy, the limits of the applicability of which can still not be drawn with certainty; but it is, in every essential point, a natural consequence of Plato's notions with regard to philosophical communication, and must therefore be found, generally, to the same extent in which this latter exists. For it is nothing but the immediate putting into practice of those methodical ideas which we developed from Plato's first principle as to the mode in which writing operates. So that the same idiosyncracy of the philosopher which justifies us in looking for a pervading connection throughout his works, does also reveal to us that which yields the surest canon for judging of their genuineness, and thus the solution of both problems grows from a common root. Now the dialogistic dress has already been represented above as the external condition of this dialogistic form, and its almost indispensable scheme, but only where, vividly conceiving the purpose of imitating oral instruction, which always has to deal with a definite subject, it further adds thereto an especial characteristic, the ad-mixture of which forms the Platonic dialogue. I speak of that mimic and dramatic quality by means of which persons and circumstances become individualized, and which, by general confession, spreads so much beauty and charm over the dialogues of Plato. His great and undisputed works plainly show us that he does not neglect this admixture even when he is most deeply

absorbed in the subject, as on the other hand they
shew us almost universally that he admits it most copiously when the subject-matter does not lead so far
into the dark solemnity of speculation. Whence we
may certainly conclude that this peculiar form can never
be totally wanting, and that even in the most insignificant trifle which he undertook, whether as a study
or an occasional piece, Plato will have applied something of this art. Moreover, the want of this is indisputably the first thing which, to the feeling of every
reader, must distinguish as unplatonic the dialogues
rejected from antiquity downwards; as it is also the
correct basis upon which that old critical judgement
rests, that all dialogues without Introductions are to be
disavowed, except that this formula expresses the fact
but very partially and imperfectly. And to the inward and essential condition of the Platonic form belongs
every thing in the composition resulting from the purpose of compelling the mind of the reader to spontaneous production of ideas; that frequent recommence-
ment of the investigation from another point of view,
provided nevertheless that all these threads do actually
unite in the common center-point; that progression, often
in appearance capricious, and only excusable from the
loose tenor which a dialogue might have, but which
nevertheless is always full of meaning and of art ; the
concealment, further, of the more important object under
one more trifling; the indirect commencement with some
individual instance ; the dialectic play with ideas, under
which, however, the relation to the whole and to the
original ideas is continually progressing : these are the
conditions some of which must necessarily be found in
all really Platonic works that have any philosophical

bearing. Meanwhile it must be evident that this character can show itself in its full light only in proportion
to the importance of the subject-matter, and we here
see first how, when we are employed upon Plato, the
task of proving the genuineness of any dialogue, and the
investigation of its right place, mutually support and
verify each other. For in any dialogue which at once
recommends itself by its language, and which manifestly
treats of Platonic subjects, the more perfectly this form
is stamped upon it, we may not only pronounce it genuine
with so much the more certainty, but since all those
arts point back to what has gone before and forward
to what is to come, it will necessarily be so much the
easier to determine to what main dialogue it belongs
or between which it lies, and in what region of the
development of the Platonic philosophy it can furnish
an illuminating point. And in like manner, conversely,
the easier it is to assign to any dialogue its place in
the list of the others, these relations must become more
marked by means of those expedients, and the dialogue
appropriates itself, with the greater certainty, to Plato.
These dialogues, therefore, in which Platonic matter is
united in proper proportion with Platonic form, and
both appear sufficiently manifest, constitute a second class
of Platonic works, which, even without looking to the
pretty valid evidence which likewise appears in support
of some of them, sufficiently authenticates itself by its
relation to, and connection with, the first. But the
more deficient a dialogue is in reference to the form,
and when the subject-matter presents itself but slightly
enough proportioned to it, the more suspicious, certainly,
the genuineness of that dialogue becomes, especially as
the other elements of the Platonic character must be

less distinctly perceptible. For even the thoughts themselves will then betray less of the spirit of Plato, and
the language also will have less opportunity to develope
itself in all its power and beauty, as so much of both
is connected with those peculiarities in the composition.
Thus, as the distinctness of the form diminishes, the
conviction of genuineness does so likewise in all respects,
until, as more suspicions and doubts come into its place,
it gradually becomes less credible that Plato, to whom
it was so easy and natural to refer from all particular
ideas and separate opinions to his great original principles,
should have brought forward in a different manner any
subject whatever in the province of philosophy, where
every one may be so treated, because he must thus,
without attaining any of his well known points and for
no purpose, have transposed himself into a forced position.
With respect to such dialogues it is therefore imperative
to bring especial proof of the possibility of their being
Platonic, and a preponderant probability at least must
be shown in favour of them to prevent their rejection,
and that with the most perfect justice. But even supposing the balance to waver, and that the matter could
not be at all decided, even this continuing uncertainty
will not throw the arranger of the Platonic works into
any embarrassment. For dialogues of this kind do in
no way belong to the list which it is his object to make
out, for, even supposing their genuineness proved, this
would only be the case when a particular object or an
especial occasion for the existence of such heterogeneous
productions was pointed out, so that in any case they
can only be occasional pieces, which from their very
nature are indifferent as regards this investigation. It
is therefore easier also to decide upon the genuineness

of all which can belong to the connected system which the arranger seeks, and all in which the investigation of their genuineness can either be not made out at all, or only upon other grounds, falls at once and of itself into a third, and for him an indifferent class. I speak not only of those pieces that are dubious from a certain misunderstanding of them, but also of those in the Platonic collection which do not fall in any degree within the province of philosophy, and whose genuineness, therefore, cannot be judged of according to the same rules with the others.

Thus, then, the privilege is reserved of investigating quite from the beginning upwards the connection of the Platonic writings, and placing them in such an order as shall possess the probability of deviating as little as may be from that in which Plato wrote them; and this undertaking is not endangered even supposing that a decided judgement upon the genuineness of many dialogues must continue in abeyance for future times, or for a sharper eyed and better furnished criticism. All therefore that now remains, since the marks of genuineness and the thence resulting different circumstances of the Platonic writings have been briefly sketched, is in like manner to lay before the reader the first principles of their connection and the arrangement resting thereupon, in the way of a preliminary survey of the whole in general. For to show in detail how every dialogue strikes into the rest, must remain in reserve for the particular introductions; while here we can only give an account of the principles which are the basis of the general plan.

If then, to continue, we keep to the somewhat contracted selection of the more important Platonic works in which alone the main thread of this connection, as has

been already mentioned, is to be fonnd perfect, there are
some of them distinguished above all the rest by the
fact that they alone contain an objective scientific exposition; the Republic for instance, the Timæus and the
Critias. Every thing coincides in assigning to these the
last places, tradition, as well as internal character though
in different degrees of the most advanced maturity and
serious old age ; and even the imperfect condition which,
viewed in connection they exhibit. But more than all
this, the nature of the thing decides the question; inasmuch as these expositions rest upon the investigations
previously pursued, with which all the dialogues are
more or less engaged; upon the nature of knowledge
generally, and of philosophical knowledge in particular;
and upon the applicability of the idea of science to the
objects treated of in those works, Man himself, and Nature. It may indeed be the case that in point of time
a long period intervened between the Republic and the
Timæus ; but it is not to be supposed that Plato during
this interval composed any whatever of the works remaining to us, or even, generally, any that would properly come into connection with them, with the exception of the Laws, if those are to be counted as part of
that connected series, for we have express testimony with
regard to these that they were written after the books
upon the Republic. But these books, together with the
Timæus and Critias, form an inseparable whole, and if
it should be said that the Republic, as properly representing ethical and political science, though written
later than those dialogues in which the nature of virtue,
its capability of being taught, and the idea of the good
are treated of, might nevertheless have been very easily
written earlier than the dialogues immediately prepar-

atory to the Timæus, those namely, which endeavour
to solve the problem of the inherence of ideas in things,
and of the kind of knowledge we possess of nature; this
would be not only as unplatonic, according to what
has been said above as any thing could be, and would
suppose the grossest ignorance of those preparatory works
in which such a separation of subjects is not to be found;
but it would thence follow in particular, that the Politicus, which is preparatory to the Republic, in exactly the
same relation as the Sophist to the Timæus, was written
earlier, and that by a considerable period than the Sophist
itself, which does, nevertheless, in conjunction with the
Politicus, constitute but one dialogue, and is in fact the
first part of it.   But the Republic, as being clearly the
earliest of the properly expositive works, at once supposes the existence of all dialogues not belonging to this
class, and this splendid structure contains, as it were let
into its foundation, the key-stones of all these noble arches
upon which it rests, and which, previous to entering that
edifice whose support they are, if one considers them
only in reference to themselves, and surveys them immediately within their own range, one might, not being
able to divine their destination, pronounce objectless and
imperfect.   If, therefore the Republic will not admit of
being separated by any means from the subsequently
annexed Timæus and Critias, whoever would make any
objection against the place they occupy in common, must
assume that Plato premised, generally, the perfected exposition, and did not add until afterwards the elementary
investigations into the principles.   But every thing, as
well the manner in which those principles are introduced
into the expositive works themselves, and in which they
are investigated in the preparatory ones, as also every

possible conception of Plato's spirit and style of thought, is so strongly repugnant to the adoption of such an inverted order, that it is hardly necessary to say anything upon that point; but we need only ask any one what dialogues he would read in this order, and then leave him to his own feelings as to the inverted process and the miserable expedient that the investigations leading back to the principles will now be necessarily instituted with persons knowing nothing of the preceding expositions, so to cut off all natural references to them. Moreover, instead of those references which he will in vain look for, other relations would spontaneously force themselves throughout upon the mind of any one reading in this order, clearly pointing to the opposite arrangement. It is hoped that no one will object that the case would, in the main, be the same with the order here proposed, inasmuch as according to this, a subject is not seldom anticipated mythically which does not appear until later in its scientific form. For the very fact of its being done only mythically does not only accurately agree with that main purpose of Plato to excite his readers to spontaneous origination of ideas, upon the recognition of which our whole arrangement rests, but it is even in itself a clear proof of how firmly convinced Plato was, that in philosophizing, properly so called, it is necessary to begin not with a composite theory but with the simple principles. Nay, whoever penetrates deeper into the study of Plato, will then, and not before, be aware how the gradual development and moulding of the Platonic myths form one fundamental myth, as well as the transition of much that is mythical into a scientific form, affords a new proof in favour of the correctness of the order in which all this may be most clearly perceived. The necessity, therefore, for assigning the last place to the constructive dialogues, is in every point of view so great, that if well-grounded historical traces were to be found of an earlier composition of the Republic prior to any one of those preparatory dialogues, though none such has yet been found, and, what is more, will not be found, we could not avoid falling into the most serious contradiction with our judgement upon Plato, and we should be much embarrassed how to reconcile this instance of unreason with his vast intelligence. As then, these constructive dialogues are indisputably the last, some, on the other hand, of the remaining ones distinguish themselves as clearly as the first; for instance, continuing to adhere only to those of the first rank, the Phædrus, Protagoras, and Parmenides. For these are contrasted with the former, first by a character of youthfulness quite peculiar to them, which may indeed be most easily recognized in the first two, but even in the last will not escape the attentive eye. Moreover by the circumstance, that as by the former all the rest are presupposed, so, conversely, many references are to be found throughout to these latter as previously existing; and even looking only to the particular thoughts, they appear in these dialogues still as it were in the first glitter and awkwardness of early youth. And further, these three dialogues are not indeed like those three last, worked up into one whole with a definite purpose and with much art, but notwithstanding, mutually connected in the closest manner by a similarity in the entire construction scarcely ever to be met with again to the same degree, by many like thoughts, and a number of particular allusions. But the most important thing yet in them is their internal matter, for in them are developed the first breathings of what is the basis of all that follows, of Logic as the instrument of Philosophy, of Ideas as its proper object, consequently of the possibility and the conditions of knowledge. These therefore, in conjunction with some dialogues attaching to them of the lesser kind, form the first, and, as it were, elementary part of the Platonic works. The others occupy the interval between these and the constructive, inasmuch as they treat progressively of the applicability of those principles, of the distinction between philosophical and common knowledge in their united application to two proposed and real sciences, that of Ethics, namely, and of Physics. In this respect also they stand in the middle between the constructive in which the practical and the theoretical are completely united, and the elementary, in which the two are kept separate more than any where else in Plato. These, then, form the second part, which is distinguished by an especial and almost difficult artificiality, as well in the construction of the particular dialogues as in their progressive connection, and which might be named for distinction's sake, the indirect method, since it commences almost universally with the juxta-position of antitheses. In these three divisions therefore, the works of Plato are here to be given to the reader; so that while each part is arranged according to its obvious characteristics, the dialogues also of the second rank occupy precisely the places which, after due consideration of every point, seems to belong to them. Only it must be allowed that with respect to this more nice arrangement, everything has not equal certainty, inasmuch as there are two things necessary to be attended to in making it, the natural progression of the development of ideas, and a variety of particular allusions and references. With respect to the works of the first rank, the first of these two is generally perfectly decisive, and is never contravened by a characteristic of the second kind. Thus, in the first part, the development of the dialogistic method is the predominant object, and hence, manifestly, the Phædrus is the first and the Parmenides the last, partly as a most perfect exposition of it, partly as a transition to the second part, because it begins to philosophize upon the relation of ideas to actual things. In the second part, the explanation of knowledge and of the process of knowing in operation is the predominant subject, and at the head of that part stands the Theætetus, beyond the possibility of a mistake, taking up as it does this question by its first root, the Sophistes with the annexed Politicus in the middle, while the Phædo and Philebus close it as transitions to the third part; the first, from the anticipatory sketch of Natural Philosophy, the second, because in its discussion of the idea of the Good, it begins to approximate to a totally constructive exposition, and passes into the direct method. The arrangement of the collateral works of the second class, is not always quite so decisive, as several, in the first place, are only enlargements upon and appendages to the same principal work, as is the case in the first part with the Laches and Charmides in reference to the Protagoras, and in these therefore we can only follow certain particular, and not always very definite, indications; and, in the second place, several of them might be transitions between the same larger dialogues, as in the second part the Gorgias with the Menon and Euthydemus collectively are preludes diverging from the Theætetus, to the Politicus : so that we must rest satisfied with an accumulation of probabilities collected as accurately as may be from every source. The third part contains no other subordinate work except the Laws, to which, certainly, not only with reference to that important triple work, but also considered in itself, we must give that name, and say that, although copiously penetrated with philosophical matter, they still form only a collateral piece, although, from their extensive range and genuine Platonic origin, they are perfectly entitled to belong to the works of the first class. Lastly, as regards those dialogues, to which with reference to the point of view taken in the arrangement, we have assigned in common a third place, although they, in point of genuineness, have a very different value, they will be distributed into appendices under all three divisions, according as either historical or internal evidence, in so far as they are Platonic, assign them a probable place, or according as the critical examination of them is facilitated particularly by comparison with this or that dialogue. For they also shall have the privilege which belongs to them, of being provided with all that can be said in a short space towards elucidating them, and bringing their cause more near to a decision.

PART I.

I. PHÆDRUS.

This dialogue usually bears as a second title, " *Or of the Beautiful;*" and has been sometimes named, " *Of Love and of the Mind.*" Indisputably all such second titles, appearing as they do to several dialogues of Plato, have arisen, probably accidentally, from a later hand, and have produced almost universally the disadvantageous effect of leading the reader upon a wrong track, and thus favouring views in part far too limited, in part entirely false, with regard to the object of the philosopher and the meaning of the work This holds especially of the superadded titles of this dialogue, which have been understood almost universally as indicating the true subject of it, have been translated and used in quotations, though love and beauty appear only in one part of the work, and could not, therefore, to an unprejudiced person, obtain as the true and proper subject of it. The omission, however, of this deceptive title will be hardly sufficient to replace the reader in that original state of absence of all prejudice ; and from this cause, therefore, as well as from a desire to lay the Platonic method as clearly as possible before the mind, on occasion of the first dialogue, this introduction must claim to extend to what may appear a somewhat disproportionate length.

The whole Dialogue, exclusive of the richly ornamented Introduction, consists of two parts, much alike in extent, but otherwise, even at first sight, very different from one another. For the first of them contains three speeches upon love, one of Lysias in favour of the position that a boy should bestow his favour upon a cold and dispassionate lover rather than an enraptured and impassioned one, and two of Socrates—the first a supplementary speech, in the same sense in which such speeches were usual in courts of justice to defend the same cause with the preceding; the other, on the contrary, a counterspeech in favour of the impassioned suitor so severely accused in the first. The second part, to leave it, preliminarily, as indefinite as possible, contains several remarks, incidentally introduced on occasion of these speeches, upon the then condition of the art of speaking, together with notices of its proper principles. And from these entirely technical investigations no return whatever is again made to the subject treated of in the speeches. Now, even from this briefly-drawn sketch, every reader must at once see that not only that particular erotic question cannot have been in Plato's mind the main subject-matter, but not even love in general. For in either case this beautiful work, worked up as it evidently is with the greatest pains, would appear deformed in a most revolting manner, utterly contravening the maxim that it must be fashioned like a living creature, having a body proportioned to the mind, with parts also in due proportion. For the whole of the second half would then be nothing but an appendage strangely tacked on, and not even tolerably well fitted, which, of itself alone, and more especially from its position, could produce no effect so sure as that of necessarily drawing off the attention as far as possible from the main subject. Moreover, supposing the last to be the case, the subject itself would be yet but very indifferently completed. For notwithstanding that in the two first speeches the relation of the lovers is treated of merely upon the grounds of pleasure and profit—in the last, on the other hand, ethically and mystically; and this separate treatment might have so easily led to the true point of dispute, with regard to the nature of love and to its higher essence—notwithstanding this, no notice whatever is taken of it in the succeeding criticism upon the speeches, and nothing is done to reconcile the opposing views. Accordingly, a subject so negligently treated could not be the proper subject-matter of the work, and nothing remained but to place the whole value of the dialogue upon the mythos in the third speech, which alone expatiates to a certain degree upon the question of love—that myth, which, of all that the dialogue presents, is most celebrated and famous—together with what is said in connection with it of the high importance and the great influence of beauty. And then we shall have to explain all that remains to be digressive matter, strangely confused and unmeaningly compiled; if, that is to say, we are to start from the subject-matter of those three speeches in order to comprehend the whole.

Now if, on the contrary, we compare the second part instead of troubling ourselves so uselessly about the first, the result seems to be that as the Art is treated of in the second part, we are to look at the speeches in the first, more with reference to the *mode* of treatment, and their value as works of art, than to the subject discussed; whence ensues an attempt, the reverse of the first, to centre the main object of the whole in that which forms the subject of the second part, the more correct notions, namely, brought forward respecting the true nature of the art of speaking. This view, which has even been already adopted by several persons, is favoured by an at least half-seriously intended declaration of Socrates, that he brings forward the speeches only as examples, and that, setting aside the correct method employed, every thing else in them is to be taken only as jest. According to that, then, we should have to pay especial attention, from the beginning throughout, to what is paradigmatic in these speeches, and we must endeavour perfectly to understand every relation existing between them and the theory advanced in the second part, which consists in the main of the three following points. Plato first attempts to make quite clear what is the proper business of the art of speaking. For, as is clearly seen from the rules adduced in the second part, and the inventions of the most celebrated rhetoricians of that most ancient school, this art was treated by the artists and teachers of that day in an exclusively empirical manner. To blind the understanding of the hearers by sophistical means, and then, in particular passages, to excite their minds emotionally—this was their whole object; as likewise an extremely deficient and uniform method of instruction in composition, with uselessly accumulated subdivisions and technical terms, and some maxims upon the use of language, leading at most only to harmony and fulness of sound, or to the production of striking and brilliant effect, made up the whole secret. And thus the art was altogether devoid of internal substance. All this then, which up to this time had passed for the art itself, is degraded by Plato to the rank of technical knack, and while he exposes in its nakedness the principle of the sophistical rhetoricians, that he who would convince need not himself know the true and right, he shews, that in order really to produce conviction, that is, to compel as it were others to certain thoughts and judgments, if this is to be done at all, however without reference to the truth, yet with that degree of certainty which alone can lay claim to the name of art—he shews, I say, that an aptitude at deceiving and undeceiving is requisite, an art of logical semblance, which can itself rest on nothing but a scientific method of comprehending similar notions under higher; and a like knowledge of the difference of notions, that dialectics, therefore, must be the true foundation of rhetoric, and that only what is connected with its principles, properly belongs to the art. With this, then, the second position stands in close connection. All those technicalities, he says, which were given out for art were borrowed only from practice in the courts of law and the popular assemblies, and referred to them, so that their trifling value must at once appear, even if they were only put forward as particular kinds, and no longer considered as the whole province of the art. Hence, therefore, Plato maintains that the art of speaking is universally the same, not only in these places, but also in written productions and oral discussions of every kind, as well scientific as civil, nay, even in the common usage of social life. By means of this extension and establishment of its province, now comprehending every species of philosophical communication, beyond its hitherto too narrowly drawn limits, on the one hand rhetoric is cleared from many grounds of reproach, and compelled to seek its principles for all these various branches far deeper, and on the other the rising artist reveals himself in the process, while a great archetype, emblematical of the species which he almost created, floats before him in his mind, and he subjects himself to strict conditions, which according to the general view he might have avoided. But as by this very extension, rhetoric, in the sense in which the word was hitherto used, is in a manner destroyed, Plato clears himself, prophetically, as it were, of the accusation of diluting it away and letting it vanish into the indefinite, which, among the moderns at least, might easily be charged upon him by those who bring with them to this investigation the common incorrect conception of Plato's hatred to the art in general. And this he does best by that declaration of his views according to which he sets up rhetoric, notwithstanding its maintained dependency upon dialectics, and even by virtue of it, to be art in a higher sense. For true art, according to him, is nothing but that practice of which again a true science, or, as our own countrymen usually call it, a theory can be made : for it is thus that Plato distinguishes art and artless dispatch. Now such a science can arise only when the classified variety, dialectically exhibited as resulting from the central notion of the art, is connected in a systematic and perfectly exhaustive manner with what results from the whole range of the means and objects. Accordingly, he demands from the art of speaking, that it enumerate all the different kinds of speeches, and fix every one and each to correspond to all the different kinds of minds, in order thus to define how every speech, under given circumstances, can and must be fashioned according to the rules of art.

From this point of view thus taken up, much contained in this work may be now more correctly understood. From it, first of all, the necessity of the examples, at least for a living composition like that of Plato's, becomes

evident, and these examples could only be either completely or as good as completely finished speeches. Whence
the propriety of their position before the theoretical part,
and the necessity of a fiction for the purpose of introducing
them, naturally follows. But in order to facilitate the
comparison, Plato needed an example of the common
illogical method no less than one of his own, and after
the last again he was obliged to accomplish ends of an
opposite nature if he wished to shew the influence of
the peculiar tendency of that period upon the whole
discussion, and at the same time to produce that logical
semblance which leads unobserved from one contradiction
to another. On this account, therefore, no one, we conceive, would wish to overlook the first of the two Socratic
speeches from a preference for the second, as it is only by
the most accurate comparison that both can be understood
aright. Thus the entirely different tone of each, according to its purpose, will become evident. For in the one
we have the pervading direction of the speech to the
understanding and to sober worldly-mindedness, the expression moreover, notwithstanding all the rhythmical
accumulation of words, preserved transparent and cold—
thus it indisputably is that a mind must be treated which
it is intended to lead to a contempt of passion by directing
its views to a late future; in the other, on the contrary,
we have the inspired tone, the exaltation of beauty to
an equal rank with the highest moral ideas, and its
close connection with the Eternal and Infinite; the
manner moreover in which indulgence is demanded for
the sensuous system, without however concealing that it
is only indulgence; thus it is that with indulgence to the
imagination a young and noble mind must be wrought
upon, which, like that of a growing Hellenic boy, springs

fresh out of the school of the poetic art. Truly it could not easily be better proved than is done by this collocation, how necessary on every occasion it is to consider in what way a given mind can be influenced to a given object. In like manner from this point of view it will appear natural that these examples should be taken from a subject appertaining to Philosophy, because in a subject of this description Plato found himself most on his own peculiar ground, and because this was at the same time necessary, in order as well to verify, practically, as it were, the theory of the extension of the Art of Speaking beyond the circle of political and civil affairs, as to suggest a fitting rule for comparison between that more narrow province, and this the more extended, the sphere of the production of splendid philosophical works. Now if Plato had determined to start from an example actually given, and that example one which had already submitted to the laws of rhetoric, it will not be risking too much as to the range of his knowledge and reading at that time, to say, that his choice must have been extremely limited. For except the declamations of the Sophist, which were indeed works so unsound that for Plato with such views and principles to place himself in comparison with them would have been productive of no honour, and which moreover, as soon as Rhetoric and Sophistry began to separate, lost their consequence more and more from that point of view, there could be little else for him to choose but these erotic rhetorical essays of Lysias, who moreover, from possessing to a certain degree fundamental principles, was a more worthy opponent than ever an orator out of the poeticising school of Gorgias.

But this is just the point at which the insufficiency even of this view must strike every one. For why should Plato have wished to confine himself by such a self-imposed law, and that too quite contrary to his own method? Or is it not usual with him to put into the mouth of his Interlocutors what they have never said, liable to the sole condition that it be like them and appropriate? And what therefore should have hindered him from composing a speech in any one's name, unless he found one at hand upon a subject for which he not only had a peculiar interest, but which also stood precisely in the closest connection with the immediate object of this dialogue. For that love is indeed a moral object, and that in the method in which it is here treated of, there lies at bottom something like an apology for Socrates who was accused of it in an unworthy sense, this would be perhaps sufficient cause for introducing it as one of those subordinate points of the second rank which we meet with not sparingly here in the introduction generally, in the transitions and in various allusions; but when anything stands in such relation to the whole as these speeches do, then it becomes incumbent upon us to discover a necessary connection between it and the main idea of the whole. Now if the main idea here were nothing but the correction of the notion of rhetoric, in that case love and beauty, which form the subject matter of these speeches, would be, as regards this point, purely accidental. But this is just Plato's method, and it is the triumph of his master-mind that in his great and rich-wrought forms nothing is without its use, and that he leaves nothing for chance or blind caprice to determine, but with him every thing is proportionate and co-operative according to his subjects' range. And how should we miss this intelligence altogether in this place, above all others, where the principles which he adduces are pronounced in the clearest manner?

Thus, therefore, it is at once evident that this is not yet the correct view, and not taken from the point from which alone a survey may be had of the whole, and every particular appear in its proper form and position, but that we must seek out another, connecting every thing still more accurately. But there are yet other reasons at hand which would not allow us to stop here. For is it likely that it could have been a principal object with Plato to compose a treatise upon the technicals of rhetoric? and would this in any way agree with his other purposes as a writer? or is it not rather the case that nothing similar ever occurs again, and the Phædrus would then stand isolated in a manner in which a far less important work, in the case of this master, could scarcely be allowed to stand? Nay more, even in the second part, though it is from this that the standing point for this view is taken, still much remains inexplicable and strange on the supposition that it is the right one. For this second part not only expatiates greatly upon love and beauty as the subject of the first, but upon the form of that part and rhetoric generally. For all that is said of rhetoric is suddenly extended to poetry and politics as well, for these too are arts, and it can escape no one that, properly speaking, even rhetoric itself is set up and treated of only as an example, and the same even is said of it almost as of the speeches delivered, that, setting aside the higher laws which must be exhibited therein, its whole operation and business is nothing but child's-play. In such wise, therefore, we are driven from

H

an outer to an inner, and as this last does itself in turn soon become an outer, we push still onwards even unto the innermost soul of the whole work, which is no other than the inward spirit of those higher laws, the art, namely, of unshackled thought and informing communication, or, dialectics. For which all else in this dialogue is but preparation, in order to bring about the discovery of it in the Socratic method by the exhibition of its spirit in a well known particular, and that one in which an exclusively scientific form was in part generally recognized, and in part easy to exhibit. Now not only does Plato intend to celebrate this art as the root of every other ramification to which that name can apply, but, while in all other arts we are indeed to recognise it, it is itself to appear to every one as something much higher and perfectly divine, which is to be learnt and practised, by no means for their sake, but for its own and for that of a divine existence. Now the original object of dialectics is found in ideas, which he therefore here describes with all the ardour of first love, and thus it is philosophy that Plato here extols, independently and wholly, as the highest of all objects, and as the foundation of every thing estimable and beautiful, and for whom he may triumphantly demand that her claims to these titles be universally recognised. And it is just because philosophy fully appears here not only as an inward state, but, in accordance with its nature, as extending and communicating itself, that it is necessary to bring to consciousness and to exhibit the *impulse* which forces it outwards from within, and which is nothing but that genuine and divine love which raises itself above every other, originating in and proceeding upon any notion of advantage, as philosophy does by its nature excel

their subordinate arts which are content to play either
with pleasure or profit. For however much the attainment of the object of that impulse must be the effect
of art and of the judgment that arranges its details,
still the impulse itself appears as something originally
existing and ever at work in the mind of the finished
and perfect man, seeking its object from without, consequently as passion and divine inspiration. Hence,
therefore, all problems are solved, and this approves
itself to be the real unity of the work—bringing out
every thing, vivifying and connecting all.

This object then, considered in connection with the
manner in which it is brought forward, irrevocably secures
to the Phædrus the first place among the works of Plato.
To this conclusion we are moreover at once led, when
we observe that in this exposition of philosophy the
consciousness of the philosophical impulse and method
is far more intimate and powerful than that of the
philosophical matter, which therefore only appears
mythically, as if, on the one hand, it were still unripe
for logical exposition, and, on the other, repressed to
a certain degree by that predominant consciousness.
Now this was very naturally the first state into which
a worthily reflecting scholar of Socrates, and one already
possessed with the art, must have been transported
by the mode of teaching pursued by that philosopher.
For these two, impulse and method, were in all his
conversations the constant and ever unchanging elements,
with which therefore the mind would be most possessed,
which, as to the matter, he used but to moot particular
questions in particular detail, without selection or connected purpose. In later times, however, Plato, in
proportion as the objects of philosophy had revealed

themselves to him more clearly, and he had practised the method more fully through all his productions and brought it to honour, would have abstained from making it the core of a composition of such extent in the manner in which he has here done. Moreover, the excessive, and almost boisterous and triumphant exultation, which at once and of itself points clearly enough to the acquisition of a newly gained good, relates only to the discovery of the first principles, and the Phædrus exhibits, less than any other dialogue, a great and already acquired readiness in the application of this method. Moreover it points in a variety of ways to the poetic essays of Plato which preceded his philosophising. For any one who holds Plato in proper estimation, will not be willing to believe that he composed poetry only in the thoughtlessness of youth, but rather that he took it up seriously, and contemplated in very early times, and upon grounds of art, all effects produced upon the mind of man. Thus the power which Socrates possessed of convincing and influencing the mind with all the apparent artlessness of his arguments, must still have appeared to Plato as a master-art never surpassed, and have filled him with admiration and love. This then, under such circumstances and in such a mind, inclined by nature to favour the notion of the unity of the two, naturally exhibited itself in a reference of philosophy to art, the process of which at the same time contained an explanation and defence of his transition from the latter to the former. And, next, his immediate choice of rhetoric, which was not his own art, is conceivable upon the grounds that, more than poetry, it aims at conviction, and because he could not compare what Socrates effected in it by the science

of dialectics, with anything nearer than what the sophists and rhetoricians thought to effect by mere empiricism.

But if such arguments, however accurately they
combine with the only true center-point of the whole,
should still appear to any one insufficient to decide
the period at which the work was written, let him
further mark the innumerable proofs of the youthfulness of the work generally. Now these are to be found
immediately in its whole style and colouring. It has
a great inclination to the epideictic—to an ostentation of
convincing power and superiority; for not only, first,
the opponent set up is conquered with little trouble,
and afterwards, in every instance in what follows, the
preceding position outbidden, but even philosophy itself, in order to give it a lustre and excite our admiration, is praised chiefly, because it leaves far behind
what men most praise and admire. Now this is
in part involved in the subject-matter; but, in Plato
subject and execution are thus necessarily consequent
one upon the other, and the spirit is youthful throughout in which that general design is applied and continually worked upwards, through ascending degrees,
till it reaches a point of extravagance. Look, first of
all, but at the second speech—that speech which
annihilates Lysias, then at the counter-speech which
crushes, still more powerfully, the two preceding; observe how in them Plato showily appropriates to himself the great triumph of the Sophists, of defending
opposite propositions one after the other, and, withal,
the elaborate display immediately made of abundance
of matter; in that every contradictory detail is despised
as regards the speech itself, and only premised in the

dialogues as prefatory to it; then the apologetic confidence, which does not even attempt to deprecate the name of Eros as regards Socrates, or assume a milder instead, but even in a prayer for health and happiness, ends with love. Further, the investigation which declares what is most beautiful in this speech to be nothing but child's-play, and rejects it along with the first as if it were nothing; the bantering challenge to Lysias; the droll, comprehensive, and almost confusing polemics against the early rhetoricians, ridiculing unsparingly even what is good in their labours, because it does not proceed from right principles—and this to a length of which he would scarcely have thought them deserving at a later period, and which does itself make a somewhat ostentatious show of extent of reading; finally, as the culminating point in this epideixis, the exalted contempt, genuinely Socratic, for all writing and all oratorical speaking. Even in the outward form this youthful spirit betrays itself, in the constantly renewed luxuriance of the secondary subjects introduced at every resting point; in an animation in the dialogue, which cannot be quite defended against charges of effort and affectation; lastly also, in a somewhat immoderate introduction of the religious, and here and there even in a certain awkwardness in the transitions, not indeed in the speeches, but in the dialogistic half.

With this view, moreover, the historical indications in the work itself accurately coincide, leaving as they do no doubt remaining as to the time in which the dialogue *plays*, so to speak. It would indeed be useless to attempt to draw any proof whatever from these, and generally, with the exception of a few cases in which the impossibility of the composition prior to a

certain period is self-evident, it would be folly to form
any conclusion upon historical grounds as to the time
at which any work of Plato was written, if we are to
grant what is maintained in Athenæus, that Phædrus
could have been no contemporary at all of Socrates.
For what writer ever allowed himself such latitude,
unless he was one in whose eyes nothing was improbable, and for whom no impropriety was too great?
Not indeed that Plato was to be bound to strict historical accuracy, or as if no offence against the order
of time is to be met with in him. On the contrary,
it may indeed be the case in dialogues which were
transposed into a period pretty remote from that of
their composition, that he starts away from, and leaves,
his hypothetical grounds, whether from error of memory and negligence, or from his knowingly sacrificing
historical truth for sake of a certain effect. But this
is one thing, and it is another to introduce, as must
here be the case, two men as the only acting personages,
who, as every one knew, were not even in existence at the
same time. And what was likely to have influenced
Plato to such a course? For one circumstance of the
Phædrus would be then of no value for the dialogue,
as there could be no want of a contemporary confidant
and admirer of Lysias among the young Athenians,
and any one to whom he had here transferred the character of Phædrus, might have also delivered the speech
spoken by him in the Symposium. Nay, what cause
could there have been for making this same impossible
interlocutor come forward in the Protagoras, where, as
a mute spectator, he only swells the accumulated crowd?
We would not therefore take this even upon the word
of Athenæus unless he communicates to us some of his

more accurate sources of information as to this Phædrus, and so unproven an accusation is not to prevent
us from treating our dialogue, in what we have to
say further, as if it were possible to draw conclusions
from historical relations contained in it. This premised,
we add that two very well known personages are there
mentioned in a very decisive manner—Lysias, namely,
and Isocrates. Lysias, in Ol. LXXXIV. 1, had travelled
at the age of fifteen years to Thurium, and returned,
as Dionysius tells us, when forty-seven years old, in the
first year of the ninety-second Olympiad, from which
period his great fame as an orator first commences.
Now if we allow still some years to pass before Phædrus can say of him, as something generally granted,
that he wrote best of all his contemporaries, this dialogue cannot have been held earlier than in the ninety-
third Olympiad. And certainly not later, for Lysias
could not well be more than fifty years old to write
of and expound love-matters without shame, as Isocrates, two and twenty years younger, could not have
been much above thirty, to be brought forward as a
young man. To this may be added the mention of
Polemarchus as a living personage, who, according to
Plutarch and the composer of the Lives of the Ten
Orators, perished in the anarchy. Now all this does
indeed point immediately only to the time at which the
dialogue may have taken place : but when considered
more accurately, we have from these grounds the further
result, that it cannot have been written much later ; in
which case it is at once self-evident, that Plato, who
at that time had not been long a scholar of Socrates,
could not as yet have written anything of this description, but that the Phædrus was the first burst of the

inspiration drawn from Socrates. For, first, every man's own feeling will tell him that the manner in which Plato introduces the speech of Lysias could only have had its proper effect while this publication was fresh in the memory of the readers of the Phædrus, and that upon the contrary supposition there would not only be a degree of awkwardness about it, but it would be difficult even to conceive how Plato should have fallen in with it. Nay, when we consider further how hardly he treats Lysias, he would have subjected himself to a heavy charge of injustice, had he at a later period in his criticism upon him taken for the basis of it an old and almost forgotten piece, and one long ago superseded by many far more perfect. Moreover to what end the mention of Polemarchus' transition to Philosophy? For, as he died so soon after it, he could scarcely have supplied an illustrious example for a later period than the one we have fixed upon. But what chiefly speaks in favour of the composition of the dialogue contemporaneously with those occurrences is the prophecy respecting Isocrates which appears towards the end of the dialogue, and which cannot possibly have been spoken retrospectively, namely that he would far surpass all rhetoricians hitherto, and rise to a higher kind of composition. For supposing what this orator afterwards performed to have answered Plato's expectations, it was in that case, to say the least of it, ridiculous to make this be predicted at a far earlier period; but if Isocrates did not come up to those expectations, Plato would in that case knowingly and purposely have either told a false prophecy of Socrates, or falsely attributed such to him. But that prophecy seems to have reference to an idea, which in several passages in this dialogue is almost expressed, that Plato would have gladly realised, by predicting its existence, an Athenian school of eloquence upon the principles of Logic in opposition to that corrupted and corrupting Sicilian school; and that he wished, if possible, to invite the support of Lysias, who is considered as standing intermediate between the two. If we regard from this point of view the manner in which Anaxagoras, Pericles and Hippocrates are here brought forward, this supposition may well find support, and even such an idea, so much of it at least as concerns the interests of his native city, can only be attributed to Plato's youth at the time.

In opposition then to all these arguments, which from so many different points all meet in the same centre, what Tennemann adduces in favour of a far later period for the composition of the Phædrus, almost the last of Plato's existence as a writer, can have little weight. For, as regards the Egyptian story, there is indeed no occasion here to suppose with Ast a proverbial mode of speaking, but Plato himself gives us a pretty clear hint that this tale was composed by himself, and in order to have done so, he need not necessarily have been in that country any more than he actually brought from Thrace the Thracian Leaf mentioned in the Charmides with the Philosophy involved in it. And as to the second ground, namely, the similarity between what is said in this dialogue of the effect of writing, and what occurs to the same purpose in the seventh of the Platonic letters; it would seem that Tennemann himself did not mean the expressions in the Phædrus to apply to the same particular case which is the basis of the discussions in that letter, and consequently that he does not maintain that the Phædrus was not written till after Plato's visit to the younger Dionysius. But he only thinks, in general, that here also disagreeable circumstances in consequence of writing must have preceded such expressions as we find in the Phædrus. But of this there is no trace at all to be found; and be the case as it may with that letter, the depreciation of writing in comparison with true and living philosophical communication is itself perfectly intelligible as a justification of Socrates' abstinence from writing, and as a sentiment inspired by that method of teaching which Plato at that time despaired of ever imitating in written treatises, though he afterwards learnt to do so, and did not end with believing to the same extent in the utter incommunicability of Philosophy, although, as we see, he was well aware from the first that it could not be learnt historically. But perhaps that author does in reality hold to another ground still behind that already brought forward; namely, that in the Phædrus so much that is Platonic appears, while he is only disposed to consider those writings of an early date which connect themselves immediately with Socrates, and in which the peculiar style of Plato is still wanting, esteeming so large a work and with such a subject as only adapted to later times. But every skilful and self-experienced person will certainly allow that true philosophizing does not commence with any particular point, but with a breathing of the whole, and that the personal character of the writer, as well as the peculiarities of his modes of thought and views of things in general, must be to be found in the first commencement of the really free and independent expression of his sentiments. Why, therefore, should not the communication of the Platonic philosophy begin thus? Or if we are to believe that Plato was not merely for a certain period a simply

passive learner, but also wrote as such, then it would
be necessary to be able to point out a marked division between these two opposite classes of his works,
a task which no one would be in a condition to perform. For the existence in the Phædrus of the germs
of nearly the whole of his system, is hardly to be
denied; but then their undeveloped state is quite as
clear, and at the same time their imperfection betrays
itself so clearly in that direct method in the conduct
of the dialogue which constitutes the peculiar superiority of Plato, throughout the continuous and uninterrupted course of the last half, that it may be expected that skilful readers will agree as to the position
to be assigned to this dialogue.

Among the grounds here adduced for this arrangement, that old tradition which distinguished the Phædrus
as the first of Plato's works, has, not improperly, considering the importance of the subject, found no place.
For Diogenes and Olympiodorus refer the origin of
this tradition to no competent testimony; on the contrary, what these authors say tends rather to favour the
hypothesis, that this arrangement was only supposed
already in early times, in order to destroy several
objections made to this dialogue; as to whether, for
instance, the language of it kept within the limits of
pure prose, or indeed whether the whole investigation was
not excusable only in consideration of the youth of the
writer. It is evident what is meant by the last, namely,
the erotic question; but in the first allegation one of
the most eminent masters of antiquity agrees, and that
in no gentle manner—I mean Dionysius. What the
nature of the case may be as regards that point, will
best appear from what still remains for us to do;

namely, to add certain preliminary elucidations concerning the particular details of the work.

The Introduction is praised by Dionysius, and without taking offence at the piece of natural description in it, he accounts it an instance of that homely and temperate style, which, as the peculiar province of the school of Socrates, belongs, he thinks, to Plato in even an eminent degree. The first speech which Phædrus reads to Socrates he clearly recognizes as a work of the celebrated orator, a point upon which no one will entertain a doubt, although an English Philologist has laid a penalty on the belief of it. Now if more had remained to us of the collection of Lysias' erotic publications, we should be better able to judge of the relation of this speech to others of that writer, as regards the art and character displayed in it. This here however is not deserving of much praise in itself; for the uniformity in the moulding of the particular propositions, as well as the mode of connecting them, could hardly be given in the translation to the vicious extent to which they exist, and the indefiniteness of expression which almost always admits of several meanings, is a *crux* for the interpreter. Now supposing the others to have been like this, the whole was an attempt, not indeed thoughtlessly entered upon, but still perfectly unsuccessful, towards an extension in the Art of Speaking. Then the first Socratic speech carries forward the principle of Lysias more thoroughly and clearly worked out. Now here Dionysius at once censures the invocation to the Muses which precedes it, thinking that it comes down suddenly like storm and tempest from a clear sky, destroying the pure prose—a tasteless piece of poetastry. And Dionysius adds that Plato means soon to acknow-

ledge himself that this is a specimen of high sounding
sentences and dithyrambs, with great pomp of words
and little meaning, when he says to Phædrus that he
should be surprised at nothing in the sequel, for that
what he is now uttering is not far short of dithyrambs. Now as to that invocation to the Muses, we
might perhaps allow an affectation in the sportive de-
rivations in it; but, looking to the whole structure,
scarcely any one would be disposed to deny its claim
to the title of prose. By the surprise, on the contrary, which Plato expresses at the dithyrambic nature
of his sentences, he certainly did not intend to express
any censure upon himself. For any one who pays attention to the passage in which this occurs, will easily
discover that it does not refer to any kind of Poetic
inspiration; but that Plato only intended, certainly not
to his own disadvantage, to attract notice to the distinction between his own rythmus and that of Lysias.
For in the latter all the periods are turned with a mo-
notonous uniformity, one like another split into ante-
theses; and the whole speech is pervaded by one and
the same extremely flat melody. In that of Plato on
the contrary, the rhythmus is in continuous gradation,
so that he begins, where his ideas are far-fetched, with
short propositions at a quick step, and as the speech advances from the general to the particular, the sentences
also become more developed and articulated; until at
last the orator, when he has reached a culminating point,
hovers around it, and as it were poises himself in a
slowly revolving period. Yet, notwithstanding, the structure of these periods appears, to us at least, perfectly
prosaic, as also the epithets are taken from the philosophical and not from the poetical province of the subject.

So that to see how far the censure of Dionysius, which can strictly refer only to the feet of the words, is grounded in truth, could be the privilege of Grecian ears alone, as it is evident that Plato's Theory upon this point, rests upon different grounds from that of Dionysius. To us, who do not inquire quite so much into this matter, the fulness of expression seems actually to reach only to the extremest limits of language unfettered by metre, and in this respect certainly Plato himself intended to be epideictic. In the second speech of Socrates, that famous Myth is, lastly, beyond doubt the most important part, for sake of which all other matter in this dialogue has been unfairly thrown into the back-ground. The consequence of this has been, that not even the Myth itself has been throughout rightly understood. For the Love has, for the most part, been taken in a far too abstract and limited sense, and much has been overlooked or childishly trifled away. Least of all has the fact been remarked, that it is the fundamental Myth from which all that succeed and enter into the whole system of the Platonic Philosophy are developed; so that the more the subject-matter of it, at advanced stages, passes from the mythic into the scientific, the remainder is ever shaped out with less pretension, and becomes more vividly mythical. So that Plato here seems most expressly to assume the privilege of interweaving Myths with the expositions of his Philosophy. Though all this cannot be here regularly proved, but must verify itself by the sequel. Now as to what relates to the particular subject of the Myth, but little definite can be adduced in illustration of the imaginative in it; and the cosmographical conceptions especially which are the basis of it, are the more difficult to explain, as the Myth rests quite on the boundary between the Natural and Supernatural. More accurate solutions of it would certainly be more welcome than that discovery which Heyne some time since communicated, that the horses in this Myth were borrowed from Parmenides, which will hardly be discovered after a perusal of the fragment referred to. For the identity in a comparison, rests not so much upon the image, as upon a similar application of it to the object. Moreover, more would be implied in that assertion than that learned person probably intended, namely, that Plato borrowed his division of the Soul from Parmenides. In our confessed uncertainty as to particulars, it may however be said in general, that several of the conceptions in this Myth seem to be worked out from one another; and that, as several expressions are derived from the mysteries, a more perfect understanding of them would probably contribute most towards an explanation. On this account a still more accurate acquaintance with the Pythagorean Philosophemes may not be supposed to be the true key even to the mythology, still less to the doctrine of the human mind, as also the Platonic doctrine of renewed recollection is hardly to be explained from Pythagoras. Moreover the bulk of this Myth is evidently treated as a by-work to add to the pomp of the whole, and to harmonize the strictly allegorical parts of it. Wherefore we must beware of entering too much into details in the explanation, and rather be satisfied with only comprehending aright those philosophical indications, which Plato himself marks as such in the delivery. It might be adduced as a consequence, sufficiently immediate and but little attended to, that in every case a man's character is not *originated* during the course of his life, but exists in him from the first. What Tiedemann however has discovered in the notion that the essentially existent is beheld, not in heaven, but in the region beyond heaven, can hardly be implied in it. But it might be most difficult to explain what is said very particularly of the various character of men according as they have been more or less penetrated by the Eternal. If therefore still greater faults do not lie concealed under the considerable varieties in the readings, the whole passage might perhaps belong to that class of decorations in which we are not to look for too much. And, generally, it is impossible to draw attention too much to the fact, how completely every thing in this dialogue is meant and applied rhetorically, so that even here, where untamed imagination has been so often dis-covered, like the wild horse as it were of the Platonic philosophy hurrying the wiser one along with it, Plato appears rather with all the judgment of a master. And even supposing that in the detail this composition carried him near the borders of a province that did not belong to him, as Dionysius even compares one passage with a passage in Pindar, still the style is in the main prosaic throughout. For to sketch an image, as is here done, first with a few strokes in the outline, and then to work it out further step by step, as regularity required, could not be endured in a poem.

With regard to the second part of the dialogue, after all that has already been said in general, there is nothing further to remark, except that, although not fully applied to practice, it was the origin of that im-proved rhetoric which dates its commencement from Aristotle, who owes much to this work. The remarks will explain particular difficulties, and thus the reader will be detained no longer in the vestibule of this splen-did and genial work.

II. LYSIS.

A sufficiently unauthenticated legend, inasmuch as Diogenes does not give us the name of its voucher, makes this dialogue one of the earliest, at least among those written before the death of Socrates. A greater degree of authority however might fairly attach to it than to the similar one respecting the Phædrus, as this latter rests only upon internal evidence, while the former is grounded upon the tradition of a fact, namely Socrates' exclamation of surprise when he saw himself in the representation given of him by Plato. Such a testimony, however, scarcely deserving as it is of the name, is not here the ground upon which its place is assigned to this dialogue; the connection decides sufficiently in favour of it, even though it were not supported by historical references. For in its subject-matter the Lysis is related to the Phædrus and the Symposium alone of all the dialogues of Plato, inasmuch as the question as to the nature and the grounds of friendship and love, which constitutes its whole content, is a secondary and subordinate object in point of form in the Phædrus, while in the Symposium it is, in form, primary and predominant. Clearly, however, it could hardly occur to ony one to place the Lysis *after* the Symposium, as in the latter the question is not only decided directly and finished to the very last stroke, but also considered in its most extensive and general relations. So that dialectical touches, like those of which the Lysis consists, could scarcely be intended to form an ornamental addition to that discussion, while to work it out as an independent whole subsequently to it, would

have been as little consistent with the rules of art as
destitute of point, because every one already had before
him in that dialogue the solution of every question
started in this. And a mere dialectical exercise, especially
one so trifling as this dialogue would then be, can hardly
be attributed to the more finished master of a later period.
It would therefore only remain to be investigated, in the
next place, whether the Lysis is to be placed before or
after the Phædrus. The latter does indeed likewise speak
decisively upon the principal question, inasmuch as it
developes at length one source of love, and goes into an
explanation of it; so that any one might fairly think, in
reference to this circumstance, that, as in the case of
the Symposium, it would be contrary to the principles
assumed to place that dialogue before the Lysis, inasmuch as the Lysis only treats of the same subject
sceptically. But the great distinction must of itself be
evident to those who know the Symposium, while to
others who do not, it may certainly be made apparent
without taking an anticipative survey of that later dialogue. For the theory respecting the source of love
is only brought forward in the Phædrus mythically; and
to think of deciding in this manner a question which
had been already at an earlier period taken within the
province of logic, would be not only contrary to the
most recognized analogy in the Platonic writings, and
to every idea of the philosophy of their author, but
even in itself a vicious and useless undertaking; because
the reproduction upon a dialectic soil of those mythical
elements among which the investigation began, must render
the subject again complicated and uncertain. To this,
moreover, the following argument may be added, one which
with many will probably be more decisive. In the Phæ-

drus the matter is treated far less generally, inasmuch as there are yet other kinds of friendship than that exclusively philosophical, which is there the subject of discussion, or than that exclusively sensuous kind from which occasion is taken to start the question; but at what point these others deviate from the former, or how far the solution admits of being applied to them, is no where pointed out. In the Lysis, on the contrary, it is friendship in general that is the subject of discussion; and to think of carrying on and bringing to a conclusion an investigation begun with such universal bearings, and which yet obtains no decisive answer—to think of doing this by means of a mythical exposition, and that relating but to one part of the subject—is an absurdity so great that it could only be ascribed to an unthinking and random writer; a description which least of all applies to Plato. The Phædrus therefore is by no means to be looked upon as growing out of the Lysis, as the former also could not fail to appear ridiculous to any one who would read it with a still lingering desire to resolve the logical doubts contained in the Lysis; but this latter clearly stands between the Phædrus and the Symposium. And upon this it may be farther asked to which of the two it stands nearest; whether it is to be looked upon as a supplement to the Phædrus, or as a note of preparation to the Symposium. To the latter it does indeed approximate in its more general and various method of treating the subject; but not to mention other grounds which will not allow of being fully understood before we come to consider the Symposium, in the Lysis any trace is so utterly wanting of what Plato wrote between the Phædrus and the Symposium; and it is itself so entirely to be understood from itself and from the Phædrus, that it occupies indisputably the place next after it, and is almost to be viewed only as a supplement to this dialogue, or as an enlarged dialectic elucidation of its subject. For what in the Phædrus is brought forward in a mythical form, that love has its source in the identity of the ideal between two persons, is here proved dialectically, though indirectly and in an enlarged sense. The latter, inasmuch as the notion of relation and affinity takes in more than that of the identity of the ideal; and indeed this notion is alluded to in the Lysis so indefinitely, that it is only by reference to the Phædrus that it can be easily understood. Indirectly, inasmuch as all other propositions resolve into contradictions. For that this is the case with the last proposition likewise, and the one particularly defended by Plato, is only apparent. Much rather is the manner in which the doubts raised against the earlier position, that resemblance is the source of friendship, are applied to this likewise, to be looked upon as the key to the whole, and one which will certainly open up the entire meaning to every one who bears in mind the hints in the Phædrus. Like is only then unprofitable to Like when a man confines himself to his own external personality, and to an interest in his own sensuous being; not to him who, taking interest in the consciousness of a spiritual existence, possible at the same time among many and for the good of many, enlarges the sphere of his being beyond those limits; a process, in the course of which, first, every man universally meets with something like and related to himself, and not at war with his own endeavours. Similar hints are also implied in the similar sceptically proposed positions as to the uselessness of the good, in so far as it is conceived, not as an antidote to the bad, but independently and for itself. Aristotle, however, seems not to have understood these allusions. And this misunderstanding of the dialectics and polemics occurring in the writings of Plato, may generally indeed be excused in his case, as his synonymous arts are of a coarser metal, and of a composition admitting of no polish. But in the present instance where the case is so easy, the source of his error seems to be that he probably knew but little of the connection more especially of the earlier Platonic writings. For several passages may be found in his ethical works, in which he appears to have had the Lysis in his mind, and all of them look as if he thought Plato's apparent indecision real, and believed that he was only unable to extricate himself partly because he overlooked the distinction between friendship and inclination, partly because he mistook his three kinds of friendship, and therefore, naturally enough, could not avoid falling into a contradiction, as often as he thought to transfer to the others what held only of one. Now it must be clear to every reader of the Lysis with what emphasis Plato, though only in his indirect method, draws attention to that distinction, as a considerable part of the dialogue is devoted to the dialectical exposition of it, and how decidedly he rejects the so-called friendship of utility, and this too certainly, dialectically considered, with the greatest justice, as this utility is never and on no occasion anything for itself, but always, and this accidentally, only in another.

Still further particulars likewise speak in favour of a very early date for the composition of the Lysis after the Phædrus. Thus, for example, we find in this dialogue also harsh transitions, a playful caprice in the connection, and occasionally a carelessness in the choice of examples; all of which gives us a strong feeling of inexperience in a composer. Thus also what occurs respecting the subject of the erotic speeches and poems of Hippothales, seems to be a continued allusion to the erotic speeches of Lysias, very probably produced by unfavourable opinions as to the conduct of Plato to that celebrated man.

It would be superfluous to think of noting in detail the whole course of the dialogue after the general view of it that has been given, inasmuch as every one must now be in a condition to judge to what point the particular lines tend, and according to what rule they must be produced in order to reach the centre-point of the whole. That many polemical particulars lie concealed in this dialogue also, every reader will divine; and one feels pretty certain that Plato would completely separate the physical application of the idea of friendship from the ethical, if not entirely reject the former. Thus it can escape no one how the secondary object—that which connects the spirit with the form, namely, to enjoin a morally erotic treatment of the object of love, is not only reached by the preliminary pieces of dialogue, but is very artfully insinuated through the whole, and very easily also, with the exception of a few particular harshnesses, which, just because they were easy to avoid, mark the beginner. The same may be said of the luxuriance in the by-work, and a certain ostentation of superfluity of matter on all points. But this little dialogue is remarkable for the manner in which it suggests the principles from which it is necessary to start in order to understand and judge of the Platonic writings, partly as a striking example, and the first of such examples, of how little ground there is for the opinion, that Plato did not, generally, mean to decide the questions to the investigation of which he gives a sceptical colouring, without writing down the meaning of the riddle in plain words, as he here observes that method in the case of a subject with regard to which he decides in two other dialogues, and that in such a manner that the attentive reader may without trouble find the decision in what looks entirely sceptical. Partly, also, it is an example of how easily Plato could give birth to dialogues of a slighter cast, which, considered in themselves, are merely dialectical, but stand in a necessary connection with something mystical without them,—planets, as it were, only borrowing their light from the greater independent bodies, and moving around them. Also of how the appearances of those dialogues cannot be understood unless their relations to the larger are rightly comprehended ; and how necessary, therefore, it must be, if we would determine the subject of such writings, or decide whether they are Platonic or not, that every possible means should be tried to fix their distance from the principal bodies, and the path in which they move. For as regards the Lysis, few would now pay much attention to the doubts which a too austere and strict criticism could raise against its genuineness—nay, it could scarce be found necessary to refer the accuser further to its imitative and dramatic form, which has so beautiful an effect, and so much of the Platonic character. Of the characters themselves there is nothing to be said ; moreover, there is no trace existing that an actual occurrence is the basis either of the subject or of the dress in which it is clothed.

III. PROTAGORAS.

To the most celebrated men of those who had at
that period come forward as instructors of the Hellenic
youth ; to Protagoras first, who of all masters of dispute
and eloquence, by reason of the fundamental principle
on which his art rested, most deserved to become the
study of a philosopher, even as he was himself called
a philosopher in ancient times and honoured as such;
to the learned Hippias, moreover, the skilled in history
and antiquity, rich in stores of art and memory ; and
to Prodicus, chiefly brought forward by reason of his
philological labours, who, though as a less important
personage, contributes to the effect of the whole ; and,
further, to the friends and admirers of these wise men,
the noblest of the Athenian youth, celebrated partly
through their fathers, partly in succeeding times by
their own deeds as generals, demagogues, and poets ;
to the sons of Pericles, namely, to his ward Alcibiades,
to Critias, to Agathon and others, who, though only present as mute spectators, exalt the pomp and splendour
of the whole ; to these it is that, together with Socrates
and a young man whom he is to recommend as a pupil
to Protagoras, this richly ornamented dialogue introduces us.   And, moreover, to the most brilliant and
luxurious house in Athens, the house of Callias, who
was the richest citizen, the friend of Pericles, as the
second husband of his mother after her separation from
Hipponicus, connected in the relation of brother-in-law
to Alcibiades, who married his sister Hipparete, recognised and ridiculed by the comic poets as the most zealous
and munificent patron of the Sophists, until his unlimited

extravagance put an end to the ancient splendour of his house, which had come down almost from the time of Solon. These are the wise and noble personages who take part in the dialogue which Socrates here details to his friend just after its occurrence, and it is not necessary to have any further previous information respecting them, as they all, and the latter especially, are reflected so clearly and distinctly in the work itself, that it is one of the first and most important sources from whence a knowledge of their characteristics may be obtained.

But the question how this company was brought together cannot be passed over, as even in the old times it was objected to the dialogue, that its author had been enabled to bestow upon it this profusion of important personages only in the most inadmissible way, by means of gross offences against the order and propriety of dates. For several points of evidence appear, which seem to argue that Plato conceived the dialogue to be held not earlier than in the ninetieth olympiad. Thus Hipponicus, the father of Callias, is never mentioned. but Protagoras lodges immediately with the latter, who appears exclusively as lord and master; and Hipponicus perished in the battle of Delos not later than the beginning of the eighty-ninth olympiad. Nay, still more decisively, there is a comedy of Pherecrates, called "The Wild Men," mentioned as having been brought out in the previous year, which adorned the Lenæan festival in the last year of the eighty-ninth olympiad. Athenæus, then, takes this as his standing point, and from it accuses Plato of two faults, namely, that Hippias the Peloponnesian could not have been staying at Athens at any other time except during the truce under Isarchus, in the first year of the eighty-ninth, against which Dacier, in her introduction

to the translation of the Protagoras, endeavours to justify
Plato; further that Plato, in the first of the ninetieth,
could not have said of Protagoras that he had come first
to Athens three days ago, as he is brought forward in the
comedy of Eupolis, the Flatterers, as already present in
the third of the eighty-ninth. But even if any one should
be disposed to agree with Dacier as regards the first point,
and in respect of the second, to reject the testimony of
a comic poet, who, as well as Plato, may have allowed
himself a fiction, still the matter is not done with, as there
are several unquestionable evidences in every way opposed
to fixing the date of the dialogue in that year, and forcing
it higher up; and it is matter of wonder that these are
not mentioned in that hostile passage of Athenæus,
although he brings them forward elsewhere. For first
Socrates is treated by Protagoras as still a young man,
and even calls himself so, which it is impossible he could
do only twenty years before his death. Moreover, Alcibiades, who only a year after that assumed by Athenæus
is called a general, is termed a downy-cheeked youth, and
Agathon, crowned as a tragic poet in the same olympiad,
a boy. Nay, what is most decisive of all, Pericles is
spoken of as still living, and his sons who died before
him in the plague are present in the company, whence
this dialogue is clearly thrown back to a date prior to
the third year of the eighty-seventh olympiad. Now as
so many minor points coincide with this last epoch, not
belonging at all to what is essential in the dialogue, as
for instance Agathon and the sons of Pericles, it is
evidently that which was most clearly in Plato's mind,
and which he really intended to adhere to in the execution of the work. But as to the evidence for a later date,
it may be asked whether the comedy of Pherecrates had

not been already produced previous to the exhibition
mentioned in Athenæus, whether in the same or in a more
imperfect form, especially as it is an exhibition at the
Lenæa that is here spoken of; for it is impossible to
entertain the notion of an oversight committed by Plato,
supposing him to have here come back to the time at which
he actually wrote. In like manner it may be doubted
whether it is absolutely necessary to conceive Hipponicus
as dead, and whether he may not have been absent abroad,
perhaps in the army before Potidæa, if the second year
of the eighty-seventh olympiad is not to be thought of,
in which Hipponicus led an army against the Tana-
græans. In any way it may sooner be conceived that
Plato transposed to a false period this one circumstance,
not unimportant for his plan, than that he purposely
pursued such a course with those of trifling magnitude
and importance; and in this case " The Wild Men "
also of Pherecrates might be fixed to this date, in order
not to leave that fabrication perfectly isolated, and to
keep the more ambiguous what could not be clearly made
out. For Plato could not have chosen a better place
for this spectacle than the house of Callias, and probably
" The Flatterers " of Eupolis were the occasion of this
idea and the temptation to such a licence. And quite as
necessary for him was that earlier period in which those
wise men were actually in the flower of their fame, and
could thus be collected at Athens; and when, moreover,
this generation of knowledge-seeking youths was not yet
devoted to the affairs of state and war. Moreover, it
might well shock Plato's feeling of propriety to represent Socrates, in his year of approaching old age, engaged
in such a prize-fight with the sophists, and to make even
Protagoras, towards whom he cannot still divest himself

of a certain respect, a butt of such Socratic irony in his actually extreme old age. And even here what Protagoras says, exaggeratingly boasting of his age, and the way in which Socrates depreciatingly mentions his own youth, may not be without its object, but intended to throw ridicule upon the standard of those who perhaps reproached even Plato with his youth. For Protagoras was banished from Athens at the beginning of the ninety-second olympiad, during the change of constitution effected by Antiphon the Rhamnusian, and died, it would seem, in his exile, according to some, seventy, according to others, ninety years old. Now if we look for the truth even between the two, although Plato in the Menon, plainly declares himself in favour of the first opinion, still, five olympiads earlier, he could not boast thus of his old age to Socrates, then nearly forty years old, without some degree of exaggeration. Therefore, I would continue, if it is thought not possible to solve the contradictions in the dates, to rest upon the point that the earlier time is that which belongs to the nature of the dialogue, and into which Plato would properly wish to transpose the reader, and that from the later date only some trifling circumstances are intermixed, perhaps unconsciously, in the way of ornament. For at any rate it is but a shallow expedient to rest satisfied with the simple supposition that different dates are mixed up with one another, and that this apparent confusion does not proceed from the method and conscience of an ancient author.

But it is time to exchange the less important investigation of the external circumstances for the consideration of the internal subject of this somewhat complicated dialogue, one perhaps not quite so thoroughly understood as it is multifariously praised. It is indeed very easy to separate the different sections and to draw out the subject of each particular one in its order; but whoever thinks that he has therewith discovered the sense of the whole, proclaiming plan and arrangement as easy and simple, can hardly suppose this dialogue in any other predicament than the very worst, and this with great injustice. For he must suppose that no arranging idea whatever is the basis of the whole, but that every thing spins out accidentally from what precedes, as much without unity as without art and purpose. On the contrary, whosoever desires not to miss the object and idea of the whole, in which much that is complex is interwoven throughout, must trace accurately the connection of every particular, and into these the reader is now to be preliminarily introduced.

1. First of all Socrates endeavours, by means of a sceptical investigation into the nature and the peculiar art of the sophists, to bring the young man who desires to be taken to Protagoras, to reflect upon his purpose. This investigation is as it were continued by Protagoras quite as indirectly, though from a different point, in a short lecture delivered after a request for it had been preferred, upon the extent and antiquity of sophistics. And in this he partly exposes the boldness of his public profession to this trade, partly deduces the thing itself as of considerable antiquity, not indeed from the most ancient philosophers, but from poets and artists. Not anything however, uninvolved or definite comes out respecting the art until Socrates, in a short dialogical section, extracts from him thus much, that political virtue is properly that which constitutes the object of his instruction.

2. Hereupon Socrates, in a continuous speech, lays down the position, slightly sketched indeed, but supported by instances and the expressions of general opinion, that no instruction can be imparted in this matter; to which Protagoras offers a counterproof, partly in a myth about the origin of men and of social life, partly also by endeavouring, in some further investigations, to turn the same instances of ordinary modes of acting, which Socrates had brought forward, to favour his own proposition.

3. On occasion of what is adduced by Protagoras, Socrates, after some premonitory hints as to the difference between an epideictic lecture and a dialogue, annexes a discussion of the latter form upon the question of the unity or plurality of the virtues, in which he first compels his opponent, who maintains their plurality, to oppose justice and piety to one another, and then when Protagoras has great difficulty in extricating himself from this dilemma, Socrates courteously breaks off, forces from him in a second course the confession that discretion also and wisdom must be identical, and at length is on the point of proving the same of justice, when Protagoras violently starting off in order to break the thread, brings forward a long, but exclusively empirical discussion upon the nature of the Good.

4. Hence arise naturally new explanations as to the nature of the dialogue, and while fresh terms have to be entered into for the contest, since the affair has taken the form of a regular philosophical prize-fight, to the increasing pleasure of the noble youths the nearer it had approached that form, Prodicus and Hippias now find opportunity for coming forward in their own way, with short speeches. And Socrates also, with regard to the proposal to choose an umpire, delivers his opinion in a

form which, with all its brevity, is distinguished above all others by the strict dialectic process observed in it.

5. According to the conditions proposed by Socrates, Protagoras has now become the questioner, and after introducing a poem of Simonides, continues the dialogue concerning virtue, without however any definite point being visible to which he would conduct by this method, but only the endeavour to involve Socrates in contradictions. Socrates, however, first, as respondent, not only repels Protagoras, but also carries on further a pleasant by-fight with Prodicus, and afterwards himself explains this poem in a continuous discourse, in which the position that all evil is only willed from error, is assumed to be the general opinion of all wise men, and also a derivation of philosophy from the worldly wisdom of the Lacedæmonians and Cretans introduced, but at last a serious tone being taken up, the discussion is brought to an end with the conclusion that by such argumentations taken from poets, nothing can be gained for the establishment of ideas.

6. Upon this, lastly, the Dialogue is again taken up, and Socrates is now the questioner in it, and in that character continues to shew that virtue is only one—knowledge, science, of that namely which is to be done. First he shews this of courage, and after removing an only apparently sound objection of Protagoras, he makes him allow, half voluntarily, that there is no good but pleasure, and no evil but pain, whence it follows, as a very easy consequence, that all virtue is nothing but a science of calculation and comparative measurement. And thus the contradiction is brought to light by Socrates himself, that on the one side Protagoras, who still maintains his ability to teach virtue, has refused

to allow that it is science, while on the other Socrates has himself been at the pains to prove this, though his purpose went to dispute every supposition in favour of the possibility of teaching Virtue.

From this short summary of the details it must be at once sufficiently clear, that even here the common methods of viewing the dialogue, inasmuch as they could not comprehend the whole, but went to satisfy themselves with a part, have as good as failed altogether. Some for instance, separating what is inseparable, as they will do even in the plastic arts, have directed their attention exclusively to what can be considered only as the colouring of the whole, the uninterrupted irony, which certainly has been admired by every reader yet of this dialogue. It cannot indeed be overlooked that Plato here allows this his peculiar talent to play in a vast range, and with great self conscious skill, whence they who put a high value upon his study of the Mimes, and his approximation to the comic, might easily take up the notion that this ironical treatment, or annihilation as it might be called of the sophists, is to be understood as the chief object of the Protagoras. This is not indeed the place for deciding whether these acquired perfections, for such at least they are represented, were valued to the same degree and in the same sense by Plato himself as they are by some of his admirers; two things however are certain, and sufficient to justify the view taken in the present instance. For, on the one hand, what every eye however inattentive universally observes in the dialogue, is far from being the highest kind of irony, either of Plato generally, or of this work in particular, but only that subordinate imitative colouring which may be met with

M

not unfrequently even among the moderns, otherwise
so little given to irony, under a more modern name.
Again it is to be remarked, that every imitation of the
peculiarities and manners of particular persons proceeds
only from an endeavour after truth in the representation of the speakers, and therefore supposes at once
that something is to be said, and what it is to be,
that consequently this ironical imitation may occur any
where in Plato, and certainly does so occur, when
any point is discussed with these opponents of Socratic
wisdom and modes of thinking, not only as mere ornament, but as a means connected with the end, in
order to make the truth of the whole palpable, and to
authenticate it by a careful removal of every thing
unnatural and exaggerated; but that for that very
reason it should never be conceived as the first or
proper object, because then in the first place the exaggeration would be unavoidable, and in the next the
philosophical object, without which certainly no larger
work of Plato is ever framed, must either have been
subordinate, or have been completely wanting.

Others on the contrary, too eager for the real
treasure, and not even fortunate discoverers because
they sought without knowing their ground, have only
adhered to one of the questions started, as if that one
were to be here decided, whether it were that of the
communicability of virtue or its unity or plurality;
for any one who thus takes up only some particular
point, must necessarily waver. And how insufficient
this proceeding is appears from the fact, that from
such a point of view several parts of the dialogue do
not admit of any explanation whatever; as for instance,
the two sources mentioned of the sophistical art and

of Philosophy, and the whole discussion respecting the poem of Simonides, moreover that even such matter as is more closely connected with those questions does not *advance* but is continually beginning again from the first in a manner almost far-fetched and certainly singular: nay, to express it in a word, how could the main point of the whole be involved in an investigation, of which it is said at the end of it, ironically indeed on the one hand, but very truly on the other, that as far as bringing it to a decision was concerned, it had been pursued poorly and confusedly enough.

Now whoever attends not only to this or that point, in this dialogue, but to every thing, to the frequently interspersed and cursory hints which in Plato least of any writer admit of being overlooked, to the change of the *form* in the different sections, to what is continually recurring in and between these sections, notwithstanding all the multiplicity of subjects—whoever does this will recognize, in this very dispute respecting the form and method, the main purpose of the whole ; the purpose, namely, to praise and ennoble the dialogistic form of Socrates, and to proclaim it as the proper form of all genuine philosophical communication, in opposition to all sophistical forms, all of which therefore make their appearance, not even the method of commentating upon passages of poets excepted. If we place ourselves in this true centre point of the work, we see first, in the most decided manner, how very closely this dialogue connects itself by manifold ramifications with the Phædrus. For as there the inward spirit of the philosophizing process was exhibited, so the outward form is here discovered, and what results, as such, is criticised. Further, as in that dialogue the investigation respecting

the method was interwoven also with the exposition of
the communicative impulse, and that not the common
one whose object it is, from a feeling of vanity, to spread
a falsely so-called and really empty knowledge, but an
impulse which is to form the mind by means of ideas,
so that every thing else is grounded upon the ethical
as the base of the Socratic philosophy; so also here,
the question regarding the possibility of satisfying that
impulse is the subject on which the different forms are
to display themselves, and submit to comparison, and
that in such a manner that in this dialogue also the
argument exclusively treats of the communication of
the ethical, which is the very point that constitutes
the meaning of the question as to the communicability
of virtue. Nay, even in what concerns the outward
conformation of the whole, a striking connection between
the two manifests itself, inasmuch as in this dialogue
also the form of a pitched contest arises agreeably to
the then condition of things; only still more vividly set
forth, as at that time the sophists were connected with
the philosophers more nearly than the orators were, so
that even the polemical turn of the Phædrus appears to
be here continued and advanced. Moreover from this
point the arrangement of the whole and of every particular
in its place intelligibly manifests itself, and that move-
ment which from almost every other point seems only
circular, now assumes, on the contrary, the appearance
of a beautiful and regular progression. For while by
the comparison of the forms the deficiency of the sophistical methods is made all the more evident the
further this dialogue advances, and exposes itself still
more in examples; of how easily epideictic discourse
lends itself to seduce the hearers from the true point in

question, and how much even that is beautiful in appearance several persons together may throw off without ever understanding one another, and how on the contrary, the dialogistic form brings the true meaning of every one to light, traces out the point of distinction, and, provided only that it is not met on one side by total absence of all meaning, discovers the original error; co-ordinately with all this, by means of the continually renewed expositions of the subject from all sides, the causes are always and continually developing themselves, which must prevent the sophists from attaining a better method, and which made them well content to frame a worse. And these causes are the absence of the genuine philosophical impulse and the base enterprises and purposes for sake of which they chiefly exercised their art. And this harmony which must work its effect, like all that is beautiful in art, even though it is not recognised upon its own grounds, is certainly for the most part the source of the extreme delight which most readers take in this perfect work. Thus the first speech of Protagoras at once discovers his self-conceit and avarice—thus in the very first piece of dialogue, where he is content to oppose the reverse of discretion to knowledge also, it becomes evident, when virtue is to be divided, and consequently the distinction between the theoretical and practical eminently obtains, that he is totally destitute of all perception of it. If however this was a piece of dulness wantonly attributed by Plato to this man, it would in that case be sufficiently devoid of art. But it refers undoubtedly to something which Plato and his contemporaries had before their eyes, it matters not whether relatively to Protagoras or some one else. For that philosopher is here less himself than the representative

of his sect. In like manner the sequel further discovers
that it fares no better with Protagoras in regard of the
distinction between the pleasant and the good. And if,
at the conclusion, when Socrates exposes to him the
great contradiction in which he is involved, we learn
that he has not reflected even in the slightest degree
upon the conditions necessary for the instruction of
others, or upon the notion of virtue in which he would
instruct them; we have been meanwhile convinced how
far removed he must continue from that method, the
grand principle of which consists in bringing the nurs-
ling of philosophy to self-consciousness, and compelling
him to independent thought. Such a method, then,
has the dialogistic proved itself meanwhile to be; it
is a method which brings all this to view, and applies
those testing points, offering them for recognition or
rejection, by overlooking which, Protagoras discovers
himself to be a person who has never recognised moral
truth, and consequently has never endeavoured to attain
moral objects as the end of his philosophy. And it is
the projection of these points and the trial whether the
right can in any way be found which is the aim of the
manifold artificial and dialectic turns which Socrates
makes, which can only be falsely accounted as technicalities and sophisms in him, by one totally unacquainted with the Platonic method. On the contrary,
if we compare them with the execution of the Phædrus,
they are the very points which at once constitute a clear
proof of Plato's advancement as a philosophical artist.
For in the Phædrus we do indeed find that indirect
process which forms as it were the essential character
of all Plato's dialogues, particularly those not immediately constructive, we find it, I say, sufficiently predom-

inant in the whole of the composition, but only very sparingly applied in the details; but in this we have it pursued no less in the details than in the whole generally, so that the Protagoras is upon the whole a more perfect attempt to imitate in writing the living and inspired language of the wise man. As also the dialectic maxims of deception and undeception delivered in the Phædrus, are put into practice with that laborious industry with which able pupils in an art, who have already made considerable progress, or rising masters in the same, seek every tolerable opportunity in their exercises for exhibiting any of the secrets they have discovered before the eyes of the skilful adept. But it is not only the practical dialectics, and the commendatory recognition of the genuine form of philosophical art which appears here further advanced than in the Phædrus, but also the scientific bearing is improved. The proposition indeed that virtue is the knowledge of what is to be done or chosen, and, consequently, that vice is only error, this proposition, however serious Plato may have been in making it, is not here put into a definite form and brought forward directly as his opinion, but, left as it is indefinite, it belongs rather to the web in which he entangles those who have not yet possessed themselves of the true idea of the good; which results in part from the evidently ironical treatment of the whole proposition, partly from the connection into which it is so easily placed with that utterly un-Socratic and un-Platonic view that the good is nothing but the pleasant, partly also from the resulting application of what in virtue might be knowledge and science to the arts of measuring and arithmetic. But at all events we here find some indirect notices tending towards what certainly must precede the

decision of the question, the more accurate definition
namely of the idea of knowledge. Thus the apparent
contradiction which Socrates himself detects, involved in
the fact that he disputes the communicability of virtue,
and yet maintains that it is knowledge, this is evidently
an enticement held out to reflect upon the relation of
knowledge to teaching, after consideration of what had
been already said in the Phædrus upon the nature of
ideas. The opposition in reference to the School of
Heraclitus between *being* (τὸ εἶναι) and *becoming* (τὸ
γίγνεσθαι) although at the same time ironical as regards
the Protagoras, has a similar tendency. As also the
subordinate question of the unity or plurality of virtue
is only a particular case belonging to the more general
investigation into the nature of unity or plurality, or
the manner in which the general ideas communicate with
particulars, so that the doctrine of ideas here begins to
pass from the mythical province into the scientific, and
by the very principles brought forward in it, the Protagoras contains, over and above its own immediate object,
the germs of several succeeding works of Plato, and that
in such a manner that it is at once clear even from this
that it is of an earlier date than all other dialogues in
which these questions are treated more at length.

Now as to the myth brought forward by Protagoras,
there is no need to number it as some have done, good-
naturedly raising it to an exalted rank, among those of
Plato's own; on the contrary, if not the property of
Protagoras himself, as seems likely, though there is no
evidence to confirm the supposition, yet the manner in
which Plato applies it makes it much more probable
that it is at all events composed in his spirit. For precisely as is natural to one of a coarsely materialistic mode

of thinking, whose philosophy does not extend beyond immediate sensuous experience, the reasoning principle in men is only viewed as a recompence for their deficient corporeal conformation, and the idea of right with the feeling of shame as requisites for a sensuous existence, and as something not introduced into the minds of men until a later period. Hence also the proof contained in this myth, because Plato could not give any other colouring to such a view, is very oratorically stated, as he does not so much *spare* investigations upon principles as make the want of them perceptible, since even what he has properly to explain is not connected with the course of the narrative, but is only adduced as a command of Zeus. It appears also strange on that account in respect of the style, and probably imitated after Protagoras. And, as to Socrates' opinion of the poem of Simonides, of which nothing but this fragment is preserved to us, namely, that it must be a censure upon the apophthegm of Pittacus, this is not to be taken merely as a jest. At least we are in possession of another poem generally ascribed. to Simonides, in which the resemblance in manner and style to this is not to be mistaken, which stands in a similar polemical relation to the epigram of Cleobulus quoted in the Phædrus, who was also himself one of the seven wise men.

IV. LACHES.

Among the smaller dialogues immediately dependent upon the Protagoras, the Laches will stand the first, because it so nearly resembles the former that it can only be looked upon as an appendix to, or enlargement

of, the last part of it. For Courage, of which it is the
immediate problem of the Laches to discover the correct idea, formed the subject of an argument in the Protagoras with reference to the disputed point of the unity
of all the virtues, or the distinction of them. Protagoras,
in maintaining the latter proposition, being reduced to a
dilemma by dint of several examples, had however brought
himself, influenced by an appearance seemingly favourable
to his views, to uphold courage as an exception to that
similarity, because in its nature it is distinct from all
other virtues ; and, even in experience is often to be met
with separate from them. In opposition to this, Socrates
had shown, that, if we look to the fact how courage exhibits itself in its development as spirit and boldness, but
that these qualities only obtain the appellation of that
virtue in so far as skill and judgment are connected with
them, we shall see that these last properly constitute the
points of distinction between courage and foolhardiness
and precipitation ; and, consequently, that that virtue
also ranges into ingenuity in calculation. Against that
proof Protagoras had defended himself in a manner, as
has been already remarked, actually worthless and foreign
to the subject, which Socrates evidently only admits because further investigation upon this track would have
led him too far from the point which he had in view.
Consequently he there opens up the investigation on
another side, inasmuch as he shows, that upon the supposition that the pleasant is generally the good, we need
only oppose the unpleasant courageously as a means
towards acquiring the pleasant, and that, consequently,
courage can be nothing else but a correct comparison of
distant pleasure with near pain ; consequently a measuring art, consequently intelligence and ingenuity. This,

when applied to the main question of the Protagoras regarding the communicability of virtue, was the conclusion of the dialogue ; but the question as to courage was clearly not exhausted with the conclusion here obtained, but on the contrary remained in a state so dislocated and unsolved that Plato could scarcely let it rest there. For he had given up the first mode of considering the question in an incomplete form, and the hypothesis in the second was not his own; in respect of which, moreover, readers of that day might as easily deceive themselves, as it has happened to those of more modern times to do. This therefore is the meaning of this little illustrative dialogue, in which, what is argued respecting courage connects itself immediately with those investigations, with the intention of pursuing them more accurately, and more from Plato's own point of view. Hence, first, it is argued that boldness does not in its operation exhaust the idea of courage, inasmuch as the province of the latter extends far beyond the fearful, properly so called, and resistance to every kind of pain, nay, even to pleasure, belongs no less to courage ; that therefore perseverance would better express the distinguishing quality of this virtue. Corrected then in this manner, the first investigation in the Protagoras is repeated and brought to the conclusion, that, on the one side neither is all perseverance courage ; nor, on the other, what is ingeniously calculated to attain a certain object or result ; inasmuch as the moral judgment that an act is courageous, is proportioned neither to the degree of perseverance, as even too much of this is censurable, nor to the degree of ingenuity displayed in the calculation. Hence, generally, courage is not to be conceived as physical strength, because in that case it must be ascribed to brutes as well as men, a supposition which Nicias, who indisputably pronounces the opinion of Plato, rejects. The second question from the Protagoras is not taken up again, until, in order to make any delusion impossible, the hypothesis that the pleasant is equivalent to the good, is removed, and a distinction established between the two. Now with a view to this, there could be no point of comparison better or more intelligible than the Art of Prophecy; for, clearly, if all morals are only a geometry of pleasure, that knowledge which is to constitute virtue, can be nothing else but a prescience of results and their actual value as sources of pleasure. From this then the knowledge of the good is here completely distinguished, and it is then first demonstrated, that in so far as courage is to be considered as such a knowledge, it can be no particular virtue distinct from other virtues, because the only principle of division, according to which, looking to the ordinary meaning of the idea this could be done, namely, that derived from *time*, does not fall under consideration in moral matters; consequently, in this place also the conclusion, that virtue is indivisible, is confirmed, as well as that the same power which produces one must also produce all the others. While therefore the investigation into the idea of courage is continued, the higher ethical ideas, which were laid down in the Protagoras, are not only confirmed by a clearer refutation of what is opposed to them, but also actually projected further, although as is usual in these Platonic dialogues of this class, and agreeable to the principles of them, this is only done imperceptibly as it were, and with unconnected strokes, that he alone may find them who has been already put into the

way of discovering them at all events of himself. For
what Laches in his innocence says of the nature of
moral wisdom, as being harmony of the mind, and
coincidence of knowledge and of life, this is the right
key to the Platonic Theory of Virtue, and to the
meaning of his opinion that it is knowledge, or, *a
knowing*. And this, we may observe in passing, is not
the only remarkable instance which tends to limit
greatly the general proposition, that Plato always announces his own opinion through Socrates; or, if not,
through the person who distinguishes himself as the
wisest, and who conducts the dialogue. For neither is
all that this personage says exclusively the opinion of
Plato, who, on the contrary makes even the leading
characters say much according to the views of the
others, in order to detect the contradictions hidden in
those views; nor is that alone the truth which the
leading character says, but much also said by others
which Plato allows to pass without contradiction, and
which the attentive reader easily distinguishes by the
peculiar tone in which it is delivered.

So much for the main subject of the dialogue, which
indeed, as regards its external dress, is there somewhat
differently arranged, though not to such a degree that
any one can mistake the references to the Protagoras
here pointed out. Much also here occurs to illustrate
and exalt the dialogistic method, and we may remember
to what a degree this was a main point in the Protagoras.
Among other matter to that effect, is a very clear explanation, brought forward, probably, to justify Plato
against misconceptions of the Lysis and Protagoras,
and tending to show that the purpose of such a dialogue could never be only to expose to another his own

ignorance, while the expositor knows nothing himself; for this is unquestionably the meaning of the passage in which Nicias censures this very point as something contemptible in Laches. So also the assertion that it must be a matter of indifference whether the teacher is young and unknown or not, is certainly a defence of Plato himself in regard of his treatment of Lysias as well as Protagoras; and the other, in opposition to those who are of opinion that age is of itself to bring understanding, has a similar object in view. It cannot be superfluous to draw the attention of the reader of Plato to such particulars, partly because they bring to light still more the connection of these dialogues, partly that he may learn in time to estimate properly the constant presence of a *purpose* in the author's mind.

This pervading connection then with the Protagoras indisputably secures to the Laches its place in the series of the dialogues of Plato, notwithstanding that Aristotle, when he speaks of courage in his ethical works, never distinctly mentions it. Nor is this circumstance to be wondered at, and it can excite no suspicion; for it would have been superfluous for one who disputes the Platonic views of the good in general as well as of virtue, to delay in particular over Plato's treatment of the detailed and popular parts of virtue, and his own objections to it. Moreover, all that is external is here so perfectly Platonic, and even in part to be explained likewise from the connection of the dialogue with the Protagoras, that not a doubt can remain upon any side in any one's mind. The richness of the by-work, the change of the speakers, the presence of mute persons, are altogether as it were a continuation of the Protagoras. And as regards the choice of persons, Lysimachus the son of Aristeides, and Melesias the son of that Thucydides who maintained for a long time the balance of power against Pericles with great ability, verify with much accuracy the remark first offered in the Protagoras, that the greatest statesmen were still incapable of instructing others in their art. Moreover they are clearly here for the additional purpose of defending youth, by an almost comically kept-up representation of well-meaning but incompetent and insipid old age; and in order to show how perfectly worthless objections grounded upon youth are, as extreme old age, most of all when it has nothing else to be proud of, is accustomed to treat even men of the ripest years depreciatingly as boys, as Lysimachus here treats Socrates. In the choice of the other persons it seems to have been a general object to repel the charge, that the Socrates of Plato only understood how to parade consequentially before boys and Sophists. Therefore there are indeed boys here, but mute; and the regular interlocutors are noble personages from among the first of their class, with whom Socrates argues upon that which they might fairly be supposed to understand; of courage, that is, with captains. And Laches may have been selected above the rest of them with the intention of ennobling Socrates as his comrade in campaign, and an eye-witness of his courage. And Nicias, of whom Plutarch says that he was by nature averse to precipitation and ambitious hopes, and only concealed his innate cowardice by chance successes in war, very appropriately defends the unusual theory of courage, which makes it more a matter of insight and ingenuity.

Only the too prolix discussion of the first question regarding the art of weapon-practice, and the very agreeable though little appropriate tale of the sickle-spear of the utterly unknown Stesilaus, are not quite to be understood, and it might be difficult to come at any other information about it than that it is a luxurious excess of that pleasantry, of which, as is said in the Phædrus, there must necessarily be an admixture in every piece of writing.

V. CHARMIDES.

Of all the particular virtues applied in common life, as Socrates enumerates them in the Protagoras, Discretion was there discussed in the most unsatisfactory manner. At first it was only ironically represented as one and the same with wisdom, and afterwards, when its relation to justice was to be discussed, Protagoras, fearing the result, shot off in another direction. Hence, the Charmides very naturally arises as a second offset from that, with the view, as was done in the Laches in the case of courage, partly of confuting this notion of discretion and reinstating it as an independent virtue in the ordinary acceptation of the term, partly with that of establishing it anew in a higher sense. On behalf of the first it is here shown at large, that the particular exhibition of outward action, in which the nature of this virtue is ordinarily made to consist, may as easily be an imperfection as a perfection, and therefore cannot in any way claim to form an unconditional ethical notion. Neither tardy caution nor bashfulness, which Socrates himself recognises as the ordinary explanations of discretion, and which are conceived as opposed to impudence and precipitation, can be, as he shows, virtues in and for themselves.   In the Laches the phenomena corresponding to courage, I mean boldness and perseverance, were less formally discussed.   In this dialogue on the other hand, what was there worked out more circumstantially, is here brought forward in a shorter and less direct form.   I speak of the proposition, that it is not by subdivision of the *object* that particular virtues can be defined, but that in the case of each and every one, we come back to the good as its sole and exclusive object.   Now as regards the particular mode of stating the idea, it is only a deceptive appearance, though one which might haunt the minds of many readers, which, in this dialogue as well as in the Laches, would lead one to believe that Plato has only gone sceptically to work.   For the view in which he gives to the one and indivisible virtue the title of discretion, is sufficiently shewn, even previously to that sceptical investigation, where he lays it down as the real health of the mind, and, in another passage, makes even Critias coincide in this position with great emphasis.   Whoever then further connects with this the general proposition : no man can be discreet without *knowing* as a consequence of it, and also what Socrates allows to pass from Critias concerning self-knowledge, it is impossible that after combining the Laches and the Protagoras with this dialogue, he should continue in doubt as to Plato's opinion.   And we would moreover leave it for the decision of readers who have thus arrived at a perfect understanding of the subject, whether setting aside the trifling advantages which this translation of ours of the Greek sophrosyne by the word *besonnenheit*, may have obtained in consequence of our former application of it in the Protagoras, Plato's idea could be expressed more appropriately in our language than by this term. That of *moderation* (Mâssigung), as it was translated by Cicero, in which he seems to have had Aristotle in his mind more than Plato, is certainly not to be used at all.

Socrates' transition from the one explanation, that discretion is self-knowledge, to the other that it is knowledge of knowledge and ignorance, might perhaps at first sight appear forced and sophistical. But if self-knowledge is knowledge of perfection and imperfection, of virtue or its opposite, and if virtue itself is a knowledge, which, rightly understood, must certainly be pre-supposed, and which Plato only ceased to repeat when the further repetition of it would have been tedious; then, certainly, self-knowledge is a knowledge conversant about knowledge or ignorance. And it is simply by means of this transition, and of the way in which this investigation prefaces the separation of the dialectic from the ethical, that the investigation of the particular notion of discretion is connected with the more general one of the nature of morals, which pervades all these dialogues, and the progress of which, moreover, is the reason why the Charmides has its place rightly assigned after the Laches. For the difference between the good and pleasure is here at once pre-supposed as recognised and granted, the required unity of knowledge and action in the province of ethics is brought nearer by the inquiry into the operation of virtue as separate and distinct from virtue itself, and above all the distinction between that higher species of knowledge, and that which is particular and empirical, is further carried out. And at the conclusion not only is the instance of the prophet repeated connectedly with the Laches, but is further outbidden by an instance of one who knows all from all times, and judges of all who know, so that the distinction between practical and technical knowledge can escape no one. Moreover the distinction taken between the knowledge *that* one knows, and the knowledge of *what* one knows, the complete difference of knowledge from perception with reference to its power of making itself its own object, and the hints given as to the relative and absolute, are very remarkable as leading notices in the work.

The fact, that all these general elucidations are disguised under apparent attempts to discover yet new explanations of the idea of discretion, is a peculiarity which to a certain degree already assimilates the Charmides in point of execution to the artificiality of the works of the second period ; while by the more enlarged and more perfectly conceived problem relative to the definition of knowledge, it prepares the way more than anything that has preceded, not only for the Parmenides, but also for the Theætetus, and again starts from the apparent separation of the theoretical from the practical, which strikes us in the Protagoras and Parmenides. Any one not satisfied with the evident allusions to the Protagoras, must at all events be convinced by this connection that the Laches and Charmides do certainly belong to this place. For otherwise it would be natural enough, to consider these smaller expositions as exercises and introductions preparatory to those larger ones of justice in the Books of the Republic. But even supposing this to be the case, still, in the first place, a corresponding exposition of wisdom would be wanting; and in the next, we may add, that that larger work evidently stands upon a different basis from these smaller ones with reference to the ethical ideas. Moreover the reader who has but rightly understood the nature of morality, as it is given in the present series, will not look in vain for proper expositions of justice and wisdom, but both may be constructed after Plato's own mind out of what is brought forward in the Laches and Charmides.

Some quite peculiar circumstance there certainly is attaching to that one explanation of discretion here advanced, which makes it consist in every one doing his own business. And even supposing that some of the sophists perhaps explained it thus, in order to give to this virtue quite a different meaning as applied to the governing and the governed: still this is not sufficient, nor is it indicated in such a manner as to justify the conclusion that it was Plato's object to refute this view. On the contrary, whoever observes the facility with which this explanation is again given up, and to the peculiarly satirical emphasis with which Socrates announces that it comes from Critias, will see that some particular allusion must be here concealed, and will hardly be able to refrain from thinking of personal relations of Critias, whether it be that in his challenges to Plato relative to the undertaking of public affairs he appealed to such arguments, or that in his notorious attempt to dissuade Socrates from teaching, he may have availed himself of a similar principle, which Plato here covers with ridicule as in itself perfectly indefinite. This would coincide very well with the probable period of the composition of the dialogue, which may be conveniently placed in the anarchy, for after the death of Critias such an allusion would be no longer in the spirit of Plato, so we should have to look already for an apologetic purpose in it. The character of Charmides is strikingly the same as Xenophon represents it, so that this comparison is no slight voucher for the imitative truth of our Author.

VI. EUTHYPHRO.

As an investigation into the idea of piety, which is likewise brought forward in the Protagoras as one of the parts of virtue, the Euthyphro connects itself with that dialogue. But when compared with the Laches and Charmides, it appears, however, in the light of a very subordinate piece, because not only does its imperfect dress stand in very disadvantageous contrast with the richness and ornament which characterize these dialogues, but even its internal substance, when compared with what we find in them, does not acquit itself much better. For in the Euthyphro we can neither point to a progressive connection of the most general ethical ideas, nor, if we go no further than the particular notion which constitutes the immediate object of the investigation, are those indirect indications to be found which make the attentive reader sufficiently well acquainted with the views of the composer ; but it is clear at once, and upon the face of the work, that the object in view is as limited as the mode of treating the argument is sceptical. Now the fact that so essential an element in the formation peculiar to the Platonic dialogues is here wanting, might fairly excite a suspicion that the present dialogue is one

of those which are to be denied a place among the works
of Plato; and this suspicion is strengthened by many
peculiarities in the execution which, instead of the already
approved and finished master, betray a not unsuccessful,
and therefore complacently consequentializing imitator,
eager to push to extremes the moderate acquisition of a
little dialectics and a somewhat superficial irony. Meanwhile, the rejection of this suspicion depends upon the
validity of the following grounds. Firstly, the dialectic
exercise contained in the Euthyphro, though not so comprehensive as that in the Charmides, is no less a natural
offset from the Protagoras than, in itself, an approximation to, and preparation for, the Parmenides. This holds
especially with regard to the development of the distinction
between what indicates the nature of an idea, or only one
of its relations, as well as with regard to the origin of
that usage of language which Plato observes throughout
in the sequel to mark this distinction. Moreover, in the
remaining works of Plato, the notion of piety is cancelled
out of the list of the four cardinal virtues, with which,
in the Protagoras, it is still associated, and in such a
manner that a particular notice on the subject is altogether necessary, and, if it were not to be found, must have
been supposed lost. Later dialogues do indeed contain
some positive expressions as to the nature of piety, and
the relation in which it stands to those virtues; but
in our author what is covert always precedes what is open
and undisguised; and even these expressions are immediately connected with the merely negativing result of
the Euthyphro. Lastly, it must be taken into consideration that this dialogue was unquestionably written between
the accusation and condemnation of Socrates, and that,
under these circumstances, Plato could hardly avoid

combining with the object of dialectically investigating the notion of piety, that of defending his master in his own peculiar manner, connected as the charge against him was with this very subject. Nay, it might be, that the more pressing the circumstances, the more easily this apologetic purpose would so far swallow up the original ethico-dialectic one, that Plato neglected to introduce explanatory hints into the sceptical discussion in his usual manner, without, however, our being able to say that he is untrue to, or that he has completely renounced himself. Thus with this undeniable complication of purposes, the alleged and unquestionable deficiencies of the little work may be explained from the urgency of the endeavour to exhibit, as far as might be possible, the common ideas in their nakedness, and the haste, it would seem, of the composition—so far at least—that as we have no traces of any follower of Socrates who composed and wrote in so Platonic a style as that exhibited in this work, and the piece can hardly be fixed in the later times of the regular imitators, I still would never venture to pronounce sentence of condemnation decisively upon it.

If, therefore, we continue to regard this dialogue as Platonic, it may be added, that while it has indeed much of the character of an occasional piece from the preponderance of the subordinate purpose, it cannot without unfairness be excluded from the list of those which connect themselves with the Protagoras, in which it is probable, indeed, that it would have filled its place more worthily without the references to Socrates, though still, if allowed a certain degree of indulgence, it may certainly maintain it.

The introduction of Euthyphro as the interlocutor is quite in the style of the Laches, in which dialogue also Socrates has to do with persons eminently skilled in the subject under discussion. Now this man was, as is manifest from some of his own expressions, a very well-known and somewhat ridiculous personage—a prophet, as it would seem, and one who professed himself especially knowing in matters relating to the gods, and who boldly defended the orthodox ideas taken from the old theological poets. One Euthyphro, indisputably the same as this, appears also in the Cratylus of Plato. The idea, then, of bringing this person into contact with Socrates, while the process against the latter was actually going on, and to exhibit him in contrast with the philosopher, by means of the piece of immorality which his zeal for piety had occasioned him to commit, was one by no means unworthy of Plato. The action brought by Euthyphro against his father, bears pretty much the stamp of a real occurrence, though it might be transferred from other times or persons. The manner, moreover, in which it is discussed, may be almost compared with the story of the sickle-spear in the Laches ; only that the suit in the Euthyphro has a far closer connection with the subject, and that neither its greater prolixity, nor the frequent recurrence to it, when the unquestionable apologetic reference is taken into consideration, can be viewed in the light of a fault.

VII. PARMENIDES.

WHO knows not how in former times the Parmenides was by many contemplated at an awful distance as a gloomy sanctuary concealing treasures of the most exalted wisdom, and those accessible only to a few? But after this fancy, however natural it might be, had been though not till lately, set aside, that falsely grounded opinion of exalted wisdom was changed into objections of such a nature, that supposing the correctness of them, the whole only becomes inconceivable in another point of view. Or is it not to be thought inconceivable that a man of Plato's genius and philosophical acuteness should either not have remarked the multiplicity of meanings in the words which involved him in the contradictions which he has accordingly written out for the world, with so much patience and without tracing their solution, or that he should have run his jokes with his still unpractised readers more mischievously than all the Sophists whom he so multifariously attacks, and that he should even have pushed the thing so far as to be in danger of fatiguing the instructed with the performance, or of disgusting them with the intention. To review, preliminarily, these objections and the different explanations of them, and to endeavour to set them aside individually or collectively, might contribute more than anything to render difficult the introduction of the reader into this dialogue, on other accounts sufficiently terrifying to many in many points of view. Hence it may be more advisable to state briefly the view which seems to be the correct one, as it may possibly approve itself sufficiently to give a standard whereby to judge of other opinions.

It is in general supposed that the Parmenides belongs to the later writings of Plato; but as this hypothesis rests upon hardly any other ground except a reluctance to give him the credit of having composed so profound a work in his youth, the reader may as easily admit the opposite assumption, preliminarily and only as hypothesis, and consider the Parmenides as belonging to the Phædrus and Protagoras. For as the Phædrus had only in general inspired and admiringly praised the philosophical impulse and its organ dialectics, while the Protagoras, artfully connecting the external and the internal, had exhibited by examples this philosophical passion and the sophistical pruriency, as well as the methods resulting from each of the two: so the Parmenides also shews itself to be a similar efflux from the Phædrus, inasmuch as it completes in another point of view what the Protagoras had begun, as a supplement to it and counterpart of it. For, in the Protagoras, the philosophical passion is considered as communicative, while in this dialogue it is represented in reference to the independent process of investigation which must precede communication: how, I mean, it looks in its purity to truth alone, and rejecting every collateral point, and all alarm at any result whatever, starts only upon the necessary assumption, that scientific knowledge is possible, and searches for it in well arranged excursions. There is, therefore, no want of opposition taken between the true and the false, but it is shown partly in Zeno, who works onwards to a definite point, the refutation of others, not without a consciousness of the inadmissibility of his weapons—to whose books, at that time generally known, the reader is almost tacitly referred; partly also in Socrates who does not yet go far enough, and from youthful apprehension, still confines himself within too narrow limits. That Plato did not by this intend to imply a censure upon his friend and master, we see, partly from the circumstance that in the earlier dialogues he attributes to him a genuine zeal for dialectics; partly, because in those pieces as well as in this he represents him as only in an earlier and imperfect stage of his philosophical career. Two things, however, may probably be looked for in this indication—on the one side, I mean, a censure upon those Socraticians who only applied themselves to ethics, and who upon that very account considered themselves more genuine scholars of the philosopher ; on the other side hints for those who, overlooking, perhaps, in the Protagoras and the dialogues belonging to it the dialectic purpose and the speculative indications, would confound Plato with the class just mentioned. As then in this opposition, one side is only just indicated, so also is the other verbally set forth only in some particular expressions in the Parmenides, but shown in the main by the quiet manner in which the investigation, from which so many terrific results come out, is brought to a conclusion, and by the strictness of the method pursued in it. Now as regards the examples of philosophical investigations here chosen, the doctrine of correct division of ideas was attempted in the same way in the Protagoras : and it is there satisfactorily shewn why the philosophy of morals is chosen with that view, and every thing reduced to the question of the communicability of virtue. From the same grounds, then, and in the same spirit, in this dialogue in which investigation in the abstract is to be exhibited, the exercise is undertaken upon the doctrine of the mutual connection of ideas, as it is only by such connection, and not by separation, that knowledge can be really extended. And it is perfectly consistent with this, that in this dialogue the philosophy of nature predominates, and the highest question in it, that, namely, of the possibility of the knowledge of things, constitutes the centre-point, around which the whole moves in distant circles. Now it can hardly escape any one's

notice that such coincidence in tendency and inward
form points to the same unaltered state of mind and
to a similar view in the author. And all that I would
regularly maintain is this, that the Parmenides has its
origin in the same aims and youthful method with the
Protagoras; not that Plato constructed it as a counterpart to the Phædrus and Protagoras, with a distinct
consciousness of doing so, which is least of all to be
ascribed to the youthful writer at that time, for now
the youngest writers are often the oldest and most reflecting. We see also in the Parmenides decidedly more
historical knowledge of science than in these two, and a
more multifarious practice in philosophical art; but still
there is a youthfulness in the manner in which these are
brought into view, and put into the mouth of the great
Parmenides himself.

Now the question of the possibility of the knowledge
of things rests on the one side immediately upon that
of the tenability and constancy of ideas, and on their
relation to the objects themselves, and consequently, it
is this point which is chiefly discussed in the first part,
which is indeed something more than an introduction.
But, as we are accustomed to see in the majority of
these dialogues hitherto translated, it is only treated of
indirectly, by a statement of the manifold difficulties
involving the consideration of ideas as something independent of the mutable, and as existing of themselves.
This however is hardly the proper place for deciding
the strange dispute about Plato's peculiar doctrine of
ideas, as this dialogue, accurately taken, can be considered as the seat of that doctrine. Only thus much
appears certain in reference to this dialogue, even if we
only consider the words with which Parmenides con-

cludes the statement of the difficulties which beset the
assumption of ideas independently, that the *substantia-
tion* of ideas, as it is called, is by no means the
matter here in dispute, and which it is the purpose of
Socrates to establish. And what is said elsewhere upon
this subject can only be brought under consideration
in its proper place. For if Plato has been generally
viewed, I do not say improperly, as a precursor of
the sacred writers, he resembles them especially in
this, that it is necessary, in judging of the doctrines
ascribed to him, whether they are his own or not, to
consider every expression in its own proper place, and
in the connection in which it is there found. There
is however much that is remarkable in the examples
under which Parmenides states his doubts, in so far as
they involve a division of ideas, which if not systema-
tically carried out, is at all events very striking. For
he divides them, first, into those which, like the moral
ideas, most easily subject themselves to the faculty of
original conception; secondly, into the physical, the objects of which are the ever recurring creations of nature,
and which therefore appear to be produced only by
observation; thirdly, into those to the objects of which
no independent and constant existence seems to belong,
inasmuch as they signify only parts of universal nature,
or transitory operations of natural powers; and, finally,
into those which represent relations only, and under
which, at last, the idea of knowledge itself is again
brought.

And to the reader who does not overlook this distinguishing character, the notion will scarcely suggest
itself that Plato had in view to contradict any particular theory as to the conception of truth, or the

existence of ideas, whether peculiar to Parmenides or Socrates; but it must be clear to him that Plato's object is generally to draw attention to the difficulties which the susceptibility of distinction does itself oppose to any one who attempts to give a general answer to the question as to what mode of existence or reality must be ascribed to ideas exclusively of the appearances which fall under our observation. But this was far from being the place in which these difficulties were to be solved, and the more so as with the preparations here made for that purpose, a whole series of successive dialogues from the Theætetus upwards is occupied with the question. Even Plato indicates them exactly in the manner which he generally pursues with questions which he is yet unable to solve by means of what he has hitherto imparted or satisfactorily investigated himself, or which suppose more profound views and a higher degree of philosophical perfection than any to which he can yet hope to have brought his readers. Meanwhile, for those who have well considered all up to this point, it will not be difficult to conceive that highest philosophical problem which already at times was haunting Plato's mind as the only means of escaping from these difficulties—we speak of discovering somewhere an original identity of thought and existence, and deriving from it that immediate connexion of man with the intelligible world, expressed preliminarily in the Phædrus by the doctrines there mythically set forth of original contemplation and recollection, connected with which and dependent upon it is a higher state of knowledge, by means of which an eminence is obtained above the subordinate matter of ideas of relation.

As, then, this first part annexes itself to the assertion of Socrates, that there is no art involved in predicating various contradictions of individual real things, but that the only process deserving admiration would be to shew the same of ideas themselves, so also upon this sentiment as upon the hinge of the whole, the second part of the dialogue turns. For Parmenides, after having subjoined to this request of Socrates that he would enter upon the investigation of ideas still further, rules as to the method of pursuing it, allows himself to be persuaded to illustrate these rules by an example, and thus actually to follow out a thesis upon a manifold and exhaustive plan; and with this view he selects the instance of unity—a choice very natural for Parmenides to make, but also considered by Plato as of great importance as regards the whole subject of the dialogue. And he is to shew what are the consequences to unity itself and all besides unity, according as the former is supposed to exist or not to exist. And with this, notwithstanding that he had not pledged himself that such would be the result, he finds himself in the strange predicament, as it were involuntarily, of enunciating manifold contradictions concerning the notion he selected. For the whole investigation separates into four parts, formed by the supposed existence or non-existence of unity, and the consequences which follow for unity itself and all besides, and each of these parts attains to two contradictory results. For while the two investigations, that into the nature of unity and that into all that remains constituting plurality, are worked out in a double series of notions related each to the other, it turns out that to each and every one of these notions none of all these predicates can belong, and then again that two opposite predicates may be applied to all: and in many cases the contradictions are accumulated still more strangely. And those results in general, as well as the detailed proofs in particular of a similar description, have given rise to the belief with many persons that the whole investigation consists of mere sophisms; and with others, who could not believe this of Plato, to the notion, that he intended only to give a proof of false dialectics, or even put into Parmenides' and Zeno's own mouth their own refutation. But to these suppositions the reader who takes a proper comprehensive survey of the whole will certainly refuse his assent. To follow up, however, and elucidate this whole, with the view of making intelligible every point brought forward in it, would be an undertaking not at all appropriate here, and if it should still appear necessary to do so after what may here be said, must at least be spared for another place. But in this the following particulars only can be noticed. First, it must by all means be remembered that Parmenides had expressly recognised the request of Socrates to institute an investigation into the nature of ideas, and that he therefore contemplates, in pursuing that investigation, unity in general, and as an abstract notion. Hence, then, it is not allowable to quit this point of view, though by so doing we might perhaps be enabled more conveniently to explain this or that particular point. It is also self-evident, that, taken in the main, the contradictory results arise chiefly from the different significations of the word *existence* or *being*, consequently from the different conditions under which the notion is brought. And it is by this in particular that the second part is connected in spirit with the first, where otherwise only an extremely loose connection would be perceptible, by the prevalent purpose, I mean, observable, of drawing attention to the different significations of *existence*, and their relation to one another and to ideas. And in this process it cannot indeed be denied, that the idea of unity is considered also according to its own separate potentialities: but this is, first, not an educt from the *idea* of unity; and, secondly, Plato indicates so clearly when this is the case, that neither can the attentive reader go wrong, nor can any one suppose in the writer the intention of deluding by this course. If however, and this cannot be denied, the idea is worked out by such predicates as do not appear applicable at all to an idea, still let it be remembered, that nothing definite had been previously established to determine in what manner an abstraction with no objective existence can be classed among ideas, or what abstraction can be so classed, and that every point is to be essayed, in order, by this dialectic process, to bring the question nearer to a decision. And this indeed would suffice for an explanation as regards the great bulk of the difficulties; the following consideration however may be further added. The most intricate developements, and those most considered as intentionally sophistical, are distinguished by the circumstance, that the train of consequences resulting from them and strictly belonging to the general series might have been discovered by a far easier method, also that nothing peculiar to unity is discovered by probing deeper in the investigation; a fact to which Parmenides himself frequently calls attention. The object therefore for which these particular parts are here, is not the immediate result, but the actual mode of proof, by means of which, as it recurs in the different parts of the investigation, Plato intends, in his own peculiar manner, to draw attention to the nature of certain ideas of relation. It is very profitable to follow this collateral object through all the turnings of the dialogue, and to see how Plato makes way towards it, and how one elucidation always refers to another. That these ideas constituted an important subject of consideration in his mind, and that he held it by all means necessary to put them in a clear point of view, may be seen from a passage in the Charmides, where he speaks of it as an important and difficult matter to investigate, whether any, and what, Ideas exist in reference to themselves alone, or only in relation to others.

Now as regards the particular train of consequences in which we have a comprehensive view of the peculiar properties of unity, it must not be forgotten, that unity is the general form of all ideas alike, which Plato himself sometimes calls unities; and that, accordingly, it is from this dialectic point that the opposition of unity to all not comprised under that term, which would otherwise have no proper keeping, is to be considered, as well as the opposing results in particular. But the different views and hypotheses which co-operate towards establishing this connection, will not be easily followed out by any one to his own satisfaction who does not first compare, with much pains and accuracy, the mutually opposing sections of the investigation with one another, as well as the modes of treating homogeneous points in particular in all the several sections. And the attentive reader will find something eminently remarkable in the attempt made at the end of the first

section, certainly the most ancient in philosophy, to construct knowledge by the reconciliation of antitheses.
But few persons have divined the antiquity of this
method, and will perhaps be disposed to recognize the
mighty dialectical and speculative mind in this slight
attempt, so similar to much that has appeared among
ourselves, sooner than in many theories of Plato properly of more importance. Still more remarkable are
two notions developed in the course of the investigation,
the one in the attempt just noticed, the other where
unity is supposed non-existent—I speak of the idea of
the infinitesimally small in time, or of someting objective existing in it, and of the idea of magnitudes
or spacial repletion without unity. They are, as regards this dialogue, the result of that peculiar manner
in which, in Plato, from the fundamental character of
his philosophy, which some have most unjustly considered to be a confusion of thought with knowledge,
speculation of the more lofty kind is combined with
the dialectic process. The manner in which this notion
of magnitude, if we may so call it, is discovered, and
the way in which, notwithstanding its obstinate resistance to all management, it is nevertheless grasped and
described, appears so deserving of admiration, that it
is difficult to conceive how a philosophical critic, who
deserves in other respects some merit in his exposition
of this dialogue, gives up, not long before this section,
on receiving notice of the subject, as if he were weary
of pursuing further this loose web of sophisms. One
should have thought that a commentator who, even in
the middle, had met with much that had less claim upon
his attention, would at least, on notice given, have
been glad to work to the end through these difficulties,

were it only to reach this remarkable discovery. Above
all, the sincerely earnest reader must be on the watch
beforehand every way, for all conclusions drawn from
the hypothesis of a non-existent unity, to which, as
constituting an indispensable supplementary part, even
Parmenides himself so significantly points. It is not
difficult to adduce still more, though of less importance—but the temptation must be withstood; perhaps
for the reason that many readers, from their own self-
search into and explanation of this investigation, in
which almost every point radiates with the germs of
whole lines of fresh investigations, and each succeeding
one, by reason of the gradually increasing and manifold significancy, admits of a more extended and comprehensive survey of all connected with it, may be
induced, sooner than they would be by deficient information, to share the notion, that this strange piece
of logical art, as far as a similarity can obtain between
philosophical and poetical creations, corresponds to those
imaginative and pregnant compositions, which, under the
modest name of *tales*, represent the inward form of things,
and the true history of the world, with a richness and a
depth which no one can ever be fully conscious of
having fathomed to the bottom; even though perhaps
many readers who go along with their author in
thought and composition, may sometimes discover particular relations which have lain concealed from the
composer himself.

And further, the reason why, in the present work
at all events, as well as in those poetical compositions,
we are not in a condition to come to a perfect understanding of every particular, is grounded upon our
ignorance of many probably existing relations. Who,

for instance, can tell whether many of those points at which we take most offence, do not refer to passages in the books of Zeno? We may divine that something like this is the case to a considerable extent, if we compare the propositions of Zeno still preserved to us with several of the passages in the Parmenides, which seem to us here superfluous and sophistical. It would be a serviceable undertaking, though one that does not belong to this place, to follow out this track further. That Plato respected Zeno very highly as a dialectician, and has here adopted his method, he himself says clearly enough; but it also seems quite as certain that he put no great value upon his genius as a philosopher as exhibited in the work here brought forward. Similarly also, in another place, where he has to deal with the Eleatic philosophers, Zeno is mentioned not independently, but only as connected with Parmenides. How far, then, the notices drawn from the higher province of speculation relate to the philosophy of Parmenides in particular, and whether, for instance, the world as deprived of unity in opposition to that grounded upon and resolving itself into it, is intended to be a fresh illustration and corroboration of the opposition which Parmenides institutes between the world of reason and the world of sense; to decide this accurately we possess, and ever shall possess, too scanty remains of the compositions of the wise Eleatic. For it might be a fallacious process to listen to testimony, since Parmenides is one of those who were earliest misunderstood, and even the means to which we must resort are still in an extremely unproven and imperfect state. Even in Plato himself there is much that will not unite with what is generally assumed from these sources; only that Parmenides is intended to contradict himself by the contradictions in which unity is involved, is a thing not to be thought of. Had Plato at that time had so little respect for him as to allow himself such liberty towards him,—that is, far less than for Protagoras or Gorgias—such a proceeding would certainly have been accompanied by the most wanton display of irony. But whatever value may be put upon certain expressions according to which Plato seems to be dissatisfied with his earlier views of Parmenides, all that can be intended by them, at the most, is that he did not just at first respect him quite so highly as he deserved. It is moreover clear enough that Plato makes Parmenides speak quite in his own spirit, that many particular dialectical strokes are borrowed at once from him, and, consequently, that this whole method does indisputably owe very much to him. And it would certainly be an injustice to look here for Plato's opinion generally upon the system of Parmenides. This work, supposing even we were to assume that Plato, at the time of its composition, had already made up his opinion upon the Eleatic philosophy, is in no degree nor in any part devoted to that object. Much rather is the main point of view on the strength of which Parmenides here comes forward, and for which in fact he conducts the dialogue, that of having been the first to make the attempt to start with dialectics, and thus enter into the province of the higher philosophy.

Plato makes an endeavour, which betrays itself clearly enough, to bring Parmenides historically also into connection with Socrates, and to derive the dialectics which he praises in him from those of the first as well as the

universal founder of the art. Hence his visible endeavour to represent the dialogue as one that actually took
place, and to put its authenticity beyond a doubt. For
otherwise it might have been a matter of perfect indifference to him to be tauntingly asked by an over-curious
critic, whence he could know this dialogue, as Socrates,
after the lapse of so many years, did certainly narrate
nothing of the kind. How far then it was possible for
this conversation, or rather for any meeting whatever of
Socrates with Parmenides to have taken place—upon that
point we cannot, I think, decide upon external grounds.
For there is in point of fact no impossibility in the
time; but the question only is at what time Parmenides was in Athens, and how far reliance is to be placed
upon the assertion that this took place in the eightieth
olympiad. Only thus much is certain, that if it is a fiction
which Plato has here allowed himself, and one moreover
of a description which is at variance with actual facts,
he might in that case either have left the matter as far
as possible obscure and indefinite, or, if he wished to
reduce it to objective certainty, he had greater licences
at his command than the considerably advanced age which
he ascribes to Parmenides; and of these he would have
unhesitatingly availed himself. To what purpose this definite description, if Plato neither knew how the circumstance had taken place, nor had calculated how it might
have taken place? But without reference to truth of fact,
and suggested only by Plato's undeniable endeavour to
gain the dialogue an appearance of historical foundation,
a circumstance is here to be brought into notice, with
regard to which no one yet seems to have entertained
any suspicion, although the general opinion of it tends
to charge Plato with an absurdity of which I should be

sorry to believe him guilty. For who, I would ask, is Cephalus who repeats the dialogue, who are Glaucon and Adimantus whom he meets, and Antipho of whom he is supposed to tell the story?

In Cephalus, first, every one thinks of the son of Lysanias and the father of Lysias, who, like the naturalized resident of that name, had travelled to Athens as a stranger. But the father of Lysias is generally a Syracusan, and this Cephalus comes from home at Clazomenæ. Yet it is difficult to believe that any other is meant. For he who as the intermediate person could bring the dialogue so far in order to repeat it in Plato's presence, and such is the supposition, must have reached an advanced period of old age, and therefore be generally known. And such a man must Cephalus, the father of Lysias, have indisputably been. Whence therefore Clazomenæ comes, let every one decide for himself from the two following cases, which seem the only possible. Either this is a fiction of Plato's; but to what purpose? in order not to make Sicilian men inquire curiously after dialogues of Plato? But that would be a somewhat ponderous and complicated process in order to remedy a more trifling evil, and one that might have been avoided with perfect ease. To introduce, then, men of Clazomenæ, and to think in so doing that on the mention of unity, the reason, and on that of the remainder (all besides unity,) the original plurality of Anaxagoras, was to be suggested to the mind? But, in the first place, this would certainly intrude itself more upon the notice, and, in the next, Cephalus need not on that account be made a Clazomenian, but need only have hospitable acquaintances there. Or Cephalus the Syracusan has, before travelling to Athens, lived a certain period at Clazomenæ, and Plato mentions this with a degree of emphasis as a circumstance not generally known. But this only in passing. The principal question is, who are Glaucon, Adimantus and Antipho? The first two, every one answers, are the well-known brothers of Plato, and Antipho is a half brother of his, not indeed otherwise known, the offspring of a second marriage, mentioned, it must be allowed, no where else except in reference to this dialogue, of his mother Perictione with one Pyrilampes, who could not therefore have been the well-known person of that name, his own uncle and the friend of Pericles. But do these things come even within the range of possibility? For it cannot, notwithstanding the uncertainty which attaches to Cephalus, be meant to be said, that Plato's brothers, in the Republic, when Cephalus appears as a person of advanced age, are young men, and here, at the period of the same Cephalus' arrival at Athens, already settled and ready to promise him their interest. But even supposing Cephalus to have been another of that name far younger, consider the strange circumstance that Plato, in order to prove the authenticity of the dialogue, makes a Cephalus relate it who has himself heard it from Plato's own younger brother; so that Plato might have had it by a far less roundabout process. And the yet much stranger circumstance that a younger brother of Plato should have heard this dialogue immediately, and while still a growing boy, from an ear-witness, whose minion he appears to have been, and, notwithstanding, should be already a man at the time of Socrates' early youth. Whoever considers these things will allow that nothing more irrational can be easily conceived, and that such a plan was calculated to make the meeting, the actual occurence of which Plato wished to warrant, a mere baby tale. Let us therefore without more ado relieve Plato from this half-brother who has been forced upon him, whom even Plutarch and Proclus appropriate to him manifestly only on the ground of this passage of ours ; and let us rather confess that we do not know who Glaucon and Adimantus were, unless perhaps Glaucon the elder and Callæschrus had yet another brother called Adimantus from whom the name was transposed to the younger. But too much already about the outward circumstances of the dialogue, as there is yet something remaining to be said upon the internal matter itself.

The dialogue, I should say, comes to such a strikingly abrupt conclusion, that it might easily be doubted whether this really is the conclusion. For to conclude such a result of the investigation, and at the same time the whole dialogue, only with a simple expression of assent, such as has occurred a hundred times in the dialogue itself, seems, whether we regard it as disproportionate or over simple, entirely unworthy of Plato. Whoever recollects how in the Protagoras also the investigation concluded with a confession of a contradiction prevailing throughout its whole course, will, in this dialogue too, expect in conclusion at least a similar indication of surprise, and an express confession that a still more searching investigation is requisite. How then such a conclusion, supposing it to have been there, could have been lost, it is difficult to conceive; for whoever had worked on through so much that was tiresome would hardly have refused to add the little that was gratifying. There remains, accordingly, scarce any other supposition except that Plato was interrupted for a considerable time by some external circumstances while he was bringing the

dialogue to a termination ; and that perhaps he did not
afterwards subjoin the conclusion, because he already
had in his mind the sketches at least of other dialogues
which were intended to approximate to the same ultimate
point by another method. And that external interruption, if the supposition is to be more accurately made
out, may have been either the flight to Megara, which
followed after the death of Socrates, or even Plato's
first journey, upon which he started from that place.
The last, according to my notion, would be the most
agreeable with probabilities. For even supposing Plato,
and this supposition is of itself hardly credible, to have
composed such a work during the unquiet times in which
Socrates' accusation was prepared and finished, in that
case, nothing could prevent him from giving it the finishing touch at Megara. It is much more probable that
it was composed at Megara, when, during Plato's stay
there, and certainly not without his having exercised
important influence upon it, the school which took its
name from the place, and devoted itself especially to
dialectics, was formed. But if any one, though with the
view of setting up a more plenary defence of the work,
should think to found still more important suppositions
upon the condition in which the end is at present found,
as that, generally, the best part and the right conclusion
are lost, and that otherwise the second part would be
put in connection with the first, and the doctrine of
ideas more accurately defined according to dialectical
investigation, we could not assent to such a view. For
whoever is convinced by the exposition as brought up
to the point at which it ceases, that the Parmenides is
a counterpiece to the Protagoras, though not without the
advancement which is never wanting in the progress from

one work of Plato's to another, will find in the work as
we at present have it, a character perfectly agreeing with
that dialogue, and will have no occasion to look for anything further. But as to the reader who is not convinced
of this, we can only lay before him the following considerations which to the reader yet unacquainted with
Plato can be verified only by the sequel. The difficulties which are here adduced in opposition to every theory
of ideas, are not to be solved in the philosophy of Plato
otherwise than by an accurate comparison of the purer
or higher knowledge with that which is empiric, and
further, by the doctrines of Original Contemplation and
Recollection; subjects, therefore, to the exposition of
which Plato has devoted a series of important dialogues
from the Theætetus upwards. Now if he is to be supposed to have already completed this in the Parmenides,
to what purpose are all these dialogues, every one of
which treats its subject as if, from the very bottom, it
had never been at all explained before? But if the
composition of the Parmenides is to be dated later than
that of these dialogues, the Theætetus, the Meno, and
even, as Tennemann assumes, than the Sophist, what an
unhappy toil it would be for one who knew how to do
better, to propose as riddles what had ceased to be such;
and to repeat with useless obscurity at a later period
what had been said clearly at an earlier? Even the
language is a proof that the place of the Parmenides
is only in the transition to the dialogues of that class,
for, partly of itself, and partly as compared with them,
it shews itself to be technical language still in a state
of earliest infancy, by its unsteady wavering, by the
manner in which it grasps, not always successfully, at
correct expression, and by the fact that it can scarcely

clench the most important distinctions in words. This circumstance occasioned great difficulties in the translation. But there was here no other expedient, unless the spirit of the whole was to be extinguished, and under the appearance of facilitating the understanding of it, the difficulty of doing so infinitely aggravated, there was, I say, no other expedient but that of observing the most accurate fidelity, and of introducing the reader altogether to the simplicity, and, if one may so speak, the helplessness of the growing philosophical language—a process by which alone a translator is prevented from attaching to his author what does not belong to him, and, on the other, his own merit in having seen the truth through all its ambiguities, and himself especially conceived it, is diminished.

APPENDIX TO PART I

I. APOLOGY OF SOCRATES.

In the general Introduction to this exposition of the works of Plato, it has already been said that when any pieces are thrown into this Appendix we are far from intending thereby at once to deny or call in question their Platonic origin. Thus also the Apology of Socrates, at all times loved and admired for the spirit which breathes through it, and the image it presents of calm moral greatness and beauty, is only found in this place because it contents itself with its peculiar object and has no scientific pretensions. The Euthyphro too has indeed an undeniable apologetic reference to the accusation brought against Socrates: but on the other hand its connection with the notions started in the Protagoras gave it a manifest right to be subjoined to that dialogue. The Apology on the contrary, as a purely occasional piece can find no place in the series of the philosophical productions of its author. And there is even one signification in which—let not the reader start—it might indeed be said that it is no work of Plato's. I mean that it is hardly a work of his *thoughts*,—any thing invented and composed by him. For if we attribute to Plato the intention of defending Socrates, we must then first

of all distinguish the times at which he might have
done so, either during his process, or at all events at
some period, how soon or how late is indifferent, after
his condemnation. In the last case then Plato's only
object could have been a defence of the principles and
sentiments of his friend and master. This however,
with one who was so fond of connecting several objects
in one work might very easily have combined with his
scientific purposes, and thus we do really find not only
particular indications of this nature scattered over his
later writings, but we shall soon come to know an
important work, and one closely enough interwoven
with his scientific labours, in which notwithstanding it
is a collateral purpose and one brought out into distinct relief to hold up to the light Socrates' conduct as
an Athenian as well as his political virtue. Now a proceeding of this kind admits of explanation, but Plato
could scarcely find occasion at a later period for a piece
which merely opposes Socrates to his actual accusers.
It must then have been during the process that Plato
composed this speech. But for what purpose? At
all events it is clear that he could do his master no
worse service than by publishing a defence in Socrates'
own name before he had defended himself in court.
For the only effect of such a defence would be to assist
the accusing parties to discover what they were to be
on their guard against and what they might neglect,
and to put the accused into the dilemma of either being
obliged to repeat much or say something else less powerful. Hence then, the more excellent the defence and
the better adapted to the character of Socrates, the
more disadvantageous it would have been to him. But
no one, I suppose, will give any weight to this hypo-

thesis. After the decision which succeeded, finally, Plato might have a twofold purpose, either simply to make the progress of the matter more generally known, and to establish a memorial of it for future times; or to place in the proper light the different parties and the method of the proceeding. Now if we examine what would have been the only reasonable means for accomplishing the latter object, we shall find that a speech not attributed to Socrates but to another advocate could alone furnish them. For the latter could then adduce much of what Socrates would be compelled to omit on account of his character, and show by the work itself that provided only the cause of the accused had been conducted by one not accustomed to despise what many even of noble birth did not despise, it would have taken quite a different course. Were there any ground whatever for an anecdote, a very improbable one it must be confessed, which Diogenes has preserved for us from an insignificant writer, Plato's more natural object would have been to make known what he would himself have said if he had not been prevented. He would then have had an opportunity here for displaying in practice those higher precepts and expedients of language the power of which he had himself been the first to discover; and he certainly would have been able to apply them with great truth and art to that point in the accusation which related to the new gods and the corruption of youth. And in like manner in the name of any other person, he would have retorted with far better effect as much or more upon the accusers of Socrates, and have spoken of his merits in a different tone. On the other hand, in a speech attributed to

Socrates himself but different from that which he actually delivered, Plato could have no other object than to show what Socrates would have voluntarily neglected or involuntarily omitted, and how his defence must have been conducted in order to produce a better effect. Not to mention then that this would have been scarcely possible without renouncing the method of Socrates, it is moreover manifest that the defence which we possess is not contrived in accordance with such a purpose. For after such a speech how should the supplement come in subsequent to the pronunciation of the verdict—a supplement which supposes a result not more favourable than the real one? It therefore only remains to suppose that the sole purpose at the bottom of this piece was to exhibit and preserve the essential points in the actual progress of the cause for those Athenians who were prevented from hearing it, and for the rest of the Hellenes, and for posterity. Are we then to conceive that in such a case and under such circumstances Plato was unable to withstand the temptation of ascribing to Socrates an artificial piece, wrought by himself, perhaps perfectly strange to Socrates, with the exception of the first principles, like a pupil in rhetoric who has an exercise set him? This we should indeed be loath to believe: rather would we assume at once that in a case like this, where nothing of his own was wanted, and he had entirely devoted himself to his friend, and especially so short a time before or after his death as this piece was certainly composed— we would assume, I say, that his departing friend must have been too sacred in his eyes to allow of his disguising him with any ornament however beautiful, and

s

his whole form too spotless and noble to be exhibited in a dress, or otherwise than a divinity, naked and enwrapt in nothing but its native beauty. Neither indeed do we find the case to have been different. For the critic in art who had at the same time undertaken to improve this speech would have found in it much to change. Thus the accusation relating to the seduction of youth is far from being repelled with the solidity with which it would have been possible to do so, and in opposition to the accusation of infidelity towards the ancient gods, the defensive power of the circumstance that Socrates did every thing in the service of Apollo, is far from being made sufficiently prominent; and any reader whose eyes are but half open will discover more weaknesses of this kind not in any way founded upon the spirit of Socrates to such a degree that Plato would have been compelled to imitate them.

Accordingly nothing is more probable than that in this speech we have as true a copy from recollection of the actual defence of Socrates as the practised memory of Plato, and the necessary distinction between a written speech and one negligently delivered, could render possible. But perhaps some one might say; If then Plato, supposing him to have composed this piece, had nevertheless no hand in it but as a scribe, why are we to insist upon this, or whence can we know even that it was Plato himself and no other friend of Socrates who was present? The questioner, if he is otherwise acquainted with the language of Plato, need only be referred to that to perceive how decidedly this defence betrays that it can only have flowed from the pen of Plato. For Socrates here speaks exactly as Plato makes him speak, and as we, according to all that remains to us cannot say that any other of his pupils did make him speak. And so little does this similarity admit of doubt, that on the contrary an observation of some importance may be founded upon it. I mean, whether certain peculiarities in the Platonic dialogue, particularly the fictitious questions and answers introduced into one proposition, and the accumulation and comprehension under some other of several particular propositions in common, often much too enlarged for this subordinate passage, together with the interruptions almost unavoidably ensuing in the construction of the period as begun—whether these, as we find them here so very prevalent, are not properly to be referred to Socrates. They appear in Plato most in those places in which he is particularly Socratic; but they are most frequent and least clear of their accompanying negligences in this dialogue and the following one, which is probably homogeneous with this. And from these considerations taken together a manifest probability arises that these forms of speech were originally copied after Socrates, and consequently are connected with the mimic arts of Plato, who endeavoured to a certain degree to imitate the language also of those whom he introduces, if they had peculiarities otherwise which justified him in so doing. And whoever tries this observation by the different works of Plato, especially according to the arrangement here established, will find it very much confirmed by them. And that other Socraticians did not attempt such an imitation is accounted for on the one hand, from the circumstance that no little art was required to bend to a certain degree these peculiarities of a negligent colloquial style to the laws of written language, and to blend them with the regulated beauty of expression; and on the other, more courage was required to meet a certain share of censure from small critics than Xenophon perhaps possessed. But to enlarge further upon this belongs not to this place.

One circumstance however is yet to be touched upon which might be brought forward against the supposition of this dialogue having come from Plato, and indeed with more plausibility than any other; I mean that it is stripped of the dialogic dress under which Plato produces all his other works, and which is not wanting even in the Menexenus, which otherwise consists in exactly the same manner as this does, of only one speech. Why, therefore, should the defence, which would so easily have admitted of this embellishment, of all the works of Plato alone dispense with it? However convincing, then, this may sound, still the preponderance of all the other arguments is too great to allow it to be sufficient to excite a suspicion; and we reply therefore as follows to the objection. It may be that the dialogic dress had not at that time become quite so much a matter of necessity to Plato as it subsequently did, and this may serve to satisfy those who are inclined to set a great value upon the dress of the Menexenus; or Plato himself separated this defence too far from his other writings to admit of his wishing to subject it to the same law. And then again, it would be in general very unworthy of Plato for us to think of considering the dialogic dress, even in the case of works where it does not penetrate very deep into the principal matter, only as an embellishment capriciously appended; on the contrary it always has a meaning and contributes to the conformation and effect of the whole. Now if this would not have been the case here why should Plato have wished forcibly to introduce it? Especially as it is extremely probable that he wished to hasten as much as possible the publication of this speech, and perhaps considered it not advisable to commit himself at that time to a public opinion as to the result of the case, which, if he had involved the speech in a dialogue it would not have been easy to avoid, or this form would have been utterly empty and unmeaning.

As to the Athenian judicial process in similar cases, we may certainly suppose all that has been contributed from various quarters for the understanding of this piece to be generally known; moreover, the speech itself explains most of what is necessary.

II. CRITO.

I HAVE already observed in the introduction to the preceding "Apology," that the Crito appears to be similarly circumstanced with that piece. For it is possible that this dialogue may not be a work regularly framed by Plato; but one which did actually take place as is here described, which Plato received from the interlocutor with Socrates as accurately as the former could give it, while he himself hardly did more than embellish and reinstate it in the well-known language of Socrates, ornamenting the beginning and the end, and perhaps filling up here and there when necessary. This view rests upon exactly similar grounds with those which have been already explained in considering the

Apology. For in this dialogue also there is the same entire absence of any philosophical object, and although the immediate occasion invited to the most important investigations into the nature of right, law, and compact, which certainly engaged Plato's attention at all times, these subjects are treated of so exclusively and solely with reference to the existing circumstances, that we easily see that the minds of the interlocutors, if the dialogue was really held, were exclusively filled with these; and if it is to be considered as a work of Plato's, in the composition of which facts had no influence, then we must attribute to it the character of a perfectly occasional piece. It is indeed expressly shewn that philosophizing has no place in it, as the particular principles are only laid down as granted without any investigation, and with reference indeed to old dialogues, but by no means such as could be sought for in other writings of Plato, a process which, in those works of Plato which have a philosophical meaning is perfectly unheard of. And what may be thought to have been the occasion of such an accidental piece, if we regard it as a work exclusively Plato's own? For in point of meaning, nothing is here given which was not already contained in the Apology. Or, if we are to believe that Plato intended to make known the fact that the friends of Socrates wished to assist Socrates to escape, but that he would not allow them to do so, and that all the rest with the exception of this historical foundation is his own invention, in that case, on closer consideration, only about the first half of the dialogue would be intelligible, the latter half not. For, on the one hand, there is nothing remarkable in this circumstance, but the manner in which it takes place; inasmuch as the result might be at once foreseen from the defence, and therefore the friends of Socrates were justified even by that, supposing them not to have undertaken anything of the kind. And on the other hand the dialogue itself is constituted exactly as one that actually took place, subject to a certain degree to chance circumstances as one of that description always is, must be constituted, but not at all like one composed with an object, or into which art in any way enters. For dialogues of the former class may easily start away from a thought after barely alluding to it, or even proceed to confirm by frequent repetition what might have been said at once definitely and expressly; while those of the latter can neither return to the same point, without addition and advancement, nor excite expectations which they do not satisfy. Now the Crito is clearly framed upon the former plan, and although the idea is in the main worked out beautifully and clearly, still in the details the connected parts are often loosely joined, uselessly interrupted, and again negligently taken up, exactly as we might suppose, generally, that none of the deficiencies as peculiar to a dialogue actually held and only told again, would be altogether wanting.

In this manner, therefore, I still hold it possible that Plato may have composed this dialogue, and think that so immediately after the death of Socrates, he may have had the same conscientious purpose in the publication of it, as in that of the " Apology". Not before a remote period, that into which, according to my views, the Phædon falls, could Plato even in what relates to the death of Socrates, pass from literal accuracy to a greater latitude in treating of those subjects, and interweave them with an independent work of art, designed for philosophical exposition. I at all events, will still endeavour, by means of this view, to reserve this dialogue for Plato, until a somewhat more able criticism than has hitherto appeared completely disproves its claims to be considered so. Two reasons in particular incline me to this opinion, first, the language, against which Ast brings no important objection, and which quite as clearly as that in the "Apology" unites all the peculiarities of the first period of the Platonic writings. And, secondly, the very strictness with which the composer confines himself to the particular circumstance which is the subject of the dialogue, and here abstains from all admixture of investigation into the first principles, an act of abstinence which was certainly not possible to small philosophers like the other Socraticians, but only to so distinguished a man, —an act by which he does at the same time expressly remove this piece out of the list of the others. Hence also the strong emphasis with which the announcement is made, that to those who do not start from the same moral principles, all deliberation in common is impossible, an emphasis to be ascribed rather to Plato, in order to explain the style and method of the dialogue, than to Socrates, who would hardly have needed it toward his friend Crito, who could only differ from him in consequences, and not in first principles.

Little value is to be put upon the story of Diogenes that Æschines was actually the interlocutor, and that Plato from dislike to him intruded Crito in that character. It is, however, very possible, that Plato allows himself in this particular to deviate from fact, and has chosen Crito because he was best secured by his age and condition against unpleasant consequences, probably,

also, died soon after the death of Socrates. We see at
all events an endeavour to avoid injuring any Athenian
friend of Socrates in the fact, that Plato only mentions
by name foreigners as having any share in the plot of
abduction. So that the circumstance is probably founded
in fact, and only the cause of it, by whom who can tell?
fictitiously superadded.

III. ION.

SOCRATES proves two things to the Athenian rhapsodist: First, that if his business of interpretation and
criticism is a science or an art, it must not confine itself
to one poet, but extend over all, because the objects are
the same in all, and the whole art of poetry one and
indivisible. Secondly, that it does not belong to the
rhapsodist generally to judge of the poet, but that this
can only be done in reference to every particular passage
by one who is acquainted, as an artist and adept, with
what is in every instance described in those passages.
Now it will be at once manifest to every reader that
it cannot have been Plato's ultimate object to put a
rhapsodist to shame in such a manner. For even they
who can never discover any purpose in Plato's writings
except, in a far too limited sense, that which is directed
towards common life and the improvement of it, cannot
overlook the circumstance that those rhapsodists, a
somewhat subordinate class of artists, who were for the
most part concerned only with the lower ranks of the
people, enjoyed no such influence upon the morals and

T

cultivation of the youth of a higher rank, that Plato should have made them an object of his notice and a butt of his irony. Nay, viewed even as a genuine Socratic dialogue, we must still look for some other and more remote purpose in it for which Socrates committed himself so far with such a man. It was therefore very natural, certainly, from the precise manner in which they refer continually from the rhapsodist to the poet, and from many very definite allusions to the Phædrus, to fall into the supposition that the rhapsodist is only to be looked upon as the shell, and that what is here said of the art of poetry must be considered to be the real kernel of the dialogue. We find also here, and that most distinctly announced, the notion of inspiration in opposition to art. But not only is this proposition brought forward in so direct a form, that it could scarcely for that very reason be considered the main purpose of the dialogue to maintain it, but it returns upon us in almost the same words as we found in the Phædrus, neither more deeply grounded, as it might be inferred from the same principles that poetry is but an artless craft, nor more definitely enunciated, so that it might in any degree be explained why, in that dialogue, art was cursorily attributed to the tragedians, and in this manner the two ideas, that of art and divine inspiration, be combined with one another. As then nothing of the kind is here to be found, how should a dialogue have been expressly written for the purpose of endowing a mere repetition of what had been already said with a few fresh examples. On the contrary, it is clear, upon more accurate consideration, that a contradiction exists in what those two main propositions about the art of poetry enunciate. For it is supposed, first,

that the art is one and indivisible; then the principle
is set up that every art is one by reason of its object,
and it is lastly notified that poetry has many objects
distinct from one another, according to which it certainly would not in that case be one.   This is upon the
whole so very much in the Platonic manner, to lead from
one proposition over to its opposite, that whoever has
remarked the gradual transition will certainly look at once
for more accurate advices upon the nature of the art
of poetry, by which alone this contradiction may be
solved, as the real object and purpose of the dialogue.
Now for him who searches carefully, there do indeed
exist in it something like the following; that the proposed object is by no means an object of the poet in
the sense in which it is his who deals with it for a
certain end according to the rules of art, but that the
principle of unity in the art of poetry must be looked for
in something else; and that the work of the poet exercises
a creative influence in the minds of the readers.   But,
first, there is a greater want of any kind of instruction
for pursuing these notices further than can be well excused, and then both they, and the consequences which
might be drawn from them, for the separation and subdivision of the arts generally, have been already quite
as clearly enunciated in the Phædrus, and certainly placed
upon a better and more dialectic foundation; so that the
dialogue does nothing for them, further than investigate
them in disconnection with the principles on which they
rest; a process which can never be of any but the very
slightest use.   Hence the question naturally upon this
presents itself, what the Ion is to do placed *after* the
Phædrus, and yet no one who compares the similar passages in the two, can conceive a wish to change the order.

For, compare as we will, the thing always assumes the appearance of the Ion having had the Phædrus in view, and not the Phædrus the Ion. Add to this, that what might lead the reader to consider the notices to which we just now alluded as the main object of the piece, is placed too much in the shade. For art is regarded almost entirely from the point of view alone that it supposes a knowledge, of its object, whereby it is distinguished from artless handicraft, but not from that which presents it as endeavouring to produce a work by means of that knowledge, whereby it disconnects itself from pure science. This latter point is touched upon in a cursory manner only, and never accompanied by a hint of the kind which in the Protagoras and its family, and even so early as in the Lysis, marked out the way with so much distinctness. And this can be neither attributed to the nature of the dress in which the dialogue is put, as it expressly ascribes the same work to the rhapsodist and the poet; nor does this confusion of the unities of the object and the work wear the appearance of purpose sufficiently to make it without going further, a competent guide. And since the conclusion comes round again, and considers the rhapsodist simply, without containing even a hint respecting the true view, we are almost compelled, from the obscurity and deficiency of the execution, to reject again the only tenable theory contained in the work.

And the same difficulties present themselves, when we consider closely, and compare particular passages in reference to subject and arrangement, as well as execution and language; for many details are so much in the peculiar spirit of Plato and in his most genuine

method, that we think we certainly recognize him in
them alone ; and then again we come sometimes upon
weaknesses such as we could scarcely ascribe to him in
his earliest stages, sometimes upon faulty resemblances
to other passages which have completely the appearance of unfortunate imitations. The annotations will
show this more accurately, as points of that kind can
be made manifest and judged of only by considering
them in the particular place where they occur. While,
then, as we contemplate this dialogue, our judgment
is thus drawn from one side to the other, and the
balance wavers unsteadily without giving a decisive kick,
two distinct theories spontaneously arise, between which
it may not be very easy to make or to keep a determined choice. For either one of Plato's pupils may
have composed the dialogue after a hasty sketch of his
master, in which some particular passages were worked
out more fully than others, or at least taking Plato's
hints and expressions as guides, whence the obscure
arrangement of the whole, as well as the various execution of the details, is satisfactorily explained : or this
dialogue does indeed come from Plato, but only as an
imperfectly executed essay, which had scarcely had the
correction of the finishing hand. The only period in
which it can claim to have been composed must be as
early as possible after the Phædrus ; and it can be
viewed only as the first essay towards the mode of treating the dialogue commenced subsequently to this work,
in which the development of details resembles the composition of the whole. But whether in this case the Ion
is to be considered a kind of prelude to some greater
work of Plato which remained unexecuted, upon the
nature of the Art of Poetry, or whether it had nothing

in view beyond a playful and polemic extension of certain sentiments expressed in the Phædrus—to attempt
to decide this further, in the present uncertainty of the
case, might be hazardous. Sooner might one be able
to maintain that the bringing out and publication
of the work were, not to say unintentional, such as
Zeno complains of in the Parmenides, but hastened
by some seductive cause or other from without. This,
since no trace of external circumstances can be found
in it, might perhaps most naturally have been that
pretty, though like a pet, somewhat spoiled and
abused comparison with the loadstone, from fondness
for which, in order to bring it on fresh and shining,
Plato may on the one hand have at that time finished
off this little exercise more hastily than would otherwise have been done, without expending any particular pains upon every particular, and on the other,
perhaps, not have been disposed to withhold the publication of it, if he did not otherwise lay any particular value upon the main subject. But even this
comparison would have found a place so appropriately
in the Phædrus, where the dependency of different
men upon different gods, and the attractions to love
thence resulting, were under discussion, that it were to
be wished Plato had discovered it at that time, and
by that means perhaps spared us this ambiguous Ion.
In any case this little dialogue, betraying as it does
so many suspicious features, and devoid of any particular philosophical tendency, could hardly lay claim
to any other place but this which we assign to it.

SUPPLEMENT.

IT is not without mature reflection that I leave this introduction to stand in the main as it was originally written ; for it does not seem to me good to extinguish in a later edition all traces of how circumspectly, and turning every thing to the best, I have gone to work with those dialogues ascribed to Plato which appeared to me at first suspicious, that my method of proceeding might be the less liable to be confounded, by attentive readers at least, with a frivolous and precipitate criticism coming in after the thing was decided upon. As for the rest, every reader who compares the annotations with the introduction will remark that I give more space to the grounds of suspicion than to the defence, which last however I thought it incumbent upon me to investigate in the case of a work which, with all its weaknesses, is not entirely without a Platonic tone ; and even now I re-frain from cancelling that defence, as it may pave the way towards explaining what is unquestionably Platonic in detail, supposing the work itself to be condemned as not genuine. But Bekker marks this and the follow-ing dialogues more decisively as ungenuine, and, in so doing, has my full assent.

IV. THE LESSER HIPPIAS.

THIS dialogue has a great similarity to the Ion, considered as well in itself and its whole design, as any one must see on a comparison of the two, as in reference to the ambiguity of its Platonic origin. For in the Hippias also we not only find combined with much that is genuinely Platonic so much that is suspicious, that one side might easily balance the other, but also in point of peculiar character each looks so like what we meet with in that dialogue that the same view which rejects or adopts the one must draw down a like sentence upon the other. For as regards, first of all, the subject-matter and what is essential in the form, each is not only worthy of the remaining works of Plato hitherto laid before the reader, but also in accurate agreement with them. The two positions which are immediately adduced, that, first, the man who is right and the man who is wrong in any matter is one and the same, namely he who knows something of it; and that again which in itself I can by no means consider, as Ast does, unsocratic, which maintains that he who errs intentionally in all things is better than he who errs unintentionally and without his knowledge;—these propositions are adduced in such a manner from the particular Homeric case, and the whole discussion so manifestly intended to draw attention to the distinction between the theoretical and the practical, consequently to the nature of the will and the moral faculty, and at the same time to point out in what sense alone virtue can be called a knowledge, that in this no one can mistake the whole style of the earlier Platonic

method of philosophizing. In like manner, especially
in the development of the second position, the gradual
transition to the opposite is so entirely in accordance
with the maxims in the Phædrus, that the spirit and
earlier period of the philosopher appears in this distinctly prominent This then supposed, the final object
of the dialogue is so similar to that of the Protagoras,
that it is impossible not to ask what is the order of
the two dialogues and what relation they have to one
another, if they are both to be established as coming
from Plato? Now if the Hippias was written after the
Protagoras, then some point ought to appear further developed or more distinctly set forth in the former than
in the latter. But we cannot discover this to be the
case : for it might indeed appear that the first part
must bring an attentive reader, advancing in his conclusions beyond the letter of what he reads, sooner than
the Protagoras could do, to certainty as to what, if
Virtue is a knowledge, is to be the object of this knowledge, namely, the Good. But in the Hippias this investigation is by no means carried forward from the
point at which it had stopped in the Protagoras ; but
it is introduced quite in a different manner, and in
both conducted negatively only.   For in the Protagoras it is only cursorily that the proposition, that
pleasure is the object of moral knowledge, is reduced
to a contradiction; in the Hippias it is argued against
it, that Virtue, in so far as it is a knowledge, is not
the knowledge of the object with which it is concerned
from time to time.   Now the fact that many persons
will find it easier to discover the positive conclusion
in the Hippias, can prove nothing in favour of the
later composition of that dialogue.   On the contrary,

it is manifest that Plato was very well satisfied with the course pursued in the Protagoras, as in the little dialogues that follow he advances so immediately upon the conclusions there drawn; and the entire idea of the communicability of Virtue is further preserved in a long series which we have before us, and is even far more intimately connected there with the whole philosophy of Plato than the somewhat partial though perhaps more purely Socratic treatment of it in the Hippias. Hence this dialogue, if it is placed after the Protagoras, a position which it always occupies, must ever interrupt the natural progression. Moreover we find neither in the Hippias any reference whatever to the Protagoras, nor in any of the appendages to the latter, any to the Hippias. And this view is quite as little confirmed by the proposition worked out in the second part of our dialogue, which maintains that the good man errs intentionally and only the bad man unintentionally. For if the Hippias were a supplement to the Protagoras this ought manifestly to have been brought into connection with the supposition there advanced, that no man errs intentionally. Now it is indeed true that to the proposition in the Hippias such a turn is given that it is inferred that if any man errs intentionally it must be the good man, when it seems to be supposed that more probably no man errs intentionally: but this would have been brought out far more prominently if it had been written by Plato in reference to the Protagoras. Hence we are always far more tempted to entertain the notion that the hypothesis in the Protagoras might be laid down naked and unsupported as it is, partly in reliance upon this position already worked out in the Hippias; therefore nothing now remains but

to place the Hippias before the Protagoras, and to regard it as the first attempt to bring forward those ideas
upon the nature of virtue in the well known and indirect method; but an attempt which did not seem to
have been sufficiently successful, and from that cause
occasioned that larger and more beautiful work. Now
it is true that all the testing of spirit and method interwoven into it, with all immediately dependent thereupon would be an addition perfectly new, but then it
is also very conceivable that something of the kind must
have occurred to Plato when he wished to improve and
discuss anew a subject already treated of. And this
view might even be brought to a higher degree of probability, if it was more accurately shown how some kind
of germ, though mostly in an extremely imperfect state,
of every thing else contained in the Protagoras may be
found in the Hippias, whether we look to the subject-
matter, or to the different modes of treating it. As
then this is the most favourable view which may be taken
of the work, and yet supposing it true, the Hippias
appears to a certain degree supported by the Protagoras, in no case could any other place be assigned it
except in this appendix.

But when details come to be more accurately investigated, this favourable view wanes again, and a
variety of doubts arise as to whether this dialogue can
in fact be the work of Plato at all. These doubts
do indeed arise immediately and at first sight only on
consideration of the dress in which the dialogue appears.
For, first, there is much here so awkward that we can
hardly attribute it to Plato, and then, in the whole
conversation about Hippias' olympic exhibition, the irony
upon the sophists is severed from the remaining subject-

matter of the dialogue in a way not to be found in Plato elsewhere; and again, the variations in the manner of the dialogue are so pointlessly introduced, that it seems scarcely possible that Plato should have so applied them even for the first time. But when once the reader's attention is taken by these particulars, he will then be led to view more in this dialogue with a suspicious eye. Many, for example, of the unquestionable resemblances to the Protagoras are open to the suspicion of imitation, when we consider that in that dialogue they arise out of the additional subject-matter not found in the Hippias, while in the Hippias they furnish only unmeaning ornament. And again, the manner particularly in which the interlocutors start with Homer looks like an expedient of some pupil unacquainted with those lyric poets, more valued by Plato; as also the complaint that it is impossible now to ask the Poet what he meant by the sentiment, is an echo of that in the Protagoras. Even Hippias seems severed away from among the personages of that dialogue to be the principal one here only for good luck, and without any particular reason, such as we can most generally produce in other dialogues. Nay more, whoever once looks closely at the whole dialogue in this light, the example it affords of the practice of dialectics, will appear to him of a remarkable kind; sometimes timid, sometimes awkward, and almost only resembling the Ion. So that many persons might easily be led to consider it best to apply to the Hippias also the same theory as to the Ion; reserving, that is, to Plato, his undeniable property in the first invention and arrangement; and recognising in the rest the after-work of some pains-taking and pretty intelligent pupil, destitute of the spirit and taste of his master. Hence Bekker has, in my opinion, done quite right in at once ascribing this dialogue also to an unknown composer; who, it is extremely probable, might be one and the same person with the composer of the Ion. On the other hand however, others may regard it as a preponderant argument in favour of the genuineness of this dialogue, that Aristotle quotes it not indeed under the name of Plato, but still just as he will frequently quote other decided works of his teacher. For to say in general that in investigations as to the genuineness of Platonic dialogues no regard is to be paid to the quotations of Aristotle—this is an answer which I would not at all events now make. But this quotation does indeed properly show only that Aristotle knew our dialogue, but does not decide that he ascribed it to Plato.

V. HIPPARCHUS.

It was not until after the exercise of long and complex consideration, that the final resolution was taken of following the example of two great masters in the art of criticism, and striking the Hipparchus out of the list of dialogues belonging to Plato; for the object which an intelligent reader can discover in the dialogue, is Platonic enough. This is, to treat the love of the good, as love of gain, or as self-interest, a notion very closely connected with those well-known propositions that there is nothing useful but the good, and that when men embrace the bad they do so only in error. Hence it might be very easy to believe that it was Plato's

purpose to start also from this idea appertaining
to common life as he did from that of discretion and
courage, and thus to penetrate to the central point of his
philosophy. As it is also the case that this notion
is very well calculated to be projected into that higher
and genuinely ethical theory relating to the love of the
good. This favourable view of the dialogue appears
to be still more corroborated by a passage almost at the
end, pretty clearly alluding to a further extension of the
principles and views brought forward in what has preceded. Accordingly it might be thought that this
dialogue, like the former, is constructed upon a design
of Plato; in such a manner however that only a small
part of it was executed, which might at the most have
borne the same relation to the whole as conceived by
Plato, as in the Lysis the preliminary dialogue does
to the rest. An example the more applicable in the
present case, because it is just from the kind of discussion the idea of the good there receives, that the
transition to an extension of it like that in the Hipparchus may very easily be conceived. Except indeed
that what is there hinted of the idea of the useful
proclaims itself to be far more Platonic than what we
have here in the Hipparchus. The dialogue would then
be a small fragment of which the commencement is wanting, and whose present conclusion must have been added
by a very unskilful hand. For no intelligent reader will
be able to discover in any thought of Plato's, however
cursorily expressed, any ground for believing him capable
of annexing such a termination, nor would any one with
even the slightest insight into the plan of the dialogue
think of concluding or interrupting it thus. And quite
as little is it Plato's custom to break in with such a

beginning; for even the Menon, notwithstanding that he there begins with the main question, is not without its introduction. Meanwhile, even though we would ascribe the beginning and the end of the dialogue to a strange hand, whose mutilation and mischief it may not be very easy to repair, the dialogue itself, we shall find, receives but too little assistance from this favourable view. For, firstly, that connection with other Platonic ideas, which is to save the piece, is never even in the slightest degree forthcoming, and the supposition of the existence of a higher ethical object, or a genuine dialectic treatment, has no foundation in anything but good-nature; since there is no dialogue of Plato, take it where you will, such that, if a portion co-extensive with the Hipparchus were selected or compiled out of it, the main branch to which that portion belongs might not be recognised by any one from infallible tokens. On the contrary, the Hipparchus as we have it, is connected with no other dialogue of Plato whatever, and is so far from being unworthy of its insignificant and unplatonic ending, that the unfavourable prejudice which the two extremities at once excite against it never meets with anything effectually calculated to remove it. For the dialectics which it exhibits are a tedious and lame performance, always revolving upon the same point on which it was fixed at the commencement, without making a single step in advance. And even supposing the plan of the dialogue to have been designed with far more enlarged views, who could think of ascribing to Plato that digression about the Pisistratidæ, with which so much that is not to the purpose is mixed up, and which could not have contributed even in the slightest degree to any conceivable

object whatever of the whole, so that it might rather
be looked upon as a specimen of antiquarian knowledge
produced by some sophist who wished to display his
erudition. But above all the Hipparchus is denounced
by the total absence of that which in the general preface,
with the assent it is hoped of every reader, was mentioned as a test of Platonic dialogues, I mean, the
individualizing of the persons who are interlocutors with
Socrates. For there is not a single trace to be found here,
whether internal or external, which might indicate more
accurately anything about the interlocutor. Nay even
the most external condition, the mention of his name,
is not satisfied by a single notice of it throughout the
dialogue ; so that the prefix of a name to his conversation seems to be only the addition of some old copyist
or perhaps grammarian, who was surprised by this unusual circumstance, while the title of the dialogue seems
only to have come from that digression about the Pisistratidæ. Thus much at least may be easily shown,
that if Plato composed the dialogue, this man was not
called Hipparchus with his consent. For how in such
a case would Socrates even at the very first mention
of the Pisistratid have abstained from noticing the similarity of his name to that of the interlocutor ?
Certainly on no supposition whatever. But the introduction of a quite indefinite and anonymous person is
not only completely at variance with the nature of the
Platonic dialogue, but here in particular it would have
been very easy for him to select extremely appropriate
characters out of those already used by him on other
occasions. So that, every thing duly considered, not
even a plan of Plato's can have been in existence
according to which some other writer has worked ;

for the plan must have contained the first outline, upon which the suitability of the person for the dialogue rested. On the other hand, the marks of an imitator, and a very poor one too, will be pointed out frequently enough in particular instances by the notes, in order to confirm the sentence of rejection from this side also, although even here only some points are indicated while the rest is left to the private observation of the philological reader. The notion from which the dialogue starts could not well be rendered otherwise than by *gewinnsucht* (avarice,) although in common life this word does not bear so bad a signification as the Greek one. For the essential characteristic of eagerly seeking to gain in trifles is more strongly implied in that word than in any other, and moreover the opposition to the ethical notion of love for the good cannot strike the ear too strongly as far as the purpose of the dialogue is concerned.

SUPPLEMENT.

Since I first wrote this introduction, further progress has been made in the case of this and of the following dialogue. That both might fairly be attributed to one and the same composer I had already hinted; and not only has no protest been entered into on the other side with a view to establish their authenticity, but even Boeckh's ingenious opinion, which ascribes both of them together with two other previously excommunicated dialogues to Simon, has not yet been met by a contradiction. For what Ast mentions in opposition to that hypothesis is by no means of much importance. Notwithstanding this I have let my cautious introduction stand as it was, partly that the history of the investigation may remain entire, partly for uniformity's sake. For the same reason also I have left the dialogue in its old place, and in the title, though I am fully of Boeckh's opinion that the original one only mentioned the subject, have nevertheless followed the text of Bekker; and this may be said in anticipation with regard to the next dialogue also.

VI. MINOS.

A FEW words again will suffice to gain assent to the rejection of the Minos as well as the Hipparchus. First, as to the reason for assigning this as its proper place, every reader must see the remarkable similarity between it, and the Hipparchus, which is so great that they seem both of them to have been turned out of the same mould. The beginning breaks in just as violently, and the end breaks off just as weakly and inappropriately, after a new investigation had apparently but just begun. So that even with regard to this sorry performance some persons have quieted themselves with the supposition, that all that is wanting to it is that it should be complete; as if such a design could ever be worked out to any good. Like the Hipparchus, again, the Minos is ornamentally disfigured in the middle by a discussion; not tending at all to advance the main subject, upon a personage of antiquity. And, what is more, this very discussion has equally given the dialogue its name, while the interlocutor is not only divested of all character and circumstance, but also nameless, and can the less be called Minos, as he no where gives even a hint that betrays him to be a stranger, and Minos was never an Athenian name. And further, whoever looks to the tenor and course of the dialogue, will recognize it as unplatonic. Nothing is ever gained by all the abundance of examples, nor anything more accurately defined by comparison with a similar idea; on the contrary, they pass with the most unsocratic carelessness from one idea to another; as from that of certainty to that of opinion, and every thing once said, however useful or tending towards a decision of the question, is always heedlessly abandoned. So that as regards the lame progress of the investigation, the Minos does indeed resemble the Hipparchus, but is far worse; this circumstance, however, excites no presumption against the supposition of an identity of composer, but is sufficiently explained by the nature of the subject. For the purpose of the dialogue generally cannot have been the investigation of an idea, but this is all show and pretence, adopted however, because no Socratic dialogue can exist without it, the main object being only a poor justification of Socrates' prejudice in favour of Crete. But this Minos has in itself a still further and more peculiar mark of spuriousness, in the pre-eminent awkwardness of the language. Instead of either seriously using the words connected with the principal word, by derivation and sound, or playing with them without injury to the investigation, and without sophistical trick, the author, like a clumsy workman, miserably entangles himself between these two processes. Again, the name of the kingly art is put abruptly and without any referential notice as a thing conceded, for the art of statemanship, and that of the kingly man for statesman. This is brought in here out of the later Platonic dialogues, out of which however the composer, whose imitation of Plato is always harping upon the most frequented places, was incapable of drawing anything more profound. But it is unnecessary to add more upon a subject clear as day to any one who will see.

VII. ALCIBIADES II.

ALREADY in ancient times, doubts were entertained of the legitimacy of this dialogue, as some persons attributed it to Xenophon. For this supposition there were indeed no particular grounds, and least of all a decisive similiarity of style; and we might almost say that it must have been at once rejected by every philologist. But it is only the more probable that there was at least some decided reason existing for denying this little work to Plato; though no such testimony is in fact wanting upon which to hang a decisive sentence of rejection. The case however of this dialogue is very different from that of those hitherto rejected or suspected. For many might probably say that it is better in many points of view, but every reader will certainly be obliged to confess that it is also far less Platonic in the thoughts, in the arrangement, and also in the execution. For, first, as regards the subject-matter, the interpreters have at various times congratulated themselves on finding here the true doctrine of Socrates upon the subject of prayer; and this is principally the reason why this place in particular has been assigned to this dialogue, in order to refer back to the Euthyphro and the Apology together. For when we talk of finding in Plato a doctrine of Socrates *pure,* this can only mean mixed up with the doctrine of other wise men, and not perfectly estranged from the manner in which Plato had once for all conceived Socrates. Now how could any one who has understood the hints in the Euthyphro and the spirit of the Apology consider it as a Socratic doctrine that the gods, without any fixed principle, and without even considering what is best, sometimes grant and sometimes deny, nay, that one might suppose the case possible of their offering, what could be dangerous for mankind to receive? or that to meet with death after the performance of brilliant exploits, or live in banishment is a great evil which a man must use great foresight to avoid? On the contrary, this is manifestly a doctrine about the gods of the nature of those of which Socrates says in the Euthyphro, that it is perhaps because he does not consent to anything of the kind, when people maintain such propositions concerning the gods, that he is calumniated and accused of impiety. And the latter view is quite as manifestly at variance with all the notions attributed to Socrates himself in the Apology, not to mention other Platonic dialogues which the composer of this clearly had before him. And again, whether the notion is Socratic or not, how poorly it is worked up. For as long as the supposition remains in existence, of inconsistency and uncertainty in the minds of the gods, of what use can it be to wait to pray for the knowledge of what is best, if they may also refuse this according as they think proper? But if it should be said that Plato by this contradiction wished to negative the former supposition, we answer that there is not at the end any indication of the contradiction, as there is in the Protagoras and other similar cases; nor again, is there in the course of the dialogue any trace of the irony which Plato in such a case never could have omitted to introduce. But more accurately considered, the doctrine of prayer, even according to the intention of the composer, is certainly not to be taken for the main subject of the dialogue, but what we find about the reasonable and unreasonable man, and about the relation of other arts and sciences to that of the good and the best.

Now this doctrine is certainly Platonic enough, and a preliminary discussion of it might fairly find a place here with reference to the dialogues soon to follow. But the manner in which it is brought forward is far from Platonic, or even Socratic; for it was, as we know, Socrates himself who said that all good, private and public, can arise only from virtue, and not conversely; while here the necessity for the knowledge of the best is itself only put upon the ground that otherwise security is endangered, and the state must prosper ill. And in like manner this method of drawing conclusions is neither moral nor scientific enough, as has already appeared up to the present point, and will appear still further in reference to the time of his later works, which manifestly enough our composer had in view. For immediately before the last result quite comes out, that those namely must rule in the state who have attained to the knowledge of the best, Socrates shoots off again to that discussion about prayer, which can however be nothing but the setting of the whole. And even before that the unity of the work is destroyed by the proposition being maintained that ignorance itself may be to a certain degree a good, a proposition which, in default of anything better, leaves still remaining an unsocial, uncultivated, aboriginal kind of life, such as forced itself upon those who misunderstood the cynical principles, of which generally many traces appear here, though not however without contradiction. The arrangement, moreover, as exhibited in the manner in which this theory about the knowledge of the best is connected with that of prayer, must appear to every reader so capricious and so entirely destitute of any art that it is not possible to tax Plato with such a work. And in like manner, as regards the execution, the un-

Platonic character of the work upon the whole is shown in the poverty of Socrates' sentences, the miserable little formulæ with which, in order to tack the dialogue on again as it is slipping through his hands, he asks Alcibiades' opinion of it, the very slight use made of Alcibiades, his want of anything like marked character, the indistinctness in all the by-work, and still more matter that might be brought forward—all this is so prominent, that particular turns, which come out Platonically enough, can excite no doubt whatever of the spuriousness of the dialogue, but only confirm the opinion that the composer had indeed read his master industriously enough, but had penetrated less into his spirit than his language, and been incapable of learning from him his peculiar secrets.

Plato is also thus acquitted cursorily of one of the worst anachronisms of which he can be accused. For it is only necessary to have a general knowledge of the dates, and decide as we may all that is questionable with reference to certain facts connected with this dialogue, it will still be found impossible that Socrates should have conversed with Alcibiades about the death of Archelaus; to say nothing of the fact that in the same dialogue the intention of murdering Pericles is without any necessity lent by supposition to Alcibiades, as if it were possible that the former should have been alive a short time after the death of Archelaus.

END OF THE FIRST PART.

PART II.

I. GORGIAS.

Like all Plato's greater dialogues up to this point laid before the reader, the following has been in regard of his principal meaning almost universally misunderstood. For we must in Plato's case especially regard a mere half apprehension of anything as an entire misunderstanding; since where the reciprocal connexion of the parts and their relation to the whole is missed, all correct insight into particulars, and all fundamental comprehension, is rendered impossible. Now, as in the Phædrus, most critics overlooked too entirely the subject of rhetoric, and for that reason could hardly form a conception of the meaning of the whole; so in the present instance, misled in like manner by a second and unquestionably later title of the dialogue, "Or upon the Art of Speaking," they have laid far too much weight on the topic of rhetoric, and taken every thing else merely for digressions and occasional investigations. Others again have looked to some other particular point, as to the doctrine set forth by Callicles, of the right of the stronger, and to its refutation by Socrates; or to the incidental remarks tending to the degradation of poetry, and have deduced as a result the ingenious notion, that the Gorgias contains the first outlines of that which has been treated, (I cannot tell whether in their opinion later or earlier) more fully in the books of the Republic. An idea which for the very reason that it is more ingenious than they are aware, conveys nothing at all definite as to the peculiar character

Y

of this work. For what important production of Plato
may not be said to contain, rightly understood, such
outlines? So much, however, is clear without further
exposition, that according to any one of these views,
the portion of the whole so prominently brought forward
must appear in very loose connexion with the rest; and
especially the inquiry upon the nature of pleasure, if
one regards the whole in this light, can hardly be viewed
but as an idle supernumerary labour, strangely pieced
on to the rest. But a reader must know little of Plato
who does not speedily detect thus much, that where
anything of this kind occurs, and withal sounding so
deep, this must undoubtedly be the weightiest of all
the topics handled, and the point from which alone everything else can also be understood in its true connexion,
and for that very reason the inner unity of the whole
can be discovered; and regarded in this light, the
Gorgias appears exactly as the work that is to be placed
at the head of the second division of the Platonic writings,
with reference to which our general Introduction maintained, that the dialogues which it includes, occupying
a middle position between the elementary and constructive
ones, treat generally, no longer as the first did, of the
method of philosophy, but of its *object*, aiming at a
complete apprehension and right decision of it. Nor
yet, as the latter, endeavour absolutely to set forth the
two real sciences, Physics and Ethics, but only by preparatory and progressive steps to fix and define them; and
that when considered either singly or in their community
of mutual dependence, they signalize themselves by a
less uniform construction than was in the first division,
but one peculiarly articifial and almost perplexing. Now
let this theory be again expressly brought forward here,

as introductory to this second class of Plato's collective
works, and if it be immediately applied to the dialogue
before us, and its position justified in accordance with
the theory, all will be said that can be adduced beforehand to facilitate its comprehension.

The intuition of the true and perfectly existent, in
other words, of the eternal and unalterable, with which,
as we have seen, every exposition of Plato's philosophy
commenced, has its opposite pole in the equally general,
and to common thought and being no less original
and underived, intuition of the imperfectly existent, ever-
flowing and mutable, which yet holds bound under its
form all action and thought as they can be apprehended
in actual, tangible, reality. Therefore the highest and
most general problem of philosophy is exclusively this—
to apprehend and fix the *essential* in that fleeting chaos,
to display it as the essential and good therein, and so
drawing forth to the full light of consciousness the
apparent contradiction between those two intuitions, to
reconcile it at the same time. This harmonizing process
necessarily resolves itself into two factors, upon whose
different relation to each other rests the difference of
the methods. Setting out from the intuition of the
perfectly existent, to advance in the exposition up to
the semblance, and thus, simultaneously with its solution,
for the first time to awaken and explain the consciousness of this contradiction; this is, in relation to philosophy,
the immediate way of proceeding. On the other hand,
starting from the consciousness of the contradiction as a
thing given, to advance to the primary intuition as the
means of its solution, and to lead up by force of the
very necessity of such a mean towards it, this is the
method which we have named the indirect or mediate,

and which being for many reasons especially suited to one who commences on ethical ground, is here placed by Plato in the centre, as the true mean of connexion and progressive formation from the original intuition, his elementary starting-post, to the constructive exposition, the goal of his systematic conclusion.

Now the relation which, in the sphere of nature, being and semblance or sensation bear to one another in this antithesis, is the same as that which in ethics exists between good, and pleasure or feeling. Therefore the principal object for the second part of Plato's works, and their common problem, will be to show, that science and art cannot be discovered, but only a deceitful semblance of both must be ever predominant, so long as these two are exchanged with each other, being with appearance, and good with pleasure. And advances are made to the solution of this problem naturally in a twofold way; yet without holding each course entirely apart in different writings: on the one hand, namely, that which hitherto had past for science and art is laid bare in its utter worthlessness: on the other, attempts are made, from the very position of knowing and acknowledging that antithesis to develop rightly the essence of science and art and their fundamental outlines. The Gorgias stands at the head of this class, because it rather limits itself, as preparatory, to the former task, than ventures upon the latter; and starting entirely from the ethical side, attacks at both ends the confusion existing herein, fixing on its inmost spirit, as the root, and its openly displayed arrogance as the fruits. The remaining dialogues observe this general distinction, they partly go farther back in the observation of the scientific in mere seeming, partly farther forwards in the idea

of true science, and partly contain other later consequences of what is here first advanced in preparation.

From this point, then, we observe a natural connection
between the two main positions demonstrated to the interlocutors with Socrates in this dialogue. The first, that
their pretensions to the possession of an art properly so
called in their art of speaking are entirely unfounded;
and the second, that they are involved in a profound
mistake in their confusion of the good with the pleasant.
And from the same point likewise the particular manner
in which each is proved, and the arrangement of the
whole, may be explained. For when it is the good that
is under consideration, and the ethical object is predominant, Truth must be considered more in reference to
art than science, if, that is, unity is to be preserved in
the work generally. And moreover, it is art in its most
general and comprehensive form that is here discussed,
for the dialogue embraces every thing connected with it,
from its greatest object, the state, to its least, the embellishment of sensuous existence. Only, as his custom
is, Plato is most fond of using the greater form as the
scheme and representation of the general, and the less,
on the other hand, as an example and illustration of the
greater ; that no one may lose himself, contrary to Plato's
purpose, in the object of the latter, which can never be
anything but a particular. For rhetoric, it is to be
observed, is here used to represent the whole would-be
art of politics, but still only to represent it, and on that
account especially, the introduction to the Protagoras is
here repeated, verbally one might almost say, in order
to draw attention the more certainly, by this change in
the application of the word, to the more closely drawn
variation from the earlier usage of it in that dialogue

and the Phædrus, and further, to what is notwithstanding here more intimated than expounded or systematised, the separation of rhetoric from sophistics, so that the former, regarded as an art under the category of the science of semblance, is to contain whatever refers to the greatest object of all art, the state, while sophistics, as is further explained elsewhere, contain the semblance of communicating with the principles themselves. For though Socrates compares rhetoric only with the administration of justice, and sophistics on the contrary with legislation, the proper sense of this indisputably is, that sophistics are to be supposed to imitate the knowledge of the first principles, from which certainly original composition and conformation proceed, and rhetoric the application of them to a given subject. The case is exactly the same, according to the ancient ideas, with gymnastics, in which outward perfection of the human body is one and the same with the principles of its preservation and production; rhetoric, on the contrary, like politics in the ordinary sense, can never be anything but a remedial art, and applies those principles to a given corruption. Here then, to discover and expose the utter superficiality of the art of speaking, Socrates has to deal with the artists themselves, Gorgias and Polus. The confusion of the pleasant with the good is shown on the other hand in Callicles, whom a similarity in disposition had made a pupil of the other two; and then in the last section in which Socrates recapitulates all that had preceded, both sets of principles are shown to originate in the same one vicious principle, and to point to the same deficiency. Still, as it is not natural to Plato to make any decisive divisions in his general plan, so neither do we here find them in particular in the different sections.

In the first, then, of these, Socrates shows to Gorgias, to whom Plato, we know not with what justice, ascribes at the outset a somewhat limited purpose in his instructions, representing that that purpose tends only to a proper conduct of political life, and in no way to the cultivation of virtue—Socrates proves to him from his own method, and that of the other rhetoricians, that justice and injustice, which nevertheless he is obliged to recognise as the objects of his art, can never be consciously contained in it, or *given* by it. To Polus however the nature and relations of the art of semblance are still more accurately exposed, and he is shown in particular that in the idea of the beautiful, which he still refuses to give up as unmeaning, and persists in assigning to it a province of its own, the commission of injustice proves to be worse than the sufferance of it, which leads immediately to a distinction between the good and the pleasant. Here again the comparison with the Protagoras comes very near, that we may be enabled to see the use which in his indirect investigations Plato makes of the idea of the beautiful; I mean, that he propounds it *formally* and hypothetically only, and, allowing it to be entered as an abstract and exclusive notion, explains dialectically its relation to other homogenous ideas as to which men are substantially agreed. In the Protagoras, now, the apparent supposition of the unity of the good and the pleasant had been made the ground-work of the argument, and there remained therefore no other instrument of distinction, but mediateness or immediateness of the pleasant and unpleasant in *time*, which however can constitute no such instrument, as is so multifariously explained in the Protagoras itself and the dialogues connected with it. In the dialogue with Polus the identity of the good and the pleasant is left less definite, and only the difference between the pleasant and useful more strongly laid down, without its being decidedly assumed (what indeed had been already contradicted in previous dialogues), that this distinction would depend only upon *time*. Whence, as soon as the distinction between the good and the pleasant is made out, the result comes out of itself, that the idea of the useful is immediately connected with the good.

In the conversation with Callicles Socrates' immediate purpose is chiefly to awaken the consciousness of that opposition, and to force his interlocutor to allow that the proposition, that all good is exhausted in the pleasant, has no support in internal consciousness, but that this hypothesis compels us to place yet a further good beyond the sphere of the pleasant. And the attempts which in conjunction with Callicles Socrates makes for accomplishing this end, and which, moreover, are especially remarkable on account of the admixture, the first as yet, of Italian wisdom, might fairly be allowed to constitute in themselves the most ingenious part of this work. I mean, when we further take into consideration the manner in which they fail and the necessity for this failure, which is as nicely calculated as from the whole description of Callicles' character it is beautifully applied, and the way in which Socrates, without having neglected, as he would have been most glad to have done, the excitement of the feeling, guards against the objection of giving himself pliable opponents; and returning to his own peculiar philosophical organ of dialectics, adduces a most important exposition of the true nature of pleasure, that it is something in perpetual flux, and can only be conceived as arising in the transition from one *becoming* state to another. All this is in fact far too ingenious, far too fully worked out and too accurately treated to allow of our considering it as only collateral matter occasionally touched upon, and the political part alone as the peculiar object of the work.

This explanation, as soon as Callicles has admitted a distinction between the pleasant and the good, though only quite in general terms, is followed by the third section, which connects and comprehends the two preceding. In this, then, Socrates, in accordance with the ethical and preparatory nature of the work, concludes with a development resting upon the disposition of the mind, and expressing it mythically. Now if a comparison is to be instituted also between this myth and that in the Phædrus, and there is to a certain extent much resemblance between the two, in so far as even this has been celebrated as a fundamental myth, it must be remembered that the future bears exactly the same relation to the will and to art in this, as the past does to science and knowledge in that, and that in the one as well as the other Time is only an image, while the essential point consists in the consideration of mind divested of personality. And thus Plato is so far from intending to set such a value upon the mythical part as might lead us to take it historically, that he connects it with the popular mythology. Nor, moreover, does the Gorgias leave the subject of love unnoticed, but in this dialogue love is quite as much the guiding principle of the political art, as it is in the Phædrus of the cultivation of the individual; only, as we must at all events suppose, relying upon the investigations pursued in the Lysis, it has already divested itself of its mythical dress.

But we need not pursue particular comparisons of this kind; only we may observe in general that a comparison with what has preceded brings us to our second result: I mean that with reference to the proof which the form may supply, the Gorgias not only belongs to the second part, but also occupies the first place in it. For in that which constitutes the main subject of the dialogue, the mode in which the particular instance, rhetoric, that is, as an example of mere semblance in art, is combined with the more general object of the whole exposition, the endeavour to investigate upon the practical side the opposition between the eternal and the mutable, in this the Gorgias, notwithstanding all its apparent similarity with the Phædrus, bears entirely the character of the second part. For in that dialogue, where philosophising was only spoken of as an impulsive feeling, and knowledge as inward intuition, the method, as a thing external, could only serve for illustration. But now when the Parmenides has so prepared the way, that it is rather the reality of knowledge together with its objects, that are to be discussed, instead of mere method, art is set up as something formed and finished, and the connection between the arts as something external, and the investigation is pursued rather with a view of discovering whether they have an object, and what it is. Nay, if we look to the mere structure, a decided transition may be pointed out from the Phædrus through the Protagoras to the Gorgias, and from this to the Euthydemus and Sophist, in which the form of utter negation comes out most strongly.

And in like manner all these dialogues are penetrated throughout by a germ, continually growing and treated only as an indirect object, of the positive, in the indication of true science and art and the objects of them, until at last it leaves this connection with the negative and comes out alone, when at the same time the whole of the indirect treatment passes into one of an opposite form. Thus, while the Gorgias clearly proves itself to belong to this series, it is quite as manifestly the first member of it, partly on account of the similarity already mentioned to the earlier method of instruction, partly because the last-mentioned combination of the negative object with the positive is far from being so ingenious and complicated as in the subsequent dialogues, the Euthydemus for instance, and Sophist. Moreover, the subdivision of the investigation under several heads, and the apparently frequent return to the commencement of the subject, are forms which appear more often in the sequel and become most important features, to which the Lysis and the little dialogues connected with the Protagoras afford but slight approximations.

Add to this, in order to fix the place of the Gorgias still more decisively, the ingenious manner in which almost all the earlier dialogues are again taken up in it, and sometimes particular points out of them, sometimes their actual results are more or less clearly interwoven with it, and, on the other hand, the perfectly unintentional way, though the skilful reader cannot overlook it, in which the germs of the following dialogues of this series already lie folded up in this. The former point has been already touched upon in general with reference to the Phædrus and Protagoras, but might still be pursued much further, and still more numerous references might be discovered in detail. Thus from the Phædrus the objection might be especially brought against Plato by other Socraticians,

that notwithstanding his apparent intention in that
dialogue of correcting the method of that species of
rhetoric which tends only to delude, and his depreciation of it, he still allows it to hold such a place,
that a person might look upon it as an object of desirable attainment. And it is precisely for this, that
in the Gorgias its only possible use, according to moral
principles, and of the necessary connection between method and thought, appears in so emphatic a form, and
is so multifariously repeated, in order to show how
impossible it is, starting from his principles, to come
to any view, with regard to this subject, different from
that here projected. And in the Protagoras the description of sophistical self-complacency might easily be
thought exaggerated, and the game too easy, when the
writer of the dialogues attributes to his opponent
such follies and absurdities. Hence in this dialogue,
when Gorgias finds himself similarly circumstanced with
Protagoras, he proves far more pliant and docile with
regard to the turnings of the dialogue, and draws less
ridicule upon himself. But, on the contrary, Plato
shews afresh in Polus at all events, that there is no
doubt that rhetorical undialectic sophists are incapable
of accomplishing anything in that art of conducting a
dialogue upon which his Socrates prides himself; a serious play with the method which, though certainly in
some degree an echo from the first series, manifestly
stands here in a far more subordinate relation than the
similar one in the Protagoras. Thus again from the
Lysis; not only is the notion of the neither good nor
bad taken up as a thing granted and acknowledged, but
also what we find in that smaller dialogue upon the
subject of love, predominant as it is, in a confined

and limited form, obtains in this, like what was said
in the Phædrus upon the nature of love generally,
an extended application, beyond mere personality, to
the more important civil relations as well, inasmuch
as with almost verbal reference to the Lysis, love for
the people and love for the boy are laid down as co-
ordinate. And thus too it is now for the first time
clearly proved, that in the Phædrus a peculiar value
was justly attributed to the doctrine, not, it must be
allowed, brought forward with sufficient clearness for
every one, which inculcates the necessity of a similarity in the ideal, or character, for the production of
love between two minds. With this, moreover, we are
to put in connection that view of Plato which supports
itself against all unmeaning disputation and persuasion,
that those, who pursue principles morally opposed, can
entertain no deliberation with one another in common;
a view which had been already enunciated verbally in
the Crito, but is here palpably exemplified in the first
discussion of Socrates with Callicles, and contains likewise from this point of view the defence of the indirect
dialectic method for the second part of the Platonic
works. Moreover, in our present dialogue, Plato makes
Socrates expressly acknowledge that the principle
brought forward in the Laches, that courage cannot
be conceived apart from knowledge, is certainly his opinion; and, in like manner, what has been declared in
the introduction to the Charmides to be the result of
that dialogue with reference to discretion. I mean that
Socrates agrees in the explanation, that discretion is
virtue, in so far as it is to be regarded as health of
the mind; this principle also here receives corroboration.
So also piety appears here, exactly as it was defined in

the Euthyphro, as justice towards the gods. All these are retrospective references, if not quite literal, still quite certain and decisive; and we are sure that whoever considers them comparatively, will never entertain the notion of inverting the arrangement, and take these dialogues for further enlargements upon points here as it were preliminarily noticed. And even as to the lesser Hippias, any one who would undertake to find a confirmation of it in the Gorgias, might do so by affirming that the supposition started at the end of the first section, that the just man always wills to act justly, appears to refer less to the general position already advanced elsewhere, that every one always wills the good, than to the principle that *willing* belongs quite as necessarily as *knowing* to the nature of justice in particular, and that this is exactly the natural result of the sceptical treatment of the idea of justice in the Hippias. But any one must see that this reference is far from being either as important or as certain as the others. For the principle itself, that the exercise of justice eminently implies the presence of volition, is a thing so generally recognised, that it may be assumed without any reference to a previous proof.

Again, the traces of a promise or preparation for the majority of the subsequent dialogues, appear quite as clearly as the references to earlier works which we have instanced above; partly in the design of the whole, partly in particular passages. The manner, for instance, in which, after the establishment of the essential distinction between the good and pleasant, the notion of a combination of the two is notwithstanding again entertained, points to a problem not yet solved, and which is interwoven with the subject of the Philetus, the last dia-

logue of this series. The manner in which the nature
of the art of counterfeit is taken up, and its province
divided according to the rules of dialectics, is the first
breathing of what we meet with in the Sophist and
Statesman so artificially and comprehensively worked
out. The stress laid upon separating and divesting
mind of personality, and the mode of exhibiting it mythically, is, as it were, a prophetic anticipation of the
Phædo. So that we may even decide from hence, how
much in this second period proceeded from the point
which we have specified as the centre point of the
Gorgias, and what on the contrary belongs, so to speak,
to a second formation, or must be referred to the point
already indicated, as contradistinguished from it. And
I speak not so much of the dialogues, as of the principal factors of the dialogues; for it is precisely in this
reconciliation of the two points of view, the theoretical
and practical, brought about as it is, without uniting
them so completely as to cancel all opposition between
the two, that the still more artificial form of the subsequent dialogues consists.

Hence, even the Gorgias, strictly taken, can only
be viewed as a moiety of the beginning of this second
part, and it is not until we have combined it with the
Theætetus that we can look upon it as constituting a
complete commencement, inasmuch as the latter treats
of the opposition between existence in the abstract and
conception, exactly as the Gorgias does that between
the good and perceptive feeling. Hence, considering
the total absence of any decisive testimony whatever as
to the period of composition, and moreover, that the
idea of the two works must arise almost simultaneously,
and they are both of considerable extent, the appearance

of the Gorgias prior to that of the Theætetus cannot be immediately and at once established. On the contrary, it is only as an inference mediately drawn from a variety of particulars, and these are nothing more than manifold references to what has preceded and to what follows, the character of a general prelude, if I may be allowed so to express myself, and that analogy, according to which every new *layer* in the philosophy of Plato commences originally with the ethical—these are the only grounds which can justify the precedence of the Gorgias, against several particular objections which might possibly be alleged against assigning it such a position.

Whoever takes up those traces and references, and is acquainted with the manner in which it is Plato's custom to mark such notices, will undoubtedly discover of himself more of the same kind copiously interwoven with the details of this dialogue. For other persons we may be allowed to draw attention to some of them only. For instance, with what in reference to the Phædrus and Protagoras appeared to us before in an apologetic light, still more matter connects itself in this dialogue which we can only understand as a review of particular declarations of opinion against such Platonic writings as had hitherto appeared. However, what might be said upon this point must always remain within the limits of supposition, and the best method therefore will be, only to give slight indications in the particular places and passages where such matter occurs. And, besides this, there is much that stands in such close connection with the Apology of Socrates, that it might be said that all the essential matter in that piece is here repeated, only so given as to be exalted above the immediate personal relation. And it looks almost as if the Apology of Socrates, changed as it thus is into a defence of the Socratic modes of thought and action, has rather changed than lost its personal relation, and become a defence of Plato. Least of all can this repetition lead us to agree so far with another writer as to believe that the Gorgias must have been written soon after the death of Socrates, because assuredly Plato would not have reproached the Athenians a second time with so detailed a history of that act of which they had long since repented. For when we recollect that this also applies naturally to the Phædo, we have these repetitions compressed within so short a period as to excite a feeling of satiety relative to the subject of which they treat; a process quite in contradiction with that richness and abundance which characterizes the Platonic composition, and which, in the present case, would have no conceivable object; nor is there any sign whatever of ridicule suffered or anger felt, for no trace appears anywhere of either, that might have driven Plato to such reproaches of his fellow citizens. On the contrary, the purpose I have indicated, of justifying himself by a retrospective view of what had lately happened, for his continual political inactivity, and at the same time of showing how fearlessly he intended to continue his philosophical course—this is a purpose which he may well be conceived to have entertained at a somewhat later period. Though indeed, as Plato, after having lived some time at Megara with the other Socraticians, does not appear to have returned to Athens, for any long time at least, what I have suggested can hardly have been the case at an earlier period than after his return from his first travels. Soon afterwards, however, he might have had abundant occasion for expression of sentiments of this kind. For in the Apology Socrates represents his own disfavour as having commenced with the calumnies of Aristophanes, and similar false reports respecting the tendency of his exertions; and thus Plato also experienced something of the same kind soon enough. Let but the reader recollect how in the Ecclesiazusæ of Aristophanes, the representation of which is usually put as early as the ninety-seventh Olympiad, the political views and new doctrines of Plato were exposed, and he will have no difficulty in conceiving how easily Plato may have apprehended a similar result. Hence, then, in order at the same time to justify to his friends and relations implicated in the concerns of public life—those friends who perhaps had hoped that his travels would have recalled him from abstract thought and brought him nearer to the world—thoroughly, I say, to justify to them his persevering withdrawal from the government of a state, in his own opinion, corrupt, as well as his own disadvantageous judgment upon the forms of it, and to show the necessity of being allowed to philosophize freely upon the art of politics; hence come those very strong expressions, outbidding anything in the Protagoras, against the most celebrated Athenian statesman of all time, with a slight reservation in favour of the living, as if they were less guilty; hence the way in which he puts into the mouth of Callicles the imputation of *Laconism* against himself, in order to show that what is so called arises at once quite naturally and spontaneously from the most simple and every-day experience.

Nay, even what he says cursorily upon the subject of poetry, may, in its more accurate application, be connected with the same circumstances. Much of the natural hatred and spite of bad persons in the possession of power towards wiser men seems brought out exactly in the form in which it is, in order to touch, with a slight justification and correction, upon what had occurred to Plato during his first stay in Sicily with the elder Dionysius. And this again leads almost to the supposition, that the example also of Archelaus, if we are not to imagine that that monarch had not already at so early a period Socraticians about his person, and proceeded with them in a similar way, was chosen with the same referential purpose, in order to show most strongly how impossible it was, that Plato, as had perhaps begun even at that time to be the opinion of some, should have sought the friendship of an unjust and oppressive despot. These however are the only traces, slight ones certainly, of the time at which the dialogue was composed; and we could indeed place but little reliance upon them, did they not coincide so admirably with the position which must be assigned to it, between and after others, the period of which may be more decisively fixed. According to this it would be right to consider it as the first or second work after Plato's return from his first journey, as soon, that is, as his school had become so firmly established, and so widely extended as to induce Aristophanes to give a comic representation of it. For unless all accounts of this journey are false, Plato can scarcely have formed, previous to it, a particular school of his own.

There is one objection however to this date, which might certainly be brought by an ingenious person, and which I will not suppress. We know of a philosophical work of Gorgias, and the question may very fairly be started, how Plato could have made Gorgias the principal person in a dialogue without uttering a syllable about this work, or noticing it by a single allusion. Put the dialogue into the period at which the process against Socrates was still going on, and we then have a very easy justification, in the supposition that at that time Plato had not yet become acquainted with it; but this supposition will not hold after his return from his travels, as he must unquestionably have made acquaintance with this work in Sicily. In this case, there are but two hypotheses from which to choose: either Plato, contrary to his usual custom in this particular, has kept so accurately to the time in which he places the dialogue, that he does not mention this work because at that period it was not yet known at Athens, and this may certainly be conceived, if as Olympiodorus says, it was written in the eighty-fourth Olympiad; or Plato did not consider this work deserving of particular notice, not so much by reason of its sophistical tendency, as, much more probably, its utterly rhetorical style; and thus he only comprehends it generally under the description of the corrupting art of counterfeit, and makes Gorgias say, probably not without a meaning, that he does not pretend to be anything but an orator.

II. THEÆTETUS.

IF the reader looks only to the difficulties which surround this dialogue considered in itself, and as it is usually understood, and to the sophistries of which it is accused by those who are uninitiated into the connection, he may perhaps wish for a fuller introduction to the understanding of it than he will here meet with. But much becomes at once clear from the place we assign to the Theætetus, and from immediate reference to what was said on the Gorgias. For when it is remembered what was there stated to be the common object of the two dialogues, and how the Gorgias is intended to pursue that object more on the practical side, the Theætetus more on the theoretical, the perplexity must at once become considerably less intricate, and some notion will be given of the real subject of the dialogue, in which, otherwise, at first sight, every thing seems to cancel the rest, and notwithstanding that knowledge is the subject of the argument, nothing apparently remains but ignorance ; so that this hitherto sealed work will be explained at the same time that the correctness of that connection, and of the general view taken of the whole, receive additional confirmation. For according to that view, the main object of the Theætetus must be to show, that no science can be found unless we completely separate Truth and Being from the Perceived and Perceptible or Apparent. Only that in this dialogue, as the sciences generally were not so strictly separated and individually defined as the arts, Plato himself having been almost the first to attempt this, the discussion does not here enter upon the whole system of the sciences, as in the Gorgias on that of the arts, but treats of their common element, or of knowledge in the strictest sense of the word. And not only this, but it was a principle of Plato, as well as his object to show, that both investigations are in their nature counterparts of one another, that the search for the good in pleasure, and that for pure knowledge in the sensuous perception, are grounded upon one and the same mode of thought, that, namely, which the Gorgias exhibits more at full. Therefore it is shown betimes, and no one will wonder how this subject came to be here introduced, what influence the doctrine tried must have upon the ideas of the good and beautiful, and upon the method of considering them —it is shown that in the mind of the follower of it, knowledge itself can only refer to pleasure, and that, as he who seeks only pleasure ends in the annihilation of all community of sentiment with others, contradictory even to the inward feelings themselves, so also he who, instead of knowledge, is content with sensuous impressions, can find no community either of men with one another, nor of men with God, but remains confined and isolated within the narrow limits of his own personal consciousness.

These allusions however to the connection between the theoretical and the practical, and consequently between the Theætetus and Gorgias, are found scattered in almost all parts of the dialogue. But the exposition of the theory, that knowledge ought not to be sought in the province of the senses—that, as the only source of pleasure is in the transition from one opposite to the other, so also perception is inconstant, and that whoever thinks to confine knowledge within its province, can never

attain any of the objects of knowledge—forms in its
gradual developement, the framework of the whole.
Hence the dialogue begins with showing that the Protagorean denial of a general standard of knowledge,
and the Heracleitic theory of the flux of all things, and
of *Becoming* alone remaining to the exclusion of all
Being, as well as the principle here tried throughout,
which sets up Perception, and Perception alone, for
knowledge, do all refer to one another, and form one
system. Socrates shows this while he supports the principles himself, and mutually upholds them by means
of each other better than their authors had done, who
in part, perhaps, less perfectly understood themselves,
and the connection of their thoughts. And it is not
before the Platonic Socrates has thus armed the theory
of Protagoras against his own preliminary objections,
as well as the nature of the subject admitted of, and
exhibited it in a different and more connected form,
that the dialogue proceeds to grapple seriously with those
theories, and to show that the whole system, in so far as
it affects to be knowledge and matter of instruction,
falls to pieces of itself, and can never attain its object.
Thus, first of all, the theory of Protagoras is attacked
on two sides, which the dialogue itself, in order to prevent any misunderstanding, pronounces victorious. First,
upon the side of the contradiction involved in the proposition which makes opinion the arbiter of knowledge.
For, as long as other men place a knowledge still *above*
opinion, that proposition destroys itself, inasmuch as
the number of those to whom a thing appears true, is
now the measure of certainty, and the predominant
opinion, by the supposition, maintains itself against
the value of opinion. Then it is shown that although

it may hold for the time being, that what appears to every one, *is*, as regards him, yet that it cannot hold for the useful, or for any thing which concerns the future*. Now should any one discover in this conclusion a contradiction to the way in which Plato has already considered the future elsewhere, when he showed that the knowledge of the future is not a particular knowledge, but that only he who is cognizant of the present can possibly be in a condition to judge of the future, he would nevertheless be mistaken. For, in the first place, Plato here places himself at the point of view of those to whom the future *is* a particular, and then the whole series of conclusions to which Plato intends, cannot still be drawn without taking the antecedent into consideration. Because, for instance, only what the physician thinks about the future fever is the truth; so also, by consequence, only what the physician thinks of the present state of health is the truth, and therefore the knowledge of it is distinct from mere perception. A consequence which Plato himself would have drawn somewhat more definitely, had he not been carried onwards by a press of accumulating investigations and applications, all of which were intended for this dialogue, as indeed he leaves throughout many conclusions in it to be drawn by the reader himself.

Next, and in a manner resembling this, the theory also of Heraclitus which had been already contained in the exposition of that of Protagoras, is attacked inde-

* See Theætet. p. 178. A.

Ἔτι τοίνον ἐνθένδε ἂν μᾶλλον πᾶς τις ὁμολογήσειε ταυτὰ ταῦτα, εἰ περὶ παντός τις τοῦ εἴδους ἐρωτῷη, ἐν ᾧ καὶ τὸ ὠφέλιμον τυγχάνει ὄν. ἔστι δέ που καὶ περὶ τὸν μέλλοντα χρόνον. ὅταν γὰρ νομοθετώμεθα, &c.

pendently, and upon such grounds that it is shown, that, according to this theory, strictly taken, neither a predicate could be found and adapted to a subject, nor a subject to a predicate, because even during the finding and the fitting, every thing ceases to be what it was, and thus, whatever resembles a knowledge or an enunciation is destroyed*. Hence an immediate though suppressed consequence brings us very close to the conclusion which Plato had in view, which is, that the subject of these untenable fluent operations is itself an untenable fluent, in which sense, as regards the immediate alterations of the body, Plato had already admitted the existence of simple and undeceiving perception. After this, lastly, the expression of the same idea, attributed immediately to Theætetus, is especially contradicted, and now we have notices pointing chiefly to that, whereby and wherein true knowledge is alone to be discovered; for Socrates shows how perception itself, properly considered, points to operations in nature and origin entirely separate from it, and how, provided only we begin with securing the notion of being, it thus becomes at once manifest, that perception on no possible supposition can attain to being, and that truth therefore must necessarily be sought beyond and without its range.

Thus, then, the dialogue is advanced as far in reference to the theories hitherto tested as is possible under the conditions of the indirect process adopted, and now takes another turn in order to consider more closely

---

* P. 182. D.

Εἴπερ ἀεὶ λέγοντος ὑπεξέρχεται, ἅτε δὴ ῥέον.—Τὸ δ', ὡς ἔοικεν, ἐφάνη, εἰ πάντα κινεῖται, πᾶσα ἀπόκρισις, περὶ ὅτου ἄν τις ἀποκρίνηται, ὁμοίως ὀρθὴ εἶναι, οὕτω τ' ἔχειν φάναι καὶ μὴ οὕτως, εἰ δὲ βούλει, γίγνεσθαι, ἵνα μὴ στήσωμεν αὐτοὺς τῷ λόγῳ.

the discovery last made. In such a manner, however, that here also all that necessarily belongs to the indirect exposition is abstracted from *ideas*, and even being and the discovery made of the immediate activity of the mind are brought back into the sphere of the senses, and into that of the individual and particular ; for it is only in this sense that conception (δόξα) is always spoken of in what follows. For with reference to the inquiry into the nature of knowledge, a new principle is set up affirming that it is right conception, and it is examined whether knowledge can lie within this more narrowly limited sphere. This investigation produces first of all, a laborious attempt to define the sphere of false conception, and from this, and simultaneously with it, that of true knowledge ; an attempt which Socrates declares at the end of it to be unsatisfactory, because false conception at last must still rest upon an incomprehensible mistaking of knowledge, whence he concludes that the latter must be found before the former. Hence too, there grows a very important consequence, though as before, not expressly drawn, that it is impossible that pure knowledge should lie within the same sphere as error, and that truth or falsehood cannot be predicated of the former, but only possession or non-possession. After this attempt then, that principle is itself very shortly dispatched by the distinction set up and generally recognised, and which, by means of the example chosen, again refers to the practical and the Gorgias—the distinction between true conception to be mediately attained, and knowledge at all times and in all things immediate.

This, again, paves the way to the last attempt here made to grasp the nature of knowledge, starting with the assumption, that it is right* conception combined with reasonable explanation. And here again by far the largest space is occupied by an accurately considered, though only incidental, investigation as to an assumed opposition, not however tenable throughout, in the relations of the simple and compound to knowledge in the sense assumed ; and then again the principle itself is very soon dispatched according to the two significations given of reasonable explanation, which Plato especially distinguishes, inasmuch as the refutation of the last is also good at the same time for the first.

Wonderfully ingenious, when we consider these particular grand divisions one with another, is the uniformity of execution in the structure of the whole and of the particular parts. To begin with what comes last : how limited in comparison with the beginning appears at the end the sphere within which knowledge is still sought, though not found ; and how near at last is what proceeds merely from sensuous impression, independent of ideas, brought to a deceptive similarity with knowledge, though it can never exalt itself to a level with it. It may be said that these three transitions from mere perception, as it is here represented, to right conception generally, and from this to such conception as is full and clear enough to furnish a reasonable explanation, give us a graduated scale for the simplest, and so to speak, the rudest up to the most refined view of common consciousness, so that it is rejected with all its pretensions to knowledge, and a question is at last started which manifestly points to the necessity of an opposite principle, but

---

* P. 201. D.

Τὴν μὲν μετὰ λόγου ἀληθῆ δόξαν ἐπιστήμην εἶναι, τὴν δὲ ἄλογον ἐκτὸς ἐπιστήμης· καὶ ὧν μὲν μή ἐστι λόγος, οὐκ ἐπιστητὰ εἶναι, οὑτωσὶ καὶ ὀνομάζων, ἃ δ' ἔχει, ἐπιστητά.

at the same time the sphere within which that lower consciousness is true is assigned to it throughout, and the element of right which it contains is conceded to it and defined, which even the terms themselves imply in which those untenable pretensions are stated. For we are by no means to believe that what is gained in the several parts of the dialogue by the production of objections which Socrates afterwards either allows to drop or to be refuted by Theætetus, or by investigations which with reference to the immediate subject of the dialogue are only incidental, we are not to believe that all this is intended to fall to the ground and come to nothing. So far from it, that all this matter is assuredly to be preserved and used: but better opportunities for noticing this in detail will occur in the notes on the particular passages. Again, each of the several parts is constructed precisely in the same manner. The Protagorean principle, for example, is more finely worked out at every fresh addition to the dialogue, and is at last confronted by the question as to opinions about time future held in time present. In like manner conception itself is continually more pointedly disengaged from perception, especially with reference to arithmetic, when every reader will certainly recollect the Platonic principle which Plato's disciples certainly did not forget, I mean that Geometry is a thing distinct from pure knowedge generally, and that the rank of the highest science does not belong to it. In like manner the idea of false conception is rid by the interposition of that of *exchanged conception**, of the rude form under which it was commonly and

---

* Ἀλλοδοξίαν τίνα οὖσαν ψευδῆ φαμὲν εἶναι δόξαν, ὅταν τις τι τῶν ὄντων ἄλλο αὖ τῶν ὄντων, ἀνταλλαξάμενος τῇ διανοίᾳ, φῇ εἶναι. οὕτω γάρ ὄν μὲν ἀεὶ δοξάζει, ἕτερον δὲ ἀνθ' ἑτέρου, καὶ ἁμαρτάνων οὗ ἐσκόπει δικαίως ἂν καλοῖτο ψευδῆ δοξάζων.

sophistically discussed. At last, however, the whole explanation given of knowledge is made to fall to pieces by the question, how even that true conception which is recognised most generally and authentically as right, can be knowledge. The same thing happens at last to the notion of the reasonable explanation which is taken up quite from the most idiomatic usage of the Greek language, and exhibited in its various gradations, but is nevertheless as regards the proper object of the dialogue rejected by the question, how it is possible that the conception of distinguishing quality can be wanting in conception generally, or the knowledge of that distinguishing quality explain knowledge generally*. In this manner, in short, every particular investigation fully and seriously pursued is most suddenly at the conclusion regularly ridiculed away, and thus we may say that the last conclusion of all suddenly turns to ridicule the subject of the whole dialogue, as far, that is, as the question was directed to the explanation of knowledge, although as is natural from the difference in the time and the age of the author, this ridicule is not so triumphantly proclaimed as in the Prothagoras; a comparison which must strike every one, as in fact the question as to the explicability of knowledge is the same theoretically as that of the communicability of virtue is practically.

The same uniformity is discoverable in yet another point of view. For almost in every discussion of any particular question in this dialogue a digression occurs in which immediate and distinct reference is made to the true and right, though these subjects nowhere come out in the discussions themselves. And thus also

* Διαφορότητος.

an extensive digression is introduced into the main
dialogue itself, containing its share of these allusions;
but which, as regards the immediate progress of the
dialogue, seems to be an extremely capricious interruption, not less violently brought in, and no better
kept within rule and rein, than that so justly censured
in the Phædrus. I speak of the whole passage preceding the last refutation of the Protagorean principle
where the distinction between the tyros in philosophy
and those in rhetoric and similar arts is pointed out,
and the divine, the true and the good, come out in the
full relief of their peculiar nature as perfectly opposed
to the narrow sphere of the personal. And indeed this
digression seems purposely placed soon after the beginning, that at all events the attentive reader may
have a clear point by means of which he may find his
way among the complicated mazes of the dialogue.

By these digressions then, the Theætetus connects
itself immediately and, among the earlier dialogues is
almost solitary in so doing, with the Parmenides as
a continuation of it, although from an opposite point
of view. And scarcely any other allusions to earlier
works occur in what belongs to the essential matter of
the dialogue. These digressions, however, are remarkable; for instance, the way in which not only the
Eleatic doctrine is opposed to the Ionian, but also
Parmenides to the other Eleatics, can scarcely be otherwise understood except as intending to imply that the
others, especially Melissus who is particularly named,
appeared to Plato to deviate as far from the truth as
the Ionians, to whom however in comparison with those
who would grasp every thing with their hands, he ascribes a truly philosophical tendency. For if, as he

expresses himself, the Ionians moved even the immove-
able, so, probably, the Eleatics were for reducing even
the untenable to rest, and Parmenides alone by his
hypothesis of an opposition between the intelligible and
apparent, of which we may regret that only rough
outlines and particular traces have come down to us,
appeared to have found, or at least to have divined
the right road, although even to his doctrine Plato has
objections to make in a subsequent dialogue. Even in
what Plato here says about Parmenides we may easily
detect the inclination to consider the doctrine of that
philosopher more thoroughly at a future opportunity,
in short an announcement of what he afterwards carried
into effect in the Sophist. At the same time however
it contains an almost tacit exposure of Zeno, who is by
no means excepted from among those whom Socrates
considers undeserving of much notice, and a hint implying how little any one should venture to make Parmenides the object of his satire, and how difficult it
was to penetrate to the real meaning of his doctrine.
Both refer manifestly enough to the dialogue of that
name, and to a variety of misapprehensions in the understanding of it which from these allusions may be
easily surmised. So again, without any particular mention of the philosopher, several of the antitheses discussed in the Parmenides reappear elsewhere in this
dialogue, in part accompanied by elucidations of what
is there barely stated as briefly as possible, so that the
position of the Theætetus between the Parmenides and
Sophist is thus in every way justified. And moreover,
besides these that are contained in the general plan,
there occur in detail several allusions to the Gorgias,
and among these too, individually considered, those

which presuppose the Gorgias have a great advantage over those which look as if the Theætetus ought to be placed before it.

In two other respects, moreover, these two counterparts especially resemble one another. One of these points of similarity is, that in both dialogues a variety of perfectly similar matter occurs incidentally. Thus also in the Theætetus important passages from the defence of Socrates are brought up, and as it were commented upon. For Plato expatiates in a peculiar manner, and one which almost warrants the conclusion that he must on some occasion have exposed a weak side in this respect, upon the extremely natural and very pardonable ignorance of a philosopher in all civil matters and usages. More skilful persons may decide whether this is to refer to that apology, or to passages in some other writings of his, or to some fact of which traces still survived. Moreover we find in several passages a manifest defence, partly of his indirect mode of speculation in general, as in the explanation of Socrates' midwife practice, partly directed against a variety of objections which must have been made to his writings, and likewise censure of the form and method in which many of his opponents probably endeavoured to confute him. Thus for example, he constantly repeats here as well as in the Gorgias, that in philosophical matters apparent consequences are not to be made the grounds of confutation, and particularly lays down the conditions under which, in the dialogue, a position of the opponent can be regarded as confuted. So that, these vivid expressions which recur so frequently in the course of the two dialogues rightly considered, we shall remark a concealed and gradually gathering indignation, which afterwards strives to vent itself thoroughly in the Euthydemus. Secondly, the two dialogues have even in their philosophical bearing some polemics in common with one another, quite of a different kind from what we meet with at an earlier period against the Sophists. For, as in the Gorgias, the philosopher especially confuted under the person of Callicles is manifestly Aristippus, in whose system the principle that nothing is naturally just, but only becomes so by capricious establishment, occupied an important place, so also the first half generally of this dialogue Aristippus is the person especially in view. That Aristippus took the impressions of the senses to be certain knowledge, that he did not notwithstanding deny the possibility of a progress towards greater perfection in knowledge, and the existence of a distinction between the philosopher and other men, we learn from all the sources of information we possess; and this furnishes us with a key to explain how and why it happens that Plato represented this doctrine as Protagorean though supported by Socrates, and we find Aristippus especially denoted by those who did not indeed follow the doctrine of Protagoras exclusively, but still ended with the principle that there is nothing just by nature; we find him with his propensity for good living represented in that long digression as one of those who do not occupy themselves with philosophy in the proper way, and some perhaps may even think fit to view that exposition of the Socratic midwifery as at the same time a protestation that that philosophy was in no way learnt from Socrates. In short, a multitude of allusions discover themselves as soon as ever we take these polemics into consideration. Every one however must also certainly admire the art with which they are interwoven with the whole, so completely without detracting from the universality of its purely scientific bearing, so that the reader, with the exception of very particular allusions which do not interfere with the progress of the whole, and which every one may easily be content to take as embellishments without thinking to find in them any thing particular, may understand the whole without having been aware of those allusions. The second half gives great occasion to suspect the presence in it of similar polemics against Antisthenes of whom we know, though only, I regret to say, in the most general way, that he maintained the principle of the impossibility of contradicting successfully any position whatever. These polemics appear to begin in this dialogue at the commencement of the section about false conception, and are elsewhere concluded under more definite and extended views. The character of this opponent and what we know of his relations to Plato make it probable that much has reference to him which appears to be defence against unscientific and rude attack. There may yet be much besides of a polemical character which it is now almost impossible to decypher, with the exception perhaps of a few scattered traces. What is said of the followers of Heraclitus is particularly strange, and it may be doubtful whether others than themselves are meant under their name, or actually themselves; in which case it is scarcely possible to avoid thinking of Plato having sojourned in Ionia, probably on that great journey, when, according to some accounts, he wished to penetrate even into Persia.

Historical testimonies upon which to determine the time of the composition of the dialogue are not to be found, with the exception of what follows immediately from the allusions to all those circumstances, that the schools of Plato as well as of most of the other Socratic philosophers had been already formed. Not much can be built upon the mention of the battle at Corinth in which Theætetus had been wounded; the most to be inferred from it would be only what is also certain upon other grounds, that the dialogue cannot have been written before the middle of the ninety-sixth olympiad. We should however by no means be warranted in concluding that the fight thus mentioned is the same which Xenophon notices in the fourth book of his Hellenics; on the contrary we might easily find just as much reason for thinking of less important events which may have taken place subsequently, when Iphicrates had the command in that quarter. We have however every reason for considering as historical, both the character of Theætetus and what is said of him, though not the literal words of the conversation held. Suidas mentions him in two characters, as a scholar of Socrates and a hearer of Plato; we see clearly that both notices refer to the same person: he also mentions him as a philosopher and mathematician, and knows that he taught at a later period in Heracleia.

So Proclus also mentions him among celebrated mathematicians. Hence it may easily be inferred that from the school of Socrates, as far as this expression may be allowed, he passed into that of Plato, and is very properly represented as quite young at the death of Socrates. From this point of view, that is a striking description which is sketched with so much fondness and put by Plato into the mouth partly of Euclides, partly of Theodorus. For what philosopher would not have been glad to possess and immortalize a young friend like this. What Theætetus here produces about the square root has very much the appearance of having been at that time something new, but whether it was a discovery of Theætetus himself, or one of Plato's with which he ornaments his pupil, I cannot take upon myself to decide. With regard to Theodorus it is not necessary to say anything, as he is sufficiently known, and the only question which could be a subject of curiosity, namely, why he is found in this place particularly, and why Socrates is so urgent with him to unite in conducting the dialogue, cannot be satisfactorily answered out of the dialogue itself. Meanwhile the more probable the fact is of his visit to Athens, the less probable the account becomes that Plato went expressly to Cyrene to learn his science from him there.

III. MENO.

If the reader bears in mind the end of the Theætetus, and compares it with the beginning of the Sophist, where manifestly the same persons again meet together with decided reference to the plan we find there concerted, it may fairly be matter of surprise to him that the Sophist does not here follow immediately upon the Theætetus. And there ought indeed to be very sufficient grounds to justify us in disregarding so clear and apparently so intentional a notice. But for this very reason these grounds are of such a kind that they cannot be perfectly understood by the reader until he can refer back from the Sophist to the Theætetus, and the matter which the present arrangement introduces between the two. Only every one must at least allow that that notice does not contain any compulsive necessity, or exclude the possibility of the insertion of several dialogues between the two just mentioned. For how easy it is to suppose that Plato may indeed have intended to produce, immediately after the Theætetus, what we now find in the Sophist, and yet have been afterwards either called upon by particular occasions first to explain certain points, or have even seen that he could not appropriately comprehend in one dialogue all that was necessary, in order to attain to the results he wished, and that he therefore subjoined intermediately several smaller ones, without however snapping the main clue after having once indicated it. Or it might even have been his original intention, when he ended the Theætetus, to continue the same persons in the Menon, making them say what we now find in this dialogue, and then he may have been subsequently influenced by some motive or other to prefer the choice of others for this purpose, and to apply the intimation formerly thrown out to a later work. In short, that external circumstance, explicable as it is in a variety of ways, should not stand in opposition to an internal necessity or even probability, as soon, that is, as it can be shown that the Menon does really connect itself immediately with the Theætetus, and must at all events be placed between that dialogue and the Sophist. And this, as far as this place admits of an elucidation of the subject, will, it is hoped, be clearly enough manifest from the following comparison.

We find the first indication in the fact that in that part of the Theætetus where the opposition between knowledge and ignorance is set up, Socrates says that he prefers setting aside for the present the states of Learning and Forgetting as lying between the two, and clearly speaks of them as if they involved a problem which he would suspend until another time, in order not to lose sight of his principal subject. Now this is precisely the problem stated in the Menon, and whoever compares attentively must at once, and on this account, give up all idea of placing the Menon before the Theætetus. Neither is it solved otherwise than Plato usually solves his problems when he does so preliminarily, I mean by a mythical hypothesis, so that we here find precisely what according to his own method, after this question had been once started, was necessary to be done. As then in the Sophist, as well as in other dialogues manifestly belonging to this series, the same question is treated more dialectically and scientifically: the Menon naturally comes to stand nearer to the Theætetus and before the others. For when Plato wrote the Menon, had as much been already done in public expositions towards the scientific solution of this question, as we shall find in subsequent dialogues, the mythical treatment of it in this dialogue would no longer have had any meaning, but Plato would have referred the reader by a different method, with which we have already been made acquainted in his writings, to the works in which this was better done. And the same conclusion will ensue from the consideration of another question which likewise pervades several of these dialogues, I mean that of the immortality of the soul. When it is considered how in the Gorgias and Theætetus this idea is first of all little more than hypothetically assumed and mythically sketched out, and then in this dialogue set up as a ground of explanation of a fact, and as it were *postulated,* how it is elsewhere, and in the Phædon particularly, demonstrated and expounded with a higher degree of scientific clearness, any one having already any however slight acquaintance with Plato's method of proceeding must allow that it is only by assigning this position to the Menon, that this continuously increasing distinctness which gradually penetrates to the very centre-point of the subject, peculiar to Plato, can enter into the discussion of this, and that the first thing which Plato had to do after that general projection, was precisely to show that he was justified in thus assuming the doctrine of immortality, in so far, that is, as the possibility of all science and communication of knowledge must stand or fall with it. However, this is certainly no proof for those who are able to consider the Phædon an earlier work than the Gorgias. But we cannot notice these opinions until we compare those two dialogues with one another according to our own arrangement. Now if it is kept in view, on the one hand, how these two questions, that of the possibility of communicating knowledge, and that of immortality, are brought into connection with one another; and on the other, how the question of the possibility of attaining to knowledge is here reduced within the other, of the possibility of attaining to virtue, and of the nature of virtue generally, it will be seen that the Menon belongs quite as immediately to the Gorgias as to the Theætetus, and that the view taken of the relation of these two dialogues to one another is still more confirmed by means of it, inasmuch as the Menon is intended to draw the two still more close together, and to interweave them with one another, and this for those readers who might not perhaps yet be able to comprehend how the main problems of the two dialogues are connected with one another, and how in each of the two what is brought forward as digression is connected with the principal subject. And this view is confirmed by all closer consideration of the Menon, which, the more nearly we take it in connection with those two dialogues does the more closely and spontaneously connect itself with them, and this so immediately that it is impossible to conceive the intervention of anything else between them. Hence scarcely anything will be necessary here but to put down the particular points. First then, the projection and development of the idea of right conception, and the distinction pointed out between it and pure knowledge properly so called, must present itself to every one as the last result of the Theætetus, though not in that place regularly and fully enunciated. And this in the Menon is not only assumed as proved and expressly put among the little of which Socrates can maintain that he *knows* it, but it is evident that the decisive treatment of the question respecting the possibility of teaching political virtue, (πολιτίκη ἀρέτη) is nothing but an immediate deduction, a corollary from the Theætetus intended to apply to the subject of the Gorgias the last results of the former. In like manner the Menon gives us an immediate continuation of the Gorgias, inasmuch as it is demonstrated in it, that the ideas of the good and of virtue can be quite as little determined by any more accurately defined method of attaining to the pleasant as by the pleasant in general, and that it is necessary to discuss the two connected ideas purely for themselves upon exclusive and original principles. And that the connection may not be overlooked, the interlocutor is introduced as a disciple of Gorgias, and expressly referred to a dialogue of Socrates with that philosopher. Moreover Menon answers precisely in the sense in which Gorgias and his friends must have understood the beautiful. And as the last result of the Theætetus is confirmatively enunciated, so also is that of the Gorgias repeated, and it is shown to be still not the last, and that it carries the investigation still higher.

The same result also appears when we look to what is, or seems to be, accidental matter; for in the Menon this is throughout so identical with what we find in those dialogues, that we are compelled to infer from them the existence of still further similar relations and connecting circumstances. The same use of mathematics for examples as in the Theætetus, nay, even the object selected in visible connection with that dialogue. For the problem which is the foundation of the Pythagorean theorem, to find the side of the double square, is precisely the instance in which the incommensurability of two lines with one another was most immediately, and certainly also first, made palpable. This consistency in the matter from which the examples are taken can be so little the result of accident, that we might rather be tempted by it to attribute to the example itself a still higher symbolical value; especially if we remember that Plato is in the habit of introducing remembrances into his works for the hearers of his immediate oral instructions. This however might remain for ever nothing but a weak supposition, or perhaps be altogether precipitate and false; but clearly this application of these subjects, which no where else appears so prominently, points to the fact, that during the composition of the two dialogues Plato was employed upon the same subject, whether it were more in a mathematical or a Pythagorean point of view. Again, the examples which occur in the Menon taken from natural philosophy are most manifestly connected with what is adduced in the Theætetus in illustration of the doctrine of Protagoras, and is intended defensively to show that Socrates did really there bring forward the doctrines of that school in the sense in which the master of it meant them. And Gorgias as a disciple of Empedocles is here expressly associated with the Pythagoreans, and moreover, attention is thus drawn to the inward connection between the dialogue which bears his name and the Theætetus. In like manner the Menon connects itself with both dialogues by the similarity of its polemics. For the allusion to Aristippus, the bosom friend of rich tyrants cannot be mistaken, when Menon the friend of the great king declares that virtue consists in the compilation of wealth, even when he makes the limitation, not, according to Xenophon's description, consistent with his own opinions, that this should only be done by legitimate methods. In like manner every reader will think of Antisthenes where it is conceded somewhat contemptuously by all and repeatedly asseverated, that a sophist cannot teach virtue, for Antisthenes maintained the positive side in a sense which did not meet Plato's views, and where his first master Gorgias is held up to him as a pattern of one who made no claims to this. Moreover the Menon has in common with the Theætetus and Gorgias a similar allusion to the accusation of Socrates. For as in the Theætetus express and somewhat gratuitous mention is made of it, and in the Gorgias it is almost prophesied, and in both dialogues much from the Apo-

logy recurs in a very remarkable manner, so here the
future accuser himself appears, and we see his anger
rise exactly as Socrates describes it in the Apology;
and these allusions are found in so similar a dress that
manifestly a similar occasion lies at the bottom of them
in this dialogue as in the two others, and the Menon
falls coincidently into the same period with those
dialogues. And this dialogue connects itself with the
Gorgias still further, and more particularly by what
Socrates extracts by questions from Anytus, and says
himself about the Athenian statesmen. For Plato assumes
the appearance of changing into a more favourable
opinion what he had maintained in the Gorgias; but
he does this apparently only, and with a sufficient
quantity of irony which at the end rings out clearly
enough. It seems, indeed, to be a regular apologetic
recantation with which Socrates presents them, intended
to convey that there have always been among the politicians of Athens many honourable and just men, and
that he would here only maintain that their virtue did
not rest upon knowledge, and that this was the cause
why they could not also teach and communicate, and
this explanation seems all the more powerful as Socrates
now comprehends under the sentence, in this its milder
application, even Aristides himself, whom he had before
exalted so far above · the rest. But this man, whom
as far as communication is concerned he was certainly
compelled to give up, remains nevertheless free from
the other objections of which no further mention is
here made, and the possibility of his so remaining is
founded upon the principle that there may be men in
whom the correct conception which they once have continues unchangeable; and it is precisely this which is

laid down as the true value of that virtue which is not accompanied by a perfectly finished reason, and consequently does not rest upon knowledge properly so called. The rest, on the other hand, of whom it has been already shown elsewhere that they cannot keep possession of the useful, are, with their true conception, which will not remain without knowledge, most gently merged into the same class with soothsayers and poets, and it is at last distinctly declared what was meant by this elsewhere, namely, that all these men are but as shadows to one, if such there be, who knows and can teach.

This leads of itself to a still further resemblance between the Menon and the Gorgias. For in the latter we found explanatory references to several earlier dialogues; and it may be said of the Menon that it touches upon almost all in the first series, and concludes and seals in so many words a large share of their common subject-matter of which the decision was as it were still left open. This holds especially of the Protagoras and the dialogues immediately connected with it, and on account of this relation much matter is again taken up, almost too literally and too fully, out of the Protagoras, which already lay at too great a distance to admit of Plato's referring to it only by one or two slight allusions. It is now shown here how much of the virtues remains, as they are ordinarily enumerated, and are no longer allowed to be comprehended in a unity of virtue, if we separate them from knowledge; and at the same time the whole dispute, in which, in the Protagoras, Socrates is not only engaged with Protagoras, but also each of the two with himself as to the identification of virtue with know-

ledge, and the possibility of communicating it, is solved
by the preliminarily established distinction between
knowledge and true conception. And in doing this it
is said that the more exalted species of virtue rests
certainly upon knowledge, though upon a higher mode
of it than that calculation of the pleasant, and is moreover thus communicable in the sense in which it
may be said generally that remembrancing, and the
excitement and reanimation of ideas, is communication;
while the ordinary political ἀρέτη is not communicable,
but rests for the most part only upon correct conception,
upon a feeling which has never penetrated up to the
point of true knowledge. If therefore, in consequence
of what was first remarked, the Menon is indispensable
to us as a strengthening key-stone of the dialogues
which form the beginning of the second series, so it
is also from those references indispensable as a key to
much not yet expressly solved in the first series.

Again, a slight degree of attention will show us
that the Menon thus becomes a fresh confirmation of
the arrangement hitherto pursued in general. For that
it solves the riddle of the Protagoras, and, not to go
beyond what is particularly mentioned, that of the
Laches also, and that hence those two dialogues must
be placed before the Menon and in connexion with one
another, is clear to every one, and no intelligent reader
will think of inverting the relation and saying that
those dialogues were later in point of composition, and
intended to be further continuations of what is here
preliminarily said. The same is true of the Phædrus,
to which dialogue sufficiently decided reference is made
by a resemblance in the diction, which, though without
anything like verbal coincidence, strikes us almost as

an enlargement upon that dialogue, though without any
abrupt deviation being admitted from the very differently pitched tone of this. Here too, no one on
comparison of two passages will find it possible to
entertain any view except that the Menon refers retrospectively to the Phædrus. Otherwise we shall be
obliged to conclude that he is resolved to recognise no
relation whatever between the mythical and philosophical
method of exposition, and intentionally to overlook what
is struggling to show itself spontaneously. This is the
view which we obtain from the somewhat complicated
relations of this dialogue, after placing ourselves upon
that chief and corner-point from which alone an accurate
survey of the whole can be made. Thus prepared, we
shall find it no difficult matter to judge how the case
may stand with two other views very different from
this. Of these views one had not up to a certain time
been even published, but only circulated in private
by learned men in some respects entitled to much
attention. It might however be produced under a
form which should give it a certain degree of probability, in my opinion, that is a far better one than
that under which Ast lately produced it. This view
undertakes to deny our dialogue to Plato, conceiving
that it contains but little philosophical matter, not
more precisely and better stated elsewhere, that it may
therefore be almost dispensed with for the understanding
of the Platonic philosophy, and is not moreover in
respect of arrangement and treatment of the subject
particularly worthy of Plato. And certainly whoever,
from not having considered the dialogue in the proper
connection, has convinced himself of the first point may
easily find many particulars to corroborate the second,

which will necessarily strike him the more in proportion
as he has less understanding of the whole. For instance,
the abrupt commencement without any introduction is
not very Platonic, and an introduction seemed here the
more necessary as we learn for the first time, and
quite unexpectedly in the middle of the dialogue, that
Anytus has been present from the beginning—a thing
which occurs no where else in Plato. Moreover, it is
only by an introduction that the turn could be justified
upon which the last part of the dialogue rests, that
Menon is in want of a teacher in civil virtue ; for we
are not prepared for this by anything in the dialogue.
Again, several harsh transitions and disproportionate
strides in the progress of the dialogue seem only capable of being explained upon the supposition of some
precipitate impetuosity in the characters of the speakers,
which however no where comes out in the dramatic
representation of them ; and the resemblance to the
Phædrus and Protagoras might seem nothing but me-
diocre imitation, the rather as it can scarcely be conceived
upon what principle Plato could have found himself
compelled to do a second time what he had already
before discovered the fruitlessness of, I mean, enquiring
after a quality of virtue, whether, that is, it is communicable or not, before investigating its nature. But of
all these objections no part will remain good in the
estimation of one who has rightly apprehended the
philosophical bearing of the dialogue, except that, with
us, he will consider the Menon as one of the more
careless and not perfectly finished expositions of Plato.
For, this granted, all particular objections shrink and
partially vanish, as they agree almost universally with
the manifold subordinate views of the dialogue which

we have pointed out, and some negligence in the execution of details is to be looked upon with indulgence,
the rather as it is probable that the larger works which
follow in connection with the Theætetus were already
floating before him in his mind and he hastened to
close with them. And truly nothing is more strange
than to desire that all the works even of a great
master should be possessed of similar perfection, or to
suppose that he cannot have produced those that are
not so. On the other hand, as to the objection that
this dialogue contains a kind of investigation which we
shall look for in vain elsewhere, this is not after all
so fatal to the cause. For by the assumption that
virtue can only be communicable when and in so far
as it is identical with knowledge, the question becomes
part of the original one, what virtue is or is not in
itself. And as to what Ast otherwise calls the un-
Platonic propositions of our dialogue, his objection is in
part tantamount to this, that he is unable to recognize
throughout that simply preparatory character of the
dialogue which prevails over the larger portion of the
subject matter, and then that he will not allow Plato
to use words in different dialogues sometimes in a more
limited, sometimes in a more extended sense, and in
some of them more scientifically, in others more in the
manner of common life. Had it pleased him to allow
this, he could not have indulged in such severe censures
upon the point that the virtue here spoken of is separated from φρόνησις, and it would not have escaped
him that it is precisely the distinction between political
virtue and virtue in a higher sense that is here to be
started. All other objections give way partly from
what has been adduced, and in part appear to me to

deserve no particular notice; where so much is undeniably excellent and Platonic, and we may confidently affirm that it would be impossible ever to discover any other probable composer of it.

The other view different from our own and opposed to it in a different manner, is that well known one which attributes to the Menon an important and distinguished value, because it is supposed to be a noble exercise in the doctrine of reason as it is called, and moreover the Socratic midwifery is practised in it with particular adroitness, and supposing it to be first intelligently prepared, much that is beautiful might be demonstrated out of it to little boys in school. Only it is a pity that Plato was not in the habit of producing exercises in logic at all, such things being rather to be found in the later compilation of little dialogues that were foisted upon him, and that if he does here seem to represent anything himself under this form, this is only done in order to disguise to a certain degree the introduction, subservient to quite different purposes, of a foreign ingredient. Pity also that we find in the more artificial dialogues far more artificial and fruitful examples of his midwifery according to the ideas which he himself lays down in the Theætetus; and he declares this to be only the first commencement of bringing conceptions to consciousness, and does moreover treat somewhat lightly the merits of mathematical elements in comparison with philosophical, upon which he is generally accustomed to exercise this art. Pity, lastly, that it is not quite so easy a matter to prepare and demonstrate this very dialogue of the Menon essentially and entirely, as has been done with particular fragments detached from it, but which then are not themselves understood in their relation to the whole. Hence again, these panegyrists are themselves involved in a learned dispute as to what may really be the opinion of Plato upon the communicability of virtue, whether he is indeed in earnest with the whole question, and whether the decision come to, that it is only attainable by divine inspiration, coincides with other expressed sentiments of the philosopher. And among the disputants are many so truly divine, that whatever they are to understand must come from divine inspiration, and that because they have taken upon themselves to consider for itself alone what depends upon something else, and they require not only a voice to warn them, but one to call upon and awaken them to hear when the author imparts the answers to their sapient questions. For had they but understood his voice themselves they would have given better attention to three passages, to the way in which he states the first question as to whether virtue is knowledge or something quite distinct and separate from it, and then to the limitation that in political $\alpha\rho\grave{\epsilon}\tau\eta$, right conception may supply the place of knowledge, and finally to the last sentiments about the true statesman.

As to the persons, Anytus the accuser of Socrates is not, as far as I know, mentioned either by Plato or Xenophon with his father's name. Diogenes and Athenæus consider the Anytus of this dialogue and the accuser of Socrates as one and the same, and generally the way in which he is here brought forward speaks too clearly in favour of the supposition that Plato had him in his mind to render it necessary to look for other vouchers. Hence, therefore, it is not necessary to inquire who the numerous authors can be in whose writings it was found stated that the accuser of Socrates was a son of Anthemion. Menon is unquestionably the same with him whom Xenophon mentions in the campaign of Cyrus, although Plato does not describe him as so abandoned a profligate. His country, his beauty, his wealth and the friendship of the Thessalian Aristippus, who cannot be supposed to be also a duplicate, are circumstances sufficiently material and to the purpose to establish the fact.

IV. EUTHYDEMUS.

In the Euthydemus, if the reader regards the part which is at once the most striking and amusing, the conversation, that is, in which Socrates and Ctesippus, the same whom we already know from the Lysis, are engaged with the two sophists, Dionysodorus and Euthydemus, and how far it is from being conducted dialectically in Plato's sense, with a view to rectifying their mutual sentiments and to the extrication of truth, but is most perfectly worked up in the style of a regular prize-fight only with a view to keeping the right in words—if he considers how perfect Plato shows himself to be, though this is but his first and solitary attempt, in exhibiting the way in which the matter of the sophistical questions that may be started continually dwindles away, while at the same time the pleasure and the pride of the actors increase, until at last the former merges into mere nonsense, and the two latter pass into the most extravagantly vain self-conceit, which confounds the ridicule of the intelligent with the assent of the simple, and only puffs itself out the more; and, lastly, if he notices the way in which the whole ends with that undisguised burst of ridicule so cheerily rung out, he will, we may be assured, at once admire the life and dramatic power of the whole, but will however afterwards discover in the subject thus exclusively regarded one not quite worthy of the author. And though no one can immediately doubt whether Plato could have composed any thing with this view, still every reader will require an occasion for the composition of a piece which can only be conceived to be occasional, and will be surprised to find it given in the series of scientific productions. But it is strange enough that attention has always been exclusively given to this sophistical dramatizing when to every reader the dialogue presents more important matter, a genuine philosophical bearing and a visible reference to other Platonic writings, in that other conversation; which, though but in an interrupted and intermitted form, Socrates carries on with Clinias, and which, like the dialogues up to this point, treats of the communicability of virtue and the nature of the most exalted knowledge.

This conversation may be regarded as an illustrative continuation of the Menon, and therefore, mediately, of the Theætetus and Gorgias, as it enlarges further, by an indirect method, upon the same subject. For the consequence which we have often only inferred from former dialogues as their proper result, without finding it verbally enunciated, is so verbally enunciated in this, and, as if it were already evident, assumed; and the problems with which the subsequent dialogues are engaged are here discovered and pointed out. By this then, if it is actually the case, the place which we have assigned to this dialogue, is sufficiently assured to it.

And of this every reader may convince himself if he considers the course of this conversation, the main points of which we will here note down in a few words. In this it is at once assumed almost at the beginning, as had been proved in the Gorgias, that pleasure is not identical with the good, and therefore that happiness which is sought as a common object, is defined, only for the purpose of keeping to the ordinary translation of the word *eudaimonia*, to be "right doing" (or, "well doing"). At the same time the conversation connects itself with the Menonic position, that every thing which is ordinarily called a good is not so in and for itself by virtue of the mere possession of it, but becomes so first by coming under the power of wisdom so as to be governed and managed by it. Accordingly the proper object of desire is defined to be knowledge, to which Plato here deliberately gives the more exalted name of wisdom, and without even mentioning that lower grade which is there called correct conception. But this is by no means a sign which can imply that this distinction had not yet been made, or that Plato contradicts himself in any way consciously or unconsciously: but the ground of it is as follows: just at the beginning, where Socrates states the problem, the two, the search, that is, after wisdom and the diligent endeavour to attain virtue, are laid down as identical or as connected in the most intimate manner. He intends therefore by this, expressly to show what he meant by what is only thrown out at last in the Menon, that it is certainly necessary to seek that virtue and statesmanship which proceed from wisdom, notwithstanding the fact that they have not yet existed, because without them those more common kinds which are satisfied with right conception, can have no permanent existence. After the proper result of the Menon has been thus enunciated and elucidated, it is now enquired further what that knowledge must be, and after it has been established, in part with reference to the Gorgias, that it must be an art which is capable at the same time both of producing and using its object, and thus several particular arts have been brought forward by way of example which satisfy these conditions, the conversation comes at last, less by the strictly scientific method of analysis and investigation, than by the unmethodical process of promiscuous adaptation, to the real political or kingly art to which all others surrender their products for its use. But now the progressive advance of the dialogue is at an end, and the conversation changes again into a hesitative kind of speculation which only starts riddles and hands them over with a few hints to the reflection of the hearer for their solution. It is in this sense then that the product of that art is investigated, and nothing is discoverable except that if in the good we are always to inquire after the *end* we must always come round in a circle; in this sense Socrates quite at the beginning started the question whether to teach wisdom and to create a passion for it belongs to the same art; and it is precisely in this sense that the relation between the true and the good, wisdom and art, is so multifariously repeated and brought to light. And thus, as was before maintained, this conversation contains, on the one hand, corroborative illustration of the preceding dialogues: on the other hand, the reader is to be excited not to rest content with the assumptions there made, as that virtue and wisdom are the useful, and thus this conversation becomes a preparatory indication pointing to the subsequent dialogues, in particular the Statesman and Philebus; and hence on their account, the Euthydemus appears to be a transitional member by no means superfluous, and here certainly, quite in its proper place.

After we have thus properly estimated the essential part of the dialogue, it then becomes easy to take up another view of the remainder also. For the question arises of itself, was Plato, whom in the dialogues immediately preceding the Euthydemus we have already found occasionally engaged in controversy with the founders of contemporary Socratic schools; was he, I say, likely now again to commence a battle, for which the time had quite gone by, against earlier sophists whose influence and exertions were suppressed without it, as soon as ever the Socratic schools had become regularly formed? and was he likely to support this superfluous contest by such an expence of demonstrative art, and to be so well pleased with himself in the execution of his task as is here manifestly the case? Who then were these men, Dionysodorus and Euthydemus, to deserve such notice and meet with such treatment? History is silent respecting them more than any other of the sophists mentioned by Plato, so that we may certainly maintain that they never formed anywhere any kind of school, nay, it would even seem that they were not generally men in very great repute. Xenophon mentions Dionysodorus and speaks of the time when he taught the art of war, whence we must conclude that it is a real fact which Socrates mentions that they did this first, though probably more as tacticians than trainers in the art of fighting, and only applied late to philosophizing sophisticism. Plato himself in the Cratylus brings forward Euthydemus, but with a sentiment flowing immediately from the principles of the Ionic philosophy, and from which moreover no such sophistical misapplication immediately ensues, so that we do not at once recognize this Euthydemus in him. Aristotle also mentions him, and that with a few positions of the same kind as we find here, though their formulæ will from their nature admit only of an ironical application, and could never be directed against philosophy; and hence Euthydemus would not have deserved so cruel a treatment for their sake. On the other hand Aristotle brings forward almost all the formulæ which here occur, several of them even verbally, without mentioning Euthydemus or his brother, but ascribing them entirely to the Eristic philosophers. Moreover, there is an important passage in our dialogue in which the catch-questions brought forward are mostly referred to the principle of Antisthenes, that there is no such thing as contradiction. Now if we compare with this several particular allusions in the dialogue, and another passage of Aristotle, where he says that Gorgias, the first instructor of Antisthenes, taught how to practise these matters, but not upon first principles, and consequently only communicated a few particular maxims and not the whole art itself, more and more light falls upon the whole, and it becomes very probable that under the name of those two sophists Plato intended rather to assail the Megarian schools and Antisthenes. He might be inclined to spare the former for old friendship's sake, which connected him with the

founder of them ; and he might prefer not mentioning
Antisthenes by name in order to avoid personality as
much as possible and to expose himself less to his
rough treatment. And in considering this point indeed
we must remember, in order to come to the right conclusion, that much was very intelligible to contemporaries, and would spontaneously obtrude itself upon their
notice, which we can only discover by laborious means,
and a variety of combinations and comparisons. From
the extravagant ridicule moreover the attentive reader
is made aware throughout of a profound and bitter
satire upon the then prevailing degeneracy among those
even who professed themselves disciples of Socrates.

Still however there remains yet something to illustrate and explain. For if we consider accurately what
it in reality is that is here criticised, and controverted
only in a spirit of ridicule, it must indeed be generally
allowed that the particular examples as they here occur
deserve nothing else; it is however not to be overlooked,
that the whole tissue of these lies and cheats was in
its nature nothing but that scepticism, which always ac-
companies the doctrine of flux and progressive incomplete existence, generally or partially taken up, in its
particular application to language. If Plato therefore
wished to treat this sophistical art independently and
for itself, it was necessary for him either to show shortly how closely it was connected with the principles
already refuted by him, or he was obliged to penetrate
deeper into its proper object,—language; and in this
also to point out together with the changeable, the unchangeable and constant. The first he certainly does,
but in such a manner that the greater part of the examples discussed have no business there. To the latter

he appears rather to point preliminarily than actually
to set to work in earnest upon the subject, which was
indeed under the circumstances scarcely possible; and
any one may see that Plato does not draw from the
various character of his examples the advantages which
present themselves for this purpose. Hence then the
inference manifestly is, that the examples there found
are not merely referable to the treatment of the subject, and have not been determined by it. What other
cause then produced them? and did Plato indulge himself in this empty trifling, and continue it so long from
mere pleasure in the exercise of dramatic power which
he applied to them? We are at least not compelled to
hold to this, and to ascribe to Plato in this dialogue
a mode of proceeding which is not generally peculiar to
him. For if we consider the particular examples according to their meaning, we shall find among them
several which have very much the appearance of alluding to attacks directed partly against the thoughts,
partly against the language and expression in Plato's
earlier writings; inasmuch as his opponents might have
twisted this point or that into nonsense by just such
sophistical tricks. And thus we again find, and certainly without feeling much surprise thereat, in this
dialogue also the same kind of polemics and extorted
self-defence which we had already found, almost gradually increasing in the immediately preceding dialogues;
which is moreover the character in which, in the introduction to the Theætetus, attention has been already
drawn to the Euthydemus.

And it is only by all this collectively considered
that the management of the whole can justify itself
before the judgment-seat of a higher criticism, or phi-

losophical spirit. For otherwise it might seem a vicious proceeding, and a disproportion destructive of all more exalted purpose, so to interweave as is here done mere ridicule of things utterly worthless, with the further advancement of genuine philosophical objects. It becomes however quite another matter when on the one side the ridicule is only the disguise of polemics which have relation to science itself, and in which, by the very method pursued personality is avoided, and on the other moreover the scientific bearing is itself less than usual, and only affords illustrations rather than delivers any thing of its own. It is moreover perfectly clear in this the first dialogue upon which we come after the Theætetus, repeated only as it is and not immediately represented, that Plato was necessarily brought back to this method from wanting to give free scope to the dramatic element which was, not possible otherwise than as a narration. Again, the construction of this dialogue has yet something peculiar in detail, not only from the two-fold internal dialogue, the members of which are quite separate from one another, but still more from the circumstance that the external one between Socrates and Crito to whom he narrates, is afterwards continued in a criticising spirit; and though such a proceeding is not to be found anywhere else, it agrees very well with the particular artificiality of this dialogue. Besides, this appendage contains further some polemics of its own, which have a different bearing from the dialogue itself, against the manner, namely, in which a certain respected class viewed and treated Philosophy, probably not without confounding it with Sophisticism. The same thing had been already alluded to in the Gorgias, but probably not properly understood by those whom it immediately concerned. Hence the practice is here in part more thoroughly attacked, and in part the person more distinctly indicated; and as the school of Isocrates was the most important of this kind at Athens, we can scarcely suppose otherwise than that the objections of this school were particularly meant.

V. CRATYLUS.

THE Cratylus has at all times given much trouble to the good and sturdy friends of Plato. For it seemed difficult to decide what opinion about language he does in reality profess; whether he is indeed of that which places the origin of language in convention and compact, and consequently looks upon all the details in it as indifferent and accidental; or of that which considering it in the light of a natural production ascribes to it inward truth and necessary correctness; or whether he may not perhaps have secretly in reserve that other opinion concerning language which suspects it to have been introduced among men by divine agency. Just as in the Menon we can never quite tell whether it is intended to be implied that virtue is simply practised *without,* and is consequently produced by custom in a kind of conventional manner, or viewed as matter of inward necessity, or whether it is to be regarded as a gift of the gods to men which comes to them according to the divine pleasure, and is properly on that account the only good. A still more difficult task was it to defend the great man in

the matter of the utterly false derivation and explanation of the words, when alas! among so many examples
there is hardly one that can meet with toleration, to
say nothing of support. For even though we may
be disposed to excuse, and regret that the admirable
philosopher, from fault of the times, was capable of
producing so little instructive or sound upon so important a subject, still this resource can never suffice,
because in fact the ignorance is too great, and even
against our inclination something like a feeling of
contempt will always enter into the surprise we feel,
that one who laid so much stress upon the obligation
we are under to know the variety and extent of our
ignorance, should have plunged into such trifling and
unmeaning play, upon a subject about which he manifestly knew nothing. On the other hand, much has
indeed been gained by the discovery of modern times,
that to Plato likewise all this was but play and jest,
and that here, as in several of his works, we are to
look for no exalted wisdom. Only even upon this view
it is again difficult to justify the profound philosopher
for such a mass of ponderous and pointless jesting, and
for his unexampled proceeding in allowing his unfortunate propensity for playing upon words to break out
in so astounding a manner; as a natural philosopher
would be astonished to come suddenly upon a complete
and prodigious layer of a rare kind of stone which
usually only appears distributed here and there in small
grains. And this discovery imposes upon us a difficult investigation, with a view, I mean, to separating
the jest from the earnest; unless Plato is to be
accused of the worst joke of all, namely, of affecting
a serious air in serious matters, and this too only for

a joke. Whoever then has embraced this latter view in a random kind of way, and thinks either to content himself with it in general, or by such a method to open up further traces for judging of or separating the details, and so taste about with a new palate among the old fruits and cates, we commend him to his employment; for us however it is necessary to strike into another road, and rather to follow out the work itself as if nothing had been said about it, and to try if it will not betray to us what it really means, as also to ascertain how we are to estimate every particular in it.

That we may then be able to consider more at our ease the more important matter, it may be advisable first to look at all the details, in order to draw attention separately to what is intended seriously, and what is jest. And first the principle which appears to be the ground-work of the whole, that language is the artificial instrument of the dialecticians, and that appellations must be given in conformity with the nature of things, does indeed sound strange when we hear it thus super-ficially stated; but it bears too great a resemblance to other investigations with which we are already acquainted, and follows too closely the fundamental laws of all Platonic speculation, to allow of our rejecting it as not seriously laid down. But the illustration which follows upon this, by means of more or less known proper names, which are referred to the condi-tion and peculiarities of persons or to circumstances in their life, this is clearly not serious in a similar sense, inasmuch as Socrates himself subsequently destroys it by the remark, that the manner in which particular individuals are named is not the same with that in which material things acquired their appellations, but that we must look in the latter case to the appellations of the various species of the general and eternal. Now this is again manifestly said in earnest, inasmuch as these names do certainly form a moiety of the core of language, as this core also, like the Greek, divided into nouns and verbs. But when again the dialogue pursues this further, and investigates the natural correctness of nouns, first in the names of the gods, which are so treated that we cannot well say, that as proper names, they would not have belonged rather to the first section, and then in those of the heavenly bodies and their relations, the elements, the virtues, the various other phænomena of the mind, and finally the poles of all thought and knowledge itself, all this, when thus taken in the gross, is manifestly jest. We infer this not only from the violent method of dealing with the words, from the total neglect of the distinction between fundamental and inflected syllables, and the commutation and transposition of letters, so that oftentimes a scarcely similar sound is produced; as well as from the unlimited share ascribed to the desire of embellishment in the then construction of words, so that, as Socrates allows, something was introduced from the very first in order to conceal the meaning, and consequently in entire contradiction to the supposed nature of language; but we recognize the jesting spirit even far more in the expressions of Socrates himself, when he ridicules this species of wisdom as an inspiration quite foreign to him, which he would follow to-day, but to-morrow would purify himself of; when by the same process he educes a similar sense out of opposite words, and shows consequently that it destroys

itself; when he appeals in one place to barbarian
origin or the destructive effects of time, and subsequently declares this himself to be the excuse of one
who would avoid giving any regular account. But this
mass of joking leads yet again to something perfectly
serious, to the distinction, I mean, between fundamental
and derivative words, to the investigation of what is
the proper object of representation in language, to the
distinction between the imitative and musical use of
the voice, and to the illustration of how in conformity
with it the original significancy must be looked for
in the letters. And this is certainly serious, because
Plato makes Socrates sketch a theory on purpose,
perfectly corresponding to those dialectic ground-forms
which he has already brought forward in the Phædrus.
But the manner again in which this is illustrated, by
way of example, in particular letters, and their meaning investigated, can hardly be taken for serious; for
the way in which Socrates sets to work in this must
appear very frivolous to any one, who, however superficially, balances the problems and solutions against one
another, as our annotations will do in the particular
passages; nay, even to Socrates himself, as he assures
us, his own method has a very vacant and ridiculous
air. And should any one be inclined to think that
all we find here wears such a harlequin and strange
dress, and is intentionally made ridiculous only because
it is intended to prove by violence that the doctrine
of Heraclitus lies at the bottom of the formation of
language, let him not disguise from himself the fact,
that in the few examples in which an Eleatic style of
thought is intended to appear there is quite as great an
accumulation of all that is random and vague. But if

there is any one to whom the grounds suggested for forming a judgment do not otherwise appear sufficient, we would recommend him, in order to decide accurately between jest and earnest, simply and exclusively to follow Euthyphro, and when *he* is a party to the sport, and the wisdom is referred to him, then let the reader consider that he is certainly in the province of jest. Moreover, from this the serious parts also will admit of being recognized, and we shall discover where they begin and how far, inaccessible to that pleasant spirit, they reach. And in whatever light we regard the dialogue we must inevitably arrive at the same conclusion, that Plato only marked out the particular details of that discussion upon language with a view of bringing forward a comedy, or whatever may be the meaning of it, but that all that is general is to be taken quite as seriously as the core of every Platonic dialogue. And this consideration must at once make every not unintelligent reader of Plato inclined to leave those details to rest at present upon their own merits as collateral matter, intelligible perhaps only from the consideration of the whole, and to begin the understanding of that whole, if it is to be rightly estimated, at the other end; and to suspect in the Cratylus a similar arrangement to that in the Euthydemus, where likewise an ironical whole and a serious investigation are strangely interwoven with one another.

Now if we consider apart the serious subject-matter of the work, the investigation into the nature of language ceases at once to appear alone entitled to that character, although it certainly presents itself most obtrusively and in a manner sufficiently strange. For the subjects of Platonic investigation generally occur in several works, and after they have been once discussed, they are subsequently viewed once or twice again from different points, or otherwise put into a clearer light, until, as being made perfectly clear, they are taken up into the great and all-comprehending work. But we have no trace whatever that this thread, of which certainly it cannot be said that it is here spun to the end, was ever again continued; and had fate grudged us the possession of this one dialogue, the subject would have been totally omitted, and we should be obliged to say that Plato's position relatively to language was that of a genuine artist; for that he understood excellently well how to use it, and to construct it for himself after a method of his own, but had nothing to say upon the subject. And this indeed even now, notwithstanding that this loss has not occurred to us, is the opinion of many persons, though it is far from being our own. For if we take notice of the manner in which he grapples to the opinion of Hermogenes, and instead of something compiled at random and confirmed only by convention, considers language as a thing which followed in its origin and process of formation an inward necessity—as a type of an idea, and as an instrument of art to be criticized and improved by the artist who uses it; and then of the way in which he compares the combination and connection of sounds with the connection and combined relations of things, and regards the two as systems running collaterally with and corresponding to one another, and which are therefore united in a higher; and how he recommends us to seek, in the physiological quality of sounds, the ground of all that is significant in language, not so much as imitation of the audible but as expression of the nature of things;—all this considered, we shall be obliged to confess that this is some of the most profound and most important matter that has ever been delivered upon the subject of language.

It is indeed true that what Socrates adduces in opposition to Cratylus, when he speaks of the necessity of assuming the presence in language of a capricious element, intelligible only upon the supposition of some kind of convention, may appear of a weaker character, and even in the light only of a subterfuge resorted to by one who was incapable of giving a satisfactory account of the matter; but it is equally certain that it only appears so because it is more difficult to understand, and required continuation to complete what is only delivered in imperfect hints. For when it is considered that this whole proof proceeds upon the principle that a better and a worse* enters into the affixing of appellatives, and this not so that the better exists in one and the worse in another language, inasmuch as every language, beginning with the first elements of speech, is something essentially peculiar, but that each appears in the same from a comparison of the variations which take place within the substance of every one, and consequently with reference to their growth and progress;—it will be seen that the capricious element in words according to Plato's peculiar

---

* Crat. p. 429. B.

ΣΩ. 'Ουδὲ δὴ ὄνομα, ὡς ἔοικε, δοκεῖ σοι κεῖσθαι τὸ μὲν χεῖρον, τὸ δὲ ἄμεινον ;

KP. Οὐ δῆτα. κ. τ. λ. Where Socrates' argument goes to prove the affirmative.—P. 432. D. he says, Θαρρῶν τοίνον, ὦ γενναῖε, ἔα καὶ ὄνομα τὸ μὲν εὖ κεῖσθαι, τὸ δὲ μή . . .

principles as to imperfect existence, must vanish as existing merely in appearance, provided only we proceed to draw further deductions, in Plato's own spirit, from what he says upon the relation of language to knowledge. In doing this, however, we shall be obliged to leave it undecided whether he establishes what he here says preliminarily only, with a view to leaving the reader to find out the further consequences himself, or whether he did in fact only see thus far and no farther upon these principles; as it must indeed be confessed that the origin of the positive element in that which is naturally necessary is not quite so easily seen in the case of less known objects. And this may be the part in which, from fault of the times, Plato has not perhaps gone quite so far as a way would lead which we might be able to point out to him, though his deficiency in this respect cannot be considered as in any way unworthy of his genius. But whatever may be the case with him, thus much is clear, as every unprejudiced person must see, that it is only by removal of the opposition between the opinion of Cratylus and that of Hermogenes that Plato's view of language is intended to come out, though the manner and means of effecting that removal are only just pointed out; and Plato himself seems to have considered further enlargement of the subject, according to these views, as something on the one side as no longer possible, and on the other as not yet so.

The more however this subject appears to be only sketched, and the discussion of it left altogether incomplete, the less claim it has, according to Plato's method, to be considered the subject of an exclusive work. We should rather be led to believe that it is started only

by way of a kind of example, something like the art
of speaking in the Phædrus. Hence then we must
look further for a ground and purpose of the dialogue
in other relations, and institute a supplementary inquiry as to whether there does not exist in the work
we are considering something beyond what has hitherto
come out that may afford instruction upon this point.
And the attentive reader will soon discover what he
seeks. For although the speculation into the theory
of language is not brought to a successful termination,
we find notwithstanding, in the very first outlines of it,
thus much at all events clearly enunciated as an immediate consequence; that the relation of language to knowledge is such, that, even assuming for a moment the
divine origin of the former, it is in every way impossible
for it to be regarded as the source of the latter, whether
original and the object of discovery, or derived and
the subject of instruction, and that if a dependent
relation is to obtain between them, language must be
considered rather as a product of knowledge, and existing conditionally through it. Now if we consider at
the same time the use that is made of etymology in
the ironical part, in order to justify from language
the Heraclitic doctrine, so that Socrates even seriously
allows that this tendency may be pointed out in language, and again the manner in which the whole is
pervaded throughout by a continuous polemical spirit
in opposition to that doctrine, with the expression of
which the dialogue concludes as it begun, assuming the
existence of something constant and self-independent,—
we have unquestionably discovered a point capable of
spreading a sufficient light over the whole, inasmuch
as it lays before us such a connection of that whole

with the preceding dialogues, that the same glance
enables us clearly to determine the purport of the work,
and also the place which it is to occupy in the series
of the productions of Plato.

For the caution which is intended to warn us, that
language cannot of itself lead to knowledge, and that
from it alone it is impossible to decide which of two
opposite views is the true one or the false, is manifestly of a polemical character, and supposes that such
a process had been on some occasions applied; and
these polemics essentially belong to that series of
efforts to establish the *reality* of knowledge, and its
eternity and impersonality, in which we see Plato engaged during this second period. Neither does it seem
to be a very difficult question where we are to look
for this process. For as on the one hand, even among
the disciples of Socrates, collaterally with the true
philosophy, mere empiricism, the offspring of lower
modes of thought, soon got the upper hand again, and
in the Gorgias and Theætetus Plato especially wages
war against this, when he shows that the idea of the
good is not abstracted from the feeling of the pleasant,
and that knowledge is not derived from sensuous perception or even from right conception, so on the other
side a system of unmeaning play again got the upper
hand among them—the play with the equally un-
substantial and exhausted forms of philosophy, which
scarcely preserves any subject to which it can attach itself
except language. This abuse can be imputed to one
only of the two opposite extremes which Plato always
has in view, that, I mean, involved in the doctrines of
the Ionic Philosophy; it must however, when taken
in connection with this, present a twofold appearance.

One, when viewed with the apprehension of the scepticism of these doctrines as to the essentiality of knowledge, and that it abused the forms of language in order to exhibit everything as in a state of inextricable confusion and inconstant variation, which is precisely the theory which Plato exposes in its nothingness in the Euthydemus, and of which the sophistical philosophy, again reviving in the Megarian and Eretrian schools, has to bear the burden and the blame. *Another*, when it is remembered that these doctrines themselves could be dogmatic, and hence felt no compunction in attempting to prove, when they could, that even language, though it may appear to grasp and keep hold of its objects, does nevertheless, in this process of affixing appellations, itself recognise, by the method pursued, the ceaseless flux of all things. But at this point we seem to be almost deserted by history. For it does not appear that language was used in any particular manner as a means for the foundation of knowledge, or as a canon whereby to judge of it, until we meet with such an application in the exaggerated grammatical tendency of the Stoic school; and it will scarcely be thought necessary to pursue this solitary trace. But, that we may not lose ourselves deeper in details and in obscure hints, when it is once remembered how largely the natural philosophy of the Stoics borrowed from Heraclitus; how Antisthenes is- to be regarded as the founder not only of the Cynics but also of the Stoics, only that these latter reverted more to Plato, from whom the former, seduced by personal differences, had separated himself more widely probably than their scientific views had rendered necessary; and when it is considered further that Antisthenes is supposed to have expounded the work of Heraclitus, without however mentioning by name any particular work upon the subject, while, on the other hand, several works of Heraclitus occur which manifestly have language for their subject;—we can scarcely feel a doubt as to who is the real object of these polemics. And hence also it is very soon explained, why, notwithstanding that the immediate object of the dialogue could only be so imperfectly discussed, the Cratylus nevertheless became an exclusive whole, and took the precise form in which we now find it. For the relation of language to knowledge, which constitutes its principal subject, manifestly rests entirely upon the doctrine adduced in the Theætetus, about the distinction between knowledge and right conception. For language, as it is actually *given*, stands here upon exactly the same ground with conception, or rather is in reality one and the same with it. Thus words are signs and types of things, and in them a closer or more indistinct, a more or less pure, a clearer or more obscure impress, is possible—thus in both error has its province traced out by confusion or exchange of relation, and both even coincide in this respect, that the attention is drawn to numbers as a particular object of consideration. Every one however who remembers the position which this distinction occupies in the Theætetus, will allow that the essential matter of the Cratylus could by no means have been taken into that dialogue as a digression. And so much the less because Plato, in order to say what was of most importance, required the result of the Menon, which we find therefore here supposed, that knowledge does not, properly speaking, pass by transference from one to another, but that discovery and learning are the same things in all men, namely, remembrance. In like manner the relation to be established between language and knowledge connects itself further and more particularly with polemics, against the strange and all-confusing denial of the possibility of error in the province of conception ; polemics which we find begun in the Theætetus, and continued in the Euthydemus. If, then, we remember moreover the temptation which presented itself to overwhelm the hostile Antisthenes with a whole body of ridicule, we see the Cratylus form itself as it were into an exclusive whole, out of the Theætetus and Euthydemus, and by means of its character, as well as what is connected with the immediate subject, secure its place in this series of the Platonic works; for it is as little devoted to *personal* polemics as the Euthydemus. Moreover it contains not only supplementary matter and illustrations of this dialogue and the Theætetus—as, for example, just at the beginning the decisively repeated declaration in opposition to Protagoras, from a point at which, in order to continue the dialogue, Plato had himself opened a loophole for the philosopher to escape through; and immediately thereupon the manner in which he describes the peculiar nature of the sophistical philosophy exposed in the Euthydemus; and further on the distinction, which also in the Theætetus is allowed to drop, between a whole and a collective mass, is explained from the opposition between quality and quantity ; and there are many particulars of the same kind. Quite as little can it be said that our dialogue only states the unity of the theoretical and practical as we have already found it stated in the Theætetus and Gorgias, and their relation to one another—although this too is done partly by particular allusions in the etymological part, which remind us very strongly of the Gorgias, partly by the manner in which the reality of the Beautiful and Good is here also at last connected with that of knowledge.——But besides all this, the Cratylus also advances the scientific object of Plato in the same way as the character of this series carries it along with it. Two things especially are here to be taken into account. First of all, the doctrine of the relation of Types to the Archetypes; where in fact language and its relation to things is only to be considered as an example, but one by which Plato did really intend to throw out a first notice of the doctrine of ideas and their relation to the material world, which is immediately preparatory to the Sophist. Secondly, as in the Euthydemus the kingly art, the object of which can only be absolutely the good, is set up as that which exists for itself in the identity of use and production, while all other arts, the object of which, whether as producing or using, is only partial, are merely its instruments and subordinate agents; so, on the other hand, dialectics are here represented as the art whose object is absolutely the true in the identity of knowledge and external expression, while every thing else connected with it, and conception and language especially, is only its instrument. Now this parallel visibly draws the connection between those apparent opposites closer together; and by being placed a step higher we at once more clearly perceive the philosopher on the summit, uniting in himself the dialectician and the statesman. Nay, in this respect the Cratylus is in a peculiar manner placed in connection with the Gorgias by means of the strange and obscure analogy, and which is certain only intelli-

gible upon the view we have taken of the whole—that
analogy which is here set up between law and language, inasmuch as it is repeatedly said that language
exists in virtue of a law, so that the law-giver and
word-maker are viewed almost as identical. This is
introduced by the circumstance, that as, according to
the saying of Hermogenes, language is to be regarded
only as the work of caprice and convention; though it
must be remembered that convention, even though tacit,
and law, merged into one another more among the
Hellenes than among us; so likewise the sophists and
the school of Aristippus explained even moral ideas to
be the offspring of caprice, and only introduced from
without by the ordinances of the law-giver, and even
by means of language itself. Plato, on the contrary,
discovers in the moral judgment the same inward necessity that he does in language, though this necessity
cannot be outwardly expressed in either, purely and
perfectly, except by one profoundly acquainted with
the nature of each. And if we pursue this indication,
a further application will reveal itself for what is said
upon the subject of the capricious element which enters
into the works of the legislator.

Now as to the etymological part, which is for the
most part ironical,—although in this likewise much that
is seriously meant may be found dispersed, if not in
the etymologies, at all events in the explanations of
them,—we should still be best able to judge how merci-
ful and just, or how unmerciful and exaggerated, the
satirical imitation is, if the works of Antisthenes that
are mentioned, especially those about the use of words,
had been preserved to us, where we should also pro-

bably meet with Euthyphro again, and obtain some information about him. For if he is not a person taken out of some satirized dialogue, it is impossible to conceive how he comes here. And, what is most important, we should then be better able to see what other allusions may be here further concealed. For it is certain that what we find in the dialogue is not all directed at the one person who is the object of the satire, but, as we have seen also in the Euthydemus, a large share is intended to be devoted to self-defence. This is here the more evident, as the playful manner in which Plato sometimes used language may have found censurers enough, especially among those who were in the habit cf availing themselves of much not very different from this play in proof of their opinions. And in this point of view too we should naturally expect to see this play here pushed to extremities, and to find our dialogue indulging in the very last degree of epideixis as it were in this kind; as strange explanations brought in from elsewhere are outdone in it by still stranger of its own.

And this etymological part has been the *crux* of the translator, and it was matter of long and perplexing deliberation with him how to extricate himself from the difficulty. The introduction generally of the Greek words appeared an intolerable expedient, and it seemed better to let the Socrates who was speaking German once for all derive German from German. On the other hand, it was not possible to do this with the proper names—in these it was necessary to preserve the original tongue; and since both methods now stand in company with one another, the reader will at all events have occasion to congratulate himself that no one exclusively pervades the whole. But as that which elsewhere occurs only in detached particulars comes out here in a mass, so on the other hand it cannot be denied that the art of dialogic composition goes somewhat back; and when we compare the Cratylus with the Euthydemus, with which it stands most nearly connected in so many respects, we shall find that in the latter the ironical and the serious parts are interwoven far more beautifully with one another. Here, on the contrary, Plato appears almost overcome by the superabundance of philological jest, so harsh and abrupt are the transitions in the latter part of the dialogue; sometimes, after short digressions, he turns back to what has gone before, as if it were something new rather than what had been already said—sometimes he does bring forward matter actually new, but for which no preparation whatever has been made and which is harshly subjoined to what immediately precedes, in a manner that might almost lead us to doubt, if we were to consider such passages as these exclusively, whether it is Platonic. This is particularly noticeable at the point from which the signification of the letters is explained. But the whole will admit no manner of doubt of its genuineness, and the most that can be said is, that Plato after that point returned to his subject with no great inclination to do so, and sketched as slightly as possible what still remained to be said. Of the persons of the dialogue, there is I fear but little to be said: Hermogenes is also known from Xenophon as a not rich brother of the rich Callias; Cratylus is mentioned not only as a pupil of Heraclitus, but also as a teacher of Plato in his youth—a piece of information which does indeed rest upon the authority of the Metaphysics of Aristotle, but has fortunately too little influence upon our dialogue to render it necessary for us to test it more accurately in this place.

VI. THE SOPHIST.

In the Sophist we distinguish at once and at the first glance two perfectly separate masses, one of which, distributed into the two extremities, starts with the idea of art, and endeavours, by continuous division and exclusion, to find the nature and true explanation of a Sophist; while the other, which forces itself into the middle of this, after the introduction of the problem of the possibility of co-existence and community in ideas, speaks of the existent and non-existent. If therefore we regard solely the construction and connection of the whole, we must look for its essential object and chief matter in that external mass, and take the internal only for a well-chosen or indispensable mean for attaining that object. For it is entirely in the natural course of the investigation concerning the Sophist, that a necessity arises of assuming the possibility of a non-existent, and of establishing something as to its admissibility; and as soon as this has been done so far that the original investigation can be continued, this investigation again comes in, and so completely fills up the dialogue that they conclude simultaneously. If, on the other hand, we look to the importance and scientific bearing of the two parts, the external falls entirely into the back-ground as something in comparison with the internal, almost insignificant; especially as the subject of it had been already touched upon in several points of view, and we do not in fact here learn anything new as to the nature of the Sophist, the novelty consisting solely in the method and combination. Hence this question is far less entitled to be considered as the subject of a work so important even in point of extent, than the other part, which is in itself so much more philosophical. For in this part not only is the nature of the non-existent, which was at that time the subject of such various dispute, discussed more thoroughly than elsewhere, and, as we may clearly see, the question solved to Plato's perfect satisfaction, but also that of positive existence itself profoundly entered into, and the methods hitherto pursued in the philosophical consideration of it, criticised in some important features. So that, looking to this circumstance, we might be disposed to look for the real subject-matter of the dialogue solely and immediately in the middle part of it, and to believe that the nearer the extremities any thing is found the more such matter passes into mere shell and setting. To this may be added, that in the method pursued in the enquiry after the nature of the Sophist, it is impossible to overlook the spirit of ridicule which indulges itself partly in pointing out the close connection between the business of the Sophist and all manner of mean occupations, and in particular in representing him in a great variety of ways as a pedlar, and then again constantly takes up anew the image of a sly beast very difficult to catch. And even the method applied of finding the object sought, merely by continuous subdivision, is here almost spoken of with contempt. For although it constitutes an important part of the dialectic art, and is elsewhere very seriously pursued and recommended by Plato, it still appears here, when the subject is jocular, to be not only negligently handled, as when, for example, first of all, exchange is made a subdivision of fighting, and then again fighting of exchange; and these two were originally placed as parallel and similar to one another, and generally a sort of caprice pervades the whole; but this process is actually ridiculed by Plato himself, inasmuch as he shows, from the very multitude of the attempts, that the nature of the subject is never discovered by these means, but only particular marks collected by which it may be known, as indeed at last, when the subject is correctly and exhaustively exhibited, he no longer starts thus from a general position, but from a determinate notion.

But on the other hand, this external part is still most closely connected with the internal, and the latter would not appear itself in its full light without the former. For, to go no further, the idea that the description of the Sophist might be a merely subordinate work, must be rejected as mistaken, simply because the statesman and philosopher are required in the same manner as the Sophist, and thus the foundation is laid of a great trilogy. This trilogy, indeed, it would seem, Plato did not perfectly execute, but the purpose of it must clearly have been to complete the exposition of the nature of these arts, and the description of the method of operation used by their masters in an entire whole, to be rendered the more vivid by the method pursued. And even in our present dialogue, the circumstance cannot escape the attentive reader, that together with the possibility of falsehood, the inclination for it and the life in it are to be represented as far removed from true knowledge and real existence. Nay, as the Sophist only appears fully by his place being definitely discovered, and not before it is so discovered, so, on the other hand, the discovery of his place is facilitated, and the dimness and obscurity of mere semblance and fallacious opinion made intelligible by starting from the well-known occupation which he pursues and can only pursue there. And thus, even here in the middle point of the second part of the Platonic works, we find a confirmation of what we said at the beginning of that part upon the peculiar form of the works belonging to it. The more closely, then, we consider this circumstance, the more we must be aware that there is here nothing to be rejected as mere shell, but that the whole dialogue is like a precious fruit of which a true connoisseur is glad to enjoy the outward peel at the same time with the fruit itself, because grown as the former is into the whole, it could not be separated without hurting the pure and proper relish of the latter.

This being supposed, we cannot now overlook the remaining characteristics in which this external part of the dialogue is pre-eminently rich. For the reader, from whom too much does not lie concealed under the cover of insignificant things, the knowledge of which is here brought forward, will see Plato, in part defending combinations made in earlier works and which had perhaps been assailed, and showing how nearly the smallest thing may be related to the largest in a particular point of view; and then again constructing words, almost extravagantly, in order to show how necessary this becomes as soon as a systematic process adopts subjects to which it has been hitherto strange, and at the same time to bring to notice a particular indifference as to the affixing of appellations; ennobling moreover the purifying Socratic process, and pointing out its proper pedagogic place; ridiculing moreover the arrogant method of the rhetoricians and politicians who used to confound things the most different, and, as if it profited nothing to distinguish such trifles, brought the true philosopher and the sophist under the same appellation. Which is just the reason why Plato introduces among the explanations characteristic of the sophist that most distinct one which describes the process of the philosopher, in which the stranger is continually left in doubt, whether he is to allow it to obtain as an explanation of what a sophist is, and on the other hand repeatedly sets up the close connection of the sophist with the demagogue.

If we look only to the inward, and in itself more philosophical, part of the dialogue, its characteristics will appear strikingly similar to those of the whole. For it begins with the question as to whether there can be a false in speech and thought, simply resolved into that of the possibility of a non-existent, and of its possessing any attributes, or whether non-existence cannot be predicated of anything. The arguments usually at that time brought forward on the positive side of the question, and with which we are already acquainted from notices of them in the Theætetus, Euthydemus and Cratylus, are here a second time advanced, strengthened and confirmed on all sides, and as soon as it is shown, from the necessity of assuming the possibility of a non-existent, that the existence of mere fallacious appearance and error must be admitted, and as what they are to be admitted, this part also is at an end, and the dialogue goes on into the investigation about the Sophist. Accordingly it would seem that with reference also to this part, what it begins and ends with, namely, the question relative to the non-existent and error, must obtain for the proper subject-matter; and on the other hand, that what is let in between the parts of this investigation and occupies the middle of it, must appear partly to be only a mean for reaching that end, partly a digression not unwillingly seized upon. But what reader, when he looks to the tenor of this digression, will not be compelled to apprehend in it immediately the most valuable and precious core of the dialogue, and that the more certainly, as here for the first time almost in the writings of Plato, the most inward sanctuary of philosophy is opened in a purely philosophical manner, and as, generally, existence is better and more noble than non-existence. For in the course of the investigation about the non-existent, exactly in the way in which this arose as a something higher in that about the Sophist, the question arises as to the community of ideas*, upon which all real thought and all life in knowledge depends; and the notion of the life of the existent, and of the necessary identity and reciprocality of existence and knowledge is most regularly disclosed. And there is not anything within the sphere of philosophy

---

* P. 251. B.

—— καὶ δή που χαίρουσιν οὐκ ἐῶντες ἀγαθὸν λέγειν ἄνθρωπον, ἀλλὰ τὸ μὲν ἀγαθὸν ἀγαθὸν, τὸν δὲ ἄνθρωπον ἄνθρωπον —— Ε. —— καὶ τιθῶμεν γε αὐτοὺς λέγειν, εἰ βούλει, πρῶτον μηδενὶ μηδὲν μηδεμίαν δύναμιν ἔχειν κοινωνίας εἰς μηδέν ——

more important, or any method peculiar to the views and method of Plato, more suitably adapted to conduct pupils and readers to the point than that which is here pursued. Let the reader but notice first how this the most inward, and, in point of extent, far from important kernel of the whole, exactly according to nature's method, forms itself into two halves externally, quite separate from one another, but quite grown together, and organically connected in the closest manner. For first, starting with the statement of the impossibility, that these persons should have reached the sphere of abstract existence who begin with mere unity, or they who continue to remain within the sphere of opposites; the real life of the existent, in which all opposites reciprocally penetrate and unite, is pointed out, and at the same time it is shown that knowledge can subsist neither without rest nor without motion, neither without station nor without flux, neither without constancy nor without progression, but in each pair requires a union of both. And let no one be misled by the apparently sceptical surprise at this required amalgamation of opposites, inasmuch as this is the last point at which the indirect method of demonstration, at the highest summit of which we here find ourselves, must terminate. And thus again, as if some quite new matter was arising, and without even the connection being pointed out, a descent is made from this sphere of the highest existence into that of opposites, which are here represented by the great one of motion and rest*, and it is shown that, first, community with opposites is founded upon the self-identity and diversity†

---

* P. 254. D.   † τὸ ταὐτὸν καὶ θάτερον.

of the existent as common properties, and that in this
sphere of diversity the existent exhibits itself necessarily, and in a variety of ways under the form of the
non-existent, so that there can never be any opposite
in respect of that highest existence itself considered as
such, but he who has not penetrated to the light of
true existence cannot, in general, advance further than
to this non-existence of true knowledge, and the ignorance of true existence. That, therefore, the nature of
all true philosophy is in fact here enunciated is a
position requiring no further elucidation for him who
is generally capable of apprehending it. Only let every
reader notice the manner in which these conclusions
are drawn, I mean, that Plato starts from the point
at which every one necessarily finds himself, the sphere
of conception, which is indeed at the same time that
of contradictory opposites, showing that the establishment in this of any propositions respecting the existent
carries with it exactly the same difficulties as the
establishment of propositions respecting the non-existent,
and that any one who thinks but to conceive or state
anything, must first acquire a title of possession by
virtue of which he can do so; and for this purpose the
glance into that higher sphere of speculation is disclosed for all who can penetrate into it, as the only
defence against the pretensions, not to be otherwise
repulsed, of sophistical contentiousness. And because
in our present dialogue the advance commences from
this point, and presses forward up to that, the highest,
immediately and without calling in the assistance of
any mythical expedient, or otherwise deserting the
course of the purest dialectics, we may fairly regard
the Sophist as the inmost core of all indirect specula-

tions of Plato, and to a certain degree as the first, and in its kind as a perfect image of the philosopher himself.

The latter moreover for the reason that as Plato himself grew as it were from the comprehensive survey and penetration of all earlier Grecian efforts in the province of philosophy, so also the inmost and most real substance of our dialogue results from a testing of the principles of all earlier philosophizing, of which we would here recall to the recollection of the reader as much as is necessary, and at the same time possible: for I regret that as to every point which it might be necessary and desirable to clear up, it does not also seem possible to do so. First of all then, that position which it is especially an object to refute, which asserts the utter impossibility of the non-existent, is referred to Parmenides as its most especial and pregnant source, and supported out of his own peculiar works, and it is accordingly demonstrated to him, with reference to existence, that it is not attainable under that higher potentiality of the unity of being and knowledge, by him who starts from simple unity without multiplicity, under the conditions of which the existent could not *be* under every form, not, consequently, both as a whole, and as in a state of progressiveness. It is in every way significant, that this refutation of Parmenides is put into the mouth of an Eleatic, and it might easily suggest itself that in what he here says, Plato only had in view a more correct explanation of the much misunderstood Parmenides; did not the expressions of the Stranger himself seem to oppose this view, and moreover he is not set up as a strict disciple of the Eleatic wisdom, but, as a dialogic personage, he forms in an extremely remarkable manner the transition as it were, from Parmenides himself to the Pythagorean Timæus. We have, therefore, certainly in this dialogue the chief *locus* of the difference between the Platonic and Eleatic philosophers, though we could by no means maintain with Simplicius, who otherwise says here and there much that is instructive about our dialogue, that in the dialogue of the Parmenides Plato adopted the existent unit from the philosopher; and in the Sophist, contradicted him throughout. Only it is a pity that we have not, I fear, enough remaining of Parmenides to enable us to conceive Plato's opinion about the philosopher, and especially for the reason that Plato nowhere expresses himself decidedly upon the philosophy of Parmenides as to the sensible world, though we might really feel ourselves authorized to refer much upon this subject to the Eleatic philosopher, notwithstanding that he is not named as the author of it. What, for instance, are we to say of those friends of the ideal who are mentioned at the last, who conceive the possibility of an imperfect existence *without* that perfect existence and separate from it, and consider man as participating in both*? It would not be surprising if many readers were to hit upon the idea that Plato here meant himself and his own doctrine; and when again, he involves this doctrine also in the perplexing contradiction in which the existent cannot be discovered, that this, on the other hand, is only pushing his indirect method to extremity. But

* P. 248. B.

Γένεσιν, τὴν δὲ οὐσίαν χωρίς που διελόμενοι λέγετε, ἤγαρ;

Καὶ σώματι μὲν ἡμᾶς γενέσει δι' αἰσθήσεως κοινωνεῖν, διὰ λογισμοῦ δὲ ψυχῇ πρὸς τὴν ὄντως οὐσίαν, ἥν ἀεὶ κατὰ ταὐτὰ ὡσαύτως ἔχειν φατέ, γένεσιν δὲ ἄλλοτε ἄλλως.

if the contradiction in this doctrine were to be removed, then also the distinction between perfect and imperfect existence must be destroyed, and thus Plato would have started from a manifestly false statement of his own doctrine. And moreover, that something is here meant which he actually intends to refute, must be obvious to every reader of any penetration, from the whole tone of the argument,—from this giant-combat, and this defence from the region of the invisible*. It is moreover easy to see that he has in view a perfectly well-known doctrine. Now we know Parmenides to have assumed the possibility of such an imperfect existence, and a world of appearance separate from perfect existence and in opposition to it, and thus, that man has communication with the one by means of perception, with the other by reason, would also be Parmenidean enough. If then we are to risk a guess as to why Parmenides is nevertheless not mentioned at all here, and it is entirely separated from the criticism upon his doctrines, we might say that in this part Plato had not so much Parmenides in his mind as other philosophers, against whom also he disputes elsewhere without naming them,—I mean the original and first Megarians. For these men in many particulars, as the ancients testify, approximated to Plato, under whose influence and co-operation their school had first formed itself, and thus, if we are to give as much liberty to critical combination as in this province it is

---

* P. 246.

Καὶ μὴν ἔοικέ γε ἐν αὐτοῖς οἷον γιγαντομαχία τις εἶναι διὰ τὴν ἀμφισβήτησιν περὶ τῆς οὐσίας πρὸς ἀλλήλους.

Οἱ μὲν εἰς γῆν ἐξ οὐρανοῦ καὶ τοῦ ἀοράτου πάντα ἕλκουσι . . . κ. τ. λ.

certainly necessary to do, traces are not wanting, that
even without the province of regular dialectics, they
adopted much out of the Eleatic system, and of this
I should be inclined to account this passage also as
an instance, unless some one can give a better founded
explanation. As opponents of the materialistic empirics,
of Democritus and Aristippus, for Plato has certainly
in his mind the latter also of the two, these philosophers might be most especially noticed. Again, no less
difficulty may seem to attend the explanation of what
precedes, whom, for instance, Plato means by those
who look upon the existent as involving multiplicity,
and in particular as double or triple, since so many
have equal pretensions to be considered, and then again
when we come to examine accurately, nothing is perfectly satisfactory. At first the reader may probably
be quite at a loss to know to what the argument is
to be referred ; but as soon as he remembers that in
the language of our dialogue Plato could not otherwise denote what Aristotle calls the setting up of these
principles, references and allusions pour in in clouds.
Least of all, however, will the appearance and tone of
the whole passage allow us to surmise the existence
of an allusion here to any thing abstruse, and advanced
only by a few less-known individuals. And quite as
little, certainly, to the Pythagoreans, although it might
otherwise be said of them, most appropriately, that *their*
existence is threefold, divided into the finite, the indefinite and the privative, but as no reference to this
school occurs anywhere else in the whole dialogue, it
is not probable that it was intended to be alluded to
in this passage; but as Aristotle also at the beginning
of his books on Physics says of all those who assume

the existence of a fundamental matter and two opposite functions, that they set up these principles, so also Plato has here especially in view the old Ionic philosophers. This seems also to receive confirmation from the circumstance of his separating those who assume a threefold from those who assume only a twofold existence, though he does this but very slightly and superficially. For it is precisely among the Ionians that so vague a description may be supposed to have existed, according as the fundamental matter was *given*, simple and independent of the functions, or conceived to be itself comprehended under the functions, as seems to have been the notion of Anaximander. It is only to the philosopher just named, that as far as we know the idea of the combat of the parts of the threefold existence with one another would apply. Should, however, this view appear still to be liable to much suspicion, as may perhaps be the case, we are on the other hand the more certain as to the later Ionic and Sicilian Muses*, that by them, Heraclitus and Empedocles are intended. Upon this point we have not only the express testimony of Simplicius, but the comparison of our passages, as well with what we know of the two men from other sources, as also with the way in which Plato expresses himself about them elsewhere is sufficient to establish the fact. Quite as undeniable, as Tennemann also has already observed, are the allusions to Antisthenes, where those philosophers are spoken of who do not admit the possibility of any community or connexion between ideas, but would take every thing independently and for itself, or who maintain the proposition that a false assertion enunciates

* P. 242. C.

nothing. These polemics cannot fail to force themselves upon the notice of those readers who have already accompanied us in the prosecution of them through several dialogues.

A more intimate relation between the Sophist and the Parmenides on the one side, and the Timæus on the other, is indicated not only externally by the more passive condition of Socrates in these three dialogues, but must also be of itself clear to every one, from the close connection in the subject-matter, even though it should be considered preliminarily, in a negative point of view alone. Hence it is natural to start the question, whether by a comparison of the three it may not be discovered from the dialogues themselves which of them was the latest and which the earliest. With respect then to the Timæus no doubt can arise as to its being the latest of these three works; but between the Sophist and Parmenides critics have certainly hesitated, and, as we have already remarked in the Introduction to that dialogue, have considered the last named as the later of the two. Now, disinclined as I am to refer by anticipation to what is to come, I would ask any one who knows the Timæus, whether the foundation of the Timæus is not laid perfectly and dialectically by the way in which here, in the Sophist, the existent is brought down within the sphere of opposites, as well as by the discussion which occurs here upon the subjects of identity and diversity, and whether it is not clear that our dialogue generally comes much nearer to the Timæus than the Parmenides does? This, however, is intended to be said preliminarily only, in order to show generally the point from which the question is to be viewed. But let the reader only compare the Sophist and Parmenides with one another, and observe whether anything whatever resembling an announcement of the dialogue named after the latter philosopher is to be found in the manner in which in the former Socrates appeals to his conversation with him; or whether, on the contrary, it is not manifest that the notice marking the age of the interlocutors * is there introduced with reference to and in justification of this dialogue, so that the whole passage has the appearance of being intended to bring the Parmenides to the recollection of the reader. If we compare further the particular corresponding passages, as for instance that about unity and totality, we shall unquestionably recognize in the Sophist a surer hand, and a more enlarged method. And we may even find the key to all that in the Parmenides appears to have a double sense, in the way in which essential existence, and existence in another sense, by participation that is, and so also the originally existent and existence in the sphere of contradictions are here kept separate: so that it would be strange to have already given the solution here, and then to have set the riddle afterwards in the Parmenides. Above all, however, let the reader but look to the first part of the Parmenides, and the problematical character of the expressions there as to the existence of ideas, and then consider whether this character could have found place, after the distinction had been so clearly referred to in the Theætetus, between knowledge and conception, and that between mere conception and appearance had been further subjoined here in the Sophist.

* P. 237. Παισὶν ἡμῖν οὖσιν.

But it may be useful here to throw a glance of comparison, not upon the Parmenides alone, but upon the remaining dialogues, with the view of availing ourselves of the opportunity of testing from this important point the arrangement we have hitherto pursued. First, then, the Sophist is manifestly the crown of all that is antisophistic in the Platonic dialogues, and no dialogue of which this is a principal component part can be conceived to have been written subsequently to the present, for it would have been as unseasonable in the author as putting the salt on after supper. So complete a process as we have here, by which the subject has its place assigned in the order of things, must from its nature be the last member in the investigation, and conclude the whole. For a work in which the dramatic character is so predominant as it is in the Protagoras, must precede a dialogue like the present, as far as mythical expositions elsewhere precede the productions of purely dialectic speculation. Moreover, the Protagoras supplies us with yet another, although subordinate point, of comparison. For what was said in that dialogue about baseness and vice is here manifestly intended to be illustrated, and protected from misconception, by the instancing of two species of it, so that we may say that, in this point of view, on the one hand, the Sophist brings the Protagoras into agreement with the Gorgias, and on the other, that it forms the transition to that ethical character which predominates in the books upon the Republic. In the Gorgias, which is indeed more anti-rhetorical than anti-sophistical, we find the application of the terms *idea*, *type*, and *imitation*, in order to explain from them the nature of what is false and bad, manifestly with the appearance of being earlier than it is here, because it is there put only hypothetically, while here it is regularly deduced and established. Moreover, the Sophist appeals to the notion of the semblance of the just as to a thing known, and sets up a connection between rhetoric and sophistry, such that they both coincide in the idea of mere appearance. And as the Euthydemus generally is presupposed in the Sophist, and every thing in which Plato could appeal to that dialogue is briefly dispatched, as, for example, that non-existence cannot be ever made the predicate of a proposition, and that it is self-evident, that when a man asserts falsely about a thing, he does not speak of the thing at all; so also, any one may easily see that much that was too shortly touched upon in the Euthydemus, is here demonstrated more at length. If we compare further what the Cratylus and Sophist have in common, we can scarcely doubt that the illustrations about *types* and *imitations* preceded the application here made of the same thought; especially if we notice the easy way in which the stranger is satisfied with the explanation, that a *type* is a second reality made to resemble a first, while in the Cratylus we find extensive explanations as to how the type can only be externally and in part the same with the archetype; and even in the manner in which in the Sophist the idea of a *type* is first introduced, we may easily observe the reference to the Cratylus. In like manner, Plato could scarcely have expressed himself so briefly as to the relation between thought and language, if he had not himself already represented words to be immediate imitations of things and actions. From these points, certainly, every appearance of an inverted order in the arrangement of the dialogues will easily admit of being destroyed. And how should Plato, just at the beginning of this dialogue, have come to consider all knowledge, not as resulting from an act of production, but of appropriation? and how, with his accuracy, should he thus have allowed himself to maintain this point without further discussion, if he could not reckon upon what the Menon was supposed to have made clear to his readers?

This short analysis will, it is hoped, suffice with reference now to much that has been already said on former occasions, fully also to justify the separation of the Sophist from the Theætetus, notwithstanding the two are placed so closely in connection with one another. For while, with regard to some of thᵌ dialogues introduced between these two, the manner of their connexion with the Theætetus has been made more clear, and how they develope themselves from it, and again with regard to others, how they are presupposed by the Sophist; these two circumstances taken in conjunction, become too evident in the case of every one of these dialogues to allow a doubt to arise as to their place with reference to these. But it is also immediately certain, that the Sophist rests upon the Theætetus, and would be perfectly unintelligible without the distinction previously established between knowledge and conception, and the suggestions in the Theætetus respecting the first, which constitute in fact a sufficient foundation for what is here said, and no other is essentially necessary. Let any one, however, conceive the Sophist to have followed immediately upon the Theætetus, and consequently to have contained in itself all that he can now take for granted out of the Menon, and

Euthydemus especially, and then say whether it would not necessarily have been a shapeless work for Plato to have composed, and if to its present difficulties such superabundance and complexity of matter had been further added, whether it would not then have been perfectly unintelligible. Only it is not here intended to be said, that in completing the plan of this dialogue, Plato projected in his mind those other dialogues purposely with a view to the future; but this is only to be understood in the sense in which one may reasonably speak of the natural course of the development of inward conceptions from one another. Hence, as to the assignation made at the end of the Theætetus and the continuous connection at the beginning of the Sophist, it is scarcely worth while entering into a more accurate explanation, as any reader, not satisfied with that given in the Introduction to the Meno, can do this for himself.

VII. THE STATESMAN.

It must be at once self-evident to every reader how the Statesman, as the second part of the trilogy announced in the Sophist, is connected with that dialogue. But although it takes place among the same persons, and annexes itself in a continued conversation as it were with the investigation concerning the Sophist, it would be too much to think of viewing the two as in reality and on that account one dialogue. There

is, on the contrary, reason to believe that some time intervened between the publication of the two, especially
if we are to give any weight to several particular sentiments in our dialogue, which have fully the appearance of being intended to defend the Sophist. Hence,
we have not hesitated to follow with the greater confidence, the old method of separating the two dialogues
from one another under the titles that have come down
to us, notwithstanding their intimate connection. And
indeed the similarity of the two is of such a nature
as to direct us rather to place them in juxta-position
as counterparts, than to admit of our conjoining them
as parts of a whole. For they do in fact, correspond
to one another in their whole construction more accurately than any other two dialogues of Plato; and
whatever difference is to be met with appears only to
be the result of the general distinction, that in the
Sophist the immediate object of the speculation is an
object of aversion; in the Statesman, on the contrary,
it is something genuine and excellent. Although even
in this respect our dialogue approximates again to the
Sophist, for collaterally with the meritorious object, it
at the same time, and with great pains, deduces and
describes the reverse; just as in the Sophist also the
meritorious object, namely, the philosopher, is at all
events sketched out collaterally with the elaborate description of its opposite. Thus then our dialogue justly
occupies the middle place in the designed trilogy, as
it does in fact form a middle term between the Sophist
and the promised description of the Philosopher, as
near as we can conceive what the character of the
latter is to be.

Even in the very first outlines it is impossible not to recognise a great coincidence between the two existing parts of this trilogy. For in the Statesman, as well as the preceding part, the object of the whole problem is a delineation, and it is to be discovered in like manner by subdivision of the whole province of art, though proceeding upon a different principle of separation. Only, as in the case of the Sophist, the whole process was not seriously meant, so also neither is it true. For scarcely, had this been an essential part of the whole, could we have attributed to Plato such errors as are here committed. For instance, under the department of Command, in so far as it is a part of the province of knowledge ;· the office of the mere publisher of commands is comprehended, in the exercise of which no knowledge, properly speaking, is necessary, and which we accordingly find afterwards numbered among the merely serving arts. Again, at the end of the whole subdividing process, swine are made to stand in closer and more direct relation to man than to horned cattle, whereupon Plato himself exhibits a little pleasantry, and afterwards tells us more seriously that man is related to other beasts as the nature of dæmons to that of man. Similarly also in the repetition of the panegyric upon the subdividing method, where it is said that this method does not concern itself with great and small, there is in what is said seriously a touch also of jest; if that were not the case, Plato would have been justly censured by that well-known bad joke of Diogenes with the plucked hen, which bears accurately enough upon one of the subdividing processes here pursued. And after the delineation has been discovered, it turns out not to be suitable, but more adapted to the dæmonic protectors of mankind in an earlier period, than to the real statesman of an historical time. For as regards the latter, much that belongs to the province of other arts must be separated from the character comprehended under that explanation, in order thus to obtain that of the art of the statesman properly so called. This separation now, because, as is clear enough from a digression upon the nature and the use of examples, and which can only be introduced in this place to defend the method employed in the Statesman and Sophist, because, I say, it is a new process, as that of subdivision itself was in the Sophist, is tried, as that method was in the preceding dialogue; first, in an insignificant instance, namely, that of the art of weaving, with which at last the statesman's art turns out to stand in the same relation as the practice of the sophist does with that of the angler and several others. The art of weaving, however, is itself explained by the former method of subdivision, and as the explanation discovers itself to be one that might have been far more easily found by immediate inspection, a digression is here subjoined upon the method of measuring great and small, and upon the measure which every thing has in itself. And upon this, every thing is separated, first from the art of weaving, and then conformably to this example, from that of statesmanship also, which is merely subservient to it, or is connected with its province, as remotely co-operating to the end and object of the art. And in this, the argument is visibly progressing as to its proper point, to the separation of the false statesman from the true, though there is nothing analogous to the former

in the art of weaving, and he is, therefore, notwithstanding all artificial preparation, by means of a discussion upon the various forms in the constitutions of
states, somewhat hardly, it might seem, attached to
that class which is only subservient to the state. And
the connection, which does not appear very clearly, is
properly this; that governors of such states as are
governed according to existing laws, if they remain
true to the supposition, that such laws are the work of
a really skilful statesman, are only servants and instruments of such a master; but, as soon as they
presume to throw off this character of servants, and
imitate the freedom of the legislator, they then become
that great and fundamentally corrupting evil, the false
and counterfeit statesman, who again, as an imitator,
and a bad imitator, corresponds accurately to the sophist,
and is, therefore, described also as the greatest sophist
and quack. We see manifestly, how the whole of that
description of the different forms of states, with the
exception perhaps, of the few passages relative to their
unequal value, is only treated as a means of discovering
the false statesman; for as soon as that character has
exhibited himself with sufficient clearness, the work of
separation is continued, in order to separate from the
statesman those officers who, according to the exercise of their respective duties come next in the general
description, so that at last, the statesman's art remains
as that which is supreme over all others, and assigns
to men all their duties, and then again by a harsh
transition, and without any natural connection being
apparent, returning to the example of the weaving art,
as in the Sophist, the philosopher was incidentally
described as a separating and analysing artist, so here

the statesman is described as a combining one, upon whom it is incumbent as his chiefest and almost only duty to connect together different, and therefore reciprocally repugnant, natures.

If now we look only to what forms the chief thread of the whole, and to the last result, these may certainly appear scanty enough. And that indeed, not only to the great mass of modern politicians, whose highest problem is ever only how they may increase the public wealth;—for how little Plato has to do with this, must at once be clear enough to these men from the beginning of that process of separation, when agriculture, as well as trade, is treated very contemptuously with reference to the state. But they also who bring with them more exalted moral and scientific views might look upon the result arrived at as barren, and this last, and only object of the statesman, although to a certain degree an important one, might still not satisfy their expectations, and the less, as it does not appear even once to be immediately mentioned to what particular end this combination of nature and that dominion over the business and affairs of the state is to refer; or under what form, whether always the same, or varying according to circumstances, the two are to be exercised. And the persons in question might next suspect, that as in the former dialogue the description of the sophist is manifestly drawn up with an eye to the then state of science, so also here, that of the statesman may be given with reference to the political relations at that time existing among the Hellenes; inasmuch as in this, the most profound as well as the noblest views are taken of the confusion and madness of parties, and certainly to relieve the state from these, or preserve it free from them, must be represented as the highest exercise of the statesman's art. Chiefly however, they might observe that in the present dialogue, exactly the same complication and composition obtain as in the one preceding, and that therefore it may not be in vain to look for the most important conclusions on points which they miss in that immediately connected main-thread, in matter which is given merely as digressive and incidental. For instance, as regards the form of the state, first of all, Plato gives us clearly enough to understand, that from the rarity of political wisdom the real state can scarcely admit of any other than the monarchical form; but if we, as he also does, leave the real state completely out of the question, and only regard the Statesman as prescribing his laws to another state which is to be an imitation, Plato then allows all three forms named to obtain as such; but from the statesman's business of combining natures or regulating duties alone, it cannot appear under what circumstances he will give to any one state any one of those forms; or when he would prefer to charge one individual, or the few, or the many, with the imitation of it. And we have therefore that digression upon the merits of the different forms, which clearly enough gives us to understand that in proportion as courage and discretion are combined in one, or in a few, power also must be concentrated in him or them; while, in proportion as the two are separated, the power also must be loose and disunited, and the state consequently weak in the same proportion as that main object of the statesman is still imperfectly accomplished in it. Again, the whole view of the statesman's art is greatly illustrated by that other digression upon the idea of measure, though introduced not in reference to the subject, but only to defend the method pursued. For it is not without reference to his principal subject that Plato so definitely explains that the statesman's art, like every other, aims in its operations at this natural proportion, founded upon, and contained in its nature, and which consequently, the true statesman as the scientific philosopher, must bear within himself, and also, together with right notions of the good and the just—for by what except by this proportion are these two to be defined? implant it in others, that he may be enabled in conformity with this, and in common with them, to mark off the outward and limiting circumference of the state, and also to assign its own to every part of it. With regard, lastly, to the highest object of the state in that great myth already mentioned, the character of the golden age is criticized according to the rule, that no wealth in natural things or facility of obtaining sustenance, can have any value unless the conversation and dealing of men with one another and with nature conducts them to knowledge ; so that at last, nothing either in themselves or in nature can remain concealed from them, which must therefore clearly be the aim of that political art which in the end, when combined with all others, may correspond to those exertions of the gods, and of the dæmonic protector.

Meanwhile, part of the similarity between the present dialogue and the Sophist consists in the fact, that the references adduced as bearing upon the immediate subject of the dialogue, do yet not exhaust the purport of these interwoven pieces, and we must, therefore, follow up that purport still further, as well as the traces admit of being indicated in a few steps. For instance the myth, which appears to have been suggested by an Egyptian tradition mentioned by Herodotus—for if any thing resembling it occurs elsewhere, as Plato does certainly suppose the single point which he forms into a great and important image to be well known by tradition, such resemblance has escaped the translator,—this myth has manifestly a far more comprehensive tendency. To explain the description there given of the relation of the Deity to the world, or to judge how far it might be available to search in it for the doctrine ascribed to Plato, that the principle of evil exists and originates in matter, would not be appropriate to this place, because the subject lies quite without the limits of the present dialogue. It may, however, be indeed remarked, that Plato here intended to lay down a comprehensive view of the historical periods of the world, and of the mighty revolutions of human affairs, and especially also, of their remarkable retrogression at particular times, in which he found even his own country involved, especially in a political point of view; and it is certainly part of the harmony of the whole, that this degeneracy also is explained from the absence of living knowledge, and from the presence in the state of that mere imitation in which the resemblance to truth vanishes, more in proportion as the imitation continues longer. But whoever considers this description, and follows it out more according to our method, would discover in it, not erroneously, the first finished expression of these views, which have already appeared at a much earlier period, and which contemplate the life of the world as alternating in opposite motions, and again reproducing itself. It is moreover remarkable, and a task very much to the purpose here, to compare this myth with that in the Protagoras. For it is hoped that every reader who pays attention on perusing this myth, to the manner in which the Protagorean one is here taken up again, will consider what was said about the latter to receive additional corroboration.

In like manner the idea of measure here, has a particular, though but slightly indicated reference to the two parts or forms of virtue as they are called, in order to prevent every possible misunderstanding, by which it might be conceived that they are only great or small in comparison with one another, so that the same action when considered with reference to one of two others would be considered courageous, and with reference to the other, of a contrary character; or indeed in comparison with the one courageous, and with the other mad and precipitous, and that it may be established that they are only virtuous, for the very reason that they have their measure in themselves. And hence the view of virtue here started connects itself immediately with that given in the Sophist, as the two species of vicious states, disproportionality and disease, are thus shown in their connection, and the simile here constantly employed with reference to the statesman obtains its proper signification, because the statesman now becomes the physician for the disease of the soul in general, inasmuch as he gradually corrects its temper, and together with true notions of the good and just, implants at the same time in all its natural abilities, which, as long as they want this essential unity must stand up in rebellion against one another, their true and proper proportion. So that now, by means of a complete adoption of true and correct conception into the idea of knowledge, from

which the former must still always proceed, that first
view returns in a more exalted sense, and raised above
all objections, which maintained that all virtue was
knowledge, and all vice ignorance. Finally, that last
elucidation also, and one which interrupts the main
thread of the dialogue, concerning the different forms
of the states as they were apprehended and framed by
the Hellenes, is very visibly intended, in connection
with comprehensive views, to explain without concealment Plato's opinion of the Hellenic States, and of the
constitution of his native town in particular, and the
extreme perverseness with which the influence of philosophers upon the states was depreciated there by the
merely oratorical demagogues, and as much as possible
obstructed by them, in order thus to justify at the
same time, and place in the proper light what he himself had in vain endeavoured to perform elsewhere, as
a framer of states and teacher of princes, and to proclaim
in defiance of all satirical censors, that though he had
not condescended to govern, he nevertheless considered
himself and every philosopher as the true statesman
and king.

This naturally leads us to observe this further
similarity between the present dialogues and the preceding one, that the former is likewise to be regarded
as the completion of one department of Platonic polemics, that, namely, against demagogues, rhetoricians,
and state-quacks, and that after the thorough handling
which they here receive, nothing more was to be brought
up against them, but the battle was to be looked upon
as now at an end. When once a species of perversity
has been so fully exposed, particular and incidental expressions may indeed be continually called forth upon

the same subject by particular occasions, when an author thinks he may never be taxed for an answer, but such expressions, however pointed they may be, will always say less than what has been said before, and hence, after such an exposure as this, by a judicious writer like Plato, they will not readily be brought forward with such freedom and unsuppressed abundance as we have been accustomed to find them in other dialogues, which do, therefore, from this circumstance prove themselves to have been earlier written. To enter into particulars upon this subject, would be to write as full and accurate a counterpart to our Introduction to the preceding dialogue, as the Statesman itself is to the Sophist. Only we would request our readers to look at all the dialogues, beginning with the Protagoras; for the particular character to which we are now calling attention runs more or less through all; and to observe, independent of the similarity of purpose in all, how also the strength and efficiency of the polemics depend upon and correspond with the gradual growth and development of the scientific ideas, and keep pace with that progress, and also, how the dramatic and ironical skill ceases here to be so prominent, and continually keeps its pretensions more in the back-ground in proportion as preparations are made for scientific speculation. And the results of this observation will infallibly suffice at the same time as a justification of our whole arrangement up to the present dialogue, if we take a retrospective survey of that arrangement from this point of view. For, first of all, it is manifest that the Statesman lays holds of the second side of the Euthydemus, and sticks to it also quite as decisively as the Sophist did to the first, and

that here as well as there, we are only reminded briefly
of what had been discussed at sufficient length in the
Euthydemus. Nay, when we recollect in what a help-
less condition Socrates and Clinias separated in that
dialogue, because they were not in a condition to
discover the kingly art, we must at the same time
observe, that the Statesman presumes what the reader
is supposed to have learnt from that helplessness. In
like manner it is clear that the present dialogue rests
upon the idea of imitation, as established in the Cratylus
and Sophist, and upon the theory of true conception,
which is continually developing itself from the Theætetus onwards; as what was said in the Gorgias upon
the perverse tendencies of common state-quackery, as
being less positive, and containing its own reasons in
itself, must necessarily have preceded what is said in
the Statesman; finally also, that the Statesman again
resumes the Protagoras, nearly in the same degree as
the Sophist does the Parmenides, and that what is
particularly said in the Protagoras of virtue in general,
and of all the virtues in detail, and in the Laches and
Charmides of courage and discretion, which are here
again brought forward as apparent opposites, must
quite as certainly have preceded what we find in the
Gorgias on the same subject; nay, that all matter of
an ethical character in the strictest sense, is here sum-
med up in a peculiar manner, and under the highest
point of view possible for Greeks, namely, a political
one, and thus preserved entire for future discussions.
Hence, then, the Statesman together with the Sophist
constitute the middle point of the second period of
the Platonic system. For in them, as regards the form
on the one hand, the combination of every thing ele-

mentary, tentative, and indirectly delivered, coincides in such a manner with the germs of pure philosophical speculation, that the two appear as one and the same. And again, as to the subject-matter, while in point of outward form physics and ethics become more distinctly separate, they are united in a peculiar manner in both dialogues. And in the Statesman this is done by the view, only mythical indeed, taken of the historical as subject to the law of nature and conformity of the world itself, and in this point of view, our myth, as it is generally regarded, is anticipatory of the Timæus, and, as such, corresponds to the approximation to the Platonic Republic.

VIII. THE BANQUET.

A PERSON having read the two preceding dialogues and now seeing the Symposium follow, might ask, looking to the beginning of the Sophist, why the Eleatic Stranger, when Socrates enquired what place the Sophist, Statesman, and Philosopher—all these occupy both independently and according to their distinction, form, and relation to one another, has answered only as relates to two of them, and not the third. And we might repeat to him on the one hand, that this Eleatic Stranger, because it would have been a sacrilegious act to describe the sophist first, has already mixed up with his attempt to discover that character, the description of the philosopher, though without naming him, as has already been remarked in the Introduction

to that dialogue; on the other hand, that Plato, independent of this anticipation, tired with the already
twice repeated and strict form, which could only be al-
leviated and enlivened by the touches of humour thrown
in, did not wish to describe the philosopher also by
the same method. Whence it arises, that the trilogy,
regarded in this point of view, does indeed continue
imperfect, but to those who consider it on less narrow
principles, it will appear in general more beautifully
and nobly completed by the dialogue now before us,
and the next that follows, the Phædon. For in these
two dialogues taken together, Plato exhibits before us
an image of a philosopher in the person of Socrates.
In the Phædon, of which we cannot here speak more
closely, he displays him as he appears in death, while
in our Symposium the same philosopher is ennobled as
he lived, by that panegyric of Alcibiades, which is manifestly the crest and crown of the whole dialogue, and
exhibits Socrates to us in the unwearied enthusiasm of
contemplation, and in joyous communication of the results, in the contempt of danger and exaltation above
external things, in the purity of all his relations, and
in his inward divinity under that light and cheerful ex-
terior; in short, in that perfect soundness of body and
mind, and, consequently, of existence generally. But if
we were to repeat all this, and no other answer, certainly,
could be given, it would strike the majority of readers
with surprise, because it is unusual to consider the two
dialogues from this point of view, and few only would
find in such an account any thing worth notice, the majority nothing; because in the two dialogues, even if
more importance is to be attributed to the description
of Socrates than is usually done, still the remaining and

larger part cannot be thrown entirely into the back-
ground, and as regards the present dialogue, it may
seem as difficult to explain how the preceding speeches
about love are to be connected with this panegyric of Alcibiades, as that panegyric with these speeches, if the
former is regarded as the principal part. But our
answer was intended to apply only to the first inquiry,
a half which does not pretend to be more than the
whole. On the contrary, the connection of the Symposium with the Phædon, as well as the place which we
assign to the former, depends no less upon the love-
speeches than upon the episode of Alcibiades, and our
opinion only goes to uphold that, from the point of
view here established, the whole may sooner appear as
really one united whole, than from any other; so that
we might maintain that whoever considers the Symposium only with reference to itself, and independently
of this connection and purport, as is usually done, sees,
as far at least as regards the composition, only as it
were the external Silenus-form, beautiful indeed, and
elegantly worked, but still extravagant and eccentric,
and not the infinitely more costly image of the god
enclosed within.

In order, then, to open the former and bring the
latter to light, we must connect the Symposium also
with the problem started in the Sophist, which announces a complete trilogy. Now, in addition to the
Sophist and the Statesman, the third object of Socrates'
enquiry is not merely the idea of knowledge and wisdom, but a philosopher, a man also like them, who,
although god-like when compared with the inferior life
of the majority of men, moves notwithstanding a man
among men. Consequently, it is not the abstract essence

and nature of wisdom that is to be described, but its
life and appearance in the mortal life of the visible
man, in which wisdom herself, for this is manifestly
Plato's principal point in all his explanations respecting philosophy, has put on mortality, and displays
herself subject to the conditions of time, as a progressive and expanding power, so that even the life of
a philosopher is far from a repose in wisdom, but an
endeavour to retain it, and, attaching it to every pro-
jecting point, to create in the whole of time and the
whole of space something upon which an immortality
may arise in the mortal. And when the name of love
is given to this endeavour, and the excitement and
living formation, not only of true conceptions of the
good and just, with which the statesman is engaged,
and of which even the great mass is susceptible, but
rather the formation of knowledge in the few who are
capable of it, is regarded as a species of procreation,
this is far from being merely a poetic comparison ; but
it was absolutely necessary that Plato should look upon
both as one and the same, and only view that spiritual
procreation as a higher order of the similar and similarly named energy, since, according to his theory, even
the natural birth was nothing but a reproduction of
the same eternal form and idea, and, consequently, the
immortality of the same in the mortal. Now that the
recipient of every means of production generally is the
beautiful, the same, that is, in whose particular life
and existence the harmony of the universe is visibly
recognised as peculiarly innate in it, this is a point
which, to any one who is not a perfect stranger to the
Hellenic nature, can require no elucidation. When,
therefore, the love that creates in the beautiful is de-

scribed, the business of the philosopher in general is described at the same time, and in order to designate *his* place in particular, it is only necessary to define the relation of *his* love and its object, to every other species and object of the same passion. Now, this easily appears to every reader to be the main subject of what Socrates here again repeats, as matter of former discussion between himself and Diotima. For it is scarcely possible that any one should be misled by the single fact, that this wise lady, when out of the more general idea of desire, she seeks for the proper idea of love in the more contracted sense, excludes the love of wisdom, with others like it, from this narrowed sphere. Or, if any one should take occasion from this circumstance to object to our explanation, let him only try whether it would have been possible to place the subject in that light which the purport of Diotima's speech required, without setting aside, by way of beginning, the endeavour after wisdom also, as coming under the general idea of desire, in order to obtain for love as its peculiar character, the desire to create. But starting from this, the whole discussion manifestly displays the uninterrupted gradation, not only from the pleasure arising from the contemplation of personal beauty, through that which every larger object, whether single or manifold, may occasion, to that immediate pleasure whose source is in the eternal beauty, which, without further contemplation of that which is particular and individual, displays itself to the mind's eye when practised and quickened by this order of training, but also, the gradation from the procreation of natural life through that of correct conception up to that participation, which ranges far beyond all master-skill in detail, in that immediate knowledge which alone beatifies and comprehends within itself all other good; so that it is to be shown how it is in philosophy only, that the greatest good is the object of that general desire for an ever-enduring possession, and to make this highest object immortal in a mortal subject, belongs to it alone as to the highest species of love.

We thus appear, accordingly, to have discovered the essential part of our whole work of art, in what Socrates says about love, and Alcibiades about Socrates. For the former exhibits to us the proper nature of the philosopher, it may be under a totally different external form, but when more closely considered almost according to the same method, by means of the establishment of a general idea, and by the separation of the other species, as in the Sophist and Statesman, the nature of these two characters is described, while the life and real actions of the philosopher, with respect to which, as regards the Sophist and the Statesman, only a few scattered traces appear in these dialogues, are exhibited before us in that last panegyric of Alcibiades, in a picture, which though only half worked out, is at least finished as far as the outlines are concerned. Yet may we not pretend so far to discover the whole in this last half, that the earlier love-speeches are to be looked upon only as embellishment, or as devoted entirely to other subordinate points; but, although it might be an unsound Eros to love any one of these speeches, or regard it, as of any importance in itself, as Eryximachus the physician describes that passion as his own, yet must they have been necessary when taken in connection with the rest, and consequently each in its place and its kind, beautiful——and, certainly, we may at all events assume, that the whole cannot be understood in its immediate connection with the rest of the works of Plato without them.

First, then, to continue, these speeches serve in a variety of ways to denote the sphere of love throughout its whole range, and to show further, how mortality begets upon mortality only what is mortal and transitory; and the desire to do this, is a morbid passion, and the left-hand love, with which we are already acquainted from other dialogues. Eryximachus, for instance, who enlarges the description given by Pausanias, mentions the cooking art, and consequently reminds us of the Gorgias, and the opposition in the constitution of man there treated of, so that we see how even that which is most opposed to philosophy in reference to its object, may still be united with it under the idea of love, as co-operative with it, and influential upon animated nature. Thus, they show also, how, if they who have not understood the real nature of the subject, but start only from the obscure feeling, collect and explain the particular phœnomena, these phœnomena all present a partial and one-sided appearance; and the particular details in them are again taken up in the speech of Socrates, who represents them as only conditionally and partially true, correcting what is wrong, and supplying what was wanting. We learn also in them, to examine by comparison what the common language of that period comprehended as belonging to the appellation of love, and to separate that which, coming under the more modern notion, does not belong to it in this place. And in this respect, particularly the speech of Eryximachus is remarkable, whose physiological and medicinal notion of love is ludicrously

introduced by means of the little interruption occasioned
by the hiccough of Aristophanes, and for that very
reason is not again particularly referred to in the speech
of Socrates. And as these speeches show us the difference between the philosopher and the not-philosopher,
in their subject-matter and ideas, so do they also, in
enunciation and expression, partly by means of a loose,
unconnected extravagance, partly by a corrupt musical
rhetoric, and the application of sophistical expedients—
both of which, in the speech of Agathon immediately
preceding that of Socrates, are pushed to the utmost.
And here also we see a new trace of connection between
our dialogue and the two preceding, in which likewise,
as we have endeavoured to show, the polemics against
the sophists as pretended dialecticians, and the rhetoricians and demagogues as pretended politicians, constitute
no small part. In like manner these speeches, of which
each is distinguished from the other by a peculiar
manner, which the translator has endeavoured as far as
possible to imitate, are certainly not deficient in Platonic polemics. For it is indeed hardly to be believed,
that these peculiarities were merely dramatic, and intended to show the manner in which the characters
introduced were generally accustomed to speak; since,
as several among them do not seem even to have been
authors, as Phædrus, Pausanias, Eryximachus, and,
supposing them to have been alive at the time of the
appearance of the Banquet, were far from being generally
known, it would have been lost labour to imitate them,
and not worth the composition. Also, the mention of
Gorgias does of itself lead us to quite different notions on
the matter. For hardly can these polemics, dramatic indeed as they plainly are, have been directed against other

than well-known orators and authors, and indeed such
as laboured after a theory which was the creation not
of philosophy, but only the instrument of a false Eros,
where one cannot avoid thinking particularly of the
later schools of Gorgias and on those of Socrates; although the myth of Aristophanes in its whole style,
the comic turn certainly excepted, so beautifully imi-
tates those of the poets themselves, that it seems to
me to bear a striking similarity to that told by Protagoras in the dialogue that bears his name. So that,
upon the whole, Sydenham may certainly have been
right when he conceived, that in this dialogue the
persons imitated may be not so much those actually
introduced to speak, as others represented under their
name, only that he himself followed too slight hints,
and was over hasty in his particular decision; wherein we will not imitate him, but leave the matter to
other learned men, so much the rather, as it belongs
not to our object to follow out such points.

But, on the other hand, without these speeches,
the relation of the Symposium to other dialogues of
Plato, namely the earliest, would not be near so open
to recognition, and there is clearly much that refers
to these dialogues intentionally introduced into it.
Every reader, for instance, will naturally be reminded
by this work of the Phædrus and Lysis, as when we
were engaged with that dialogue we were compelled
to refer in anticipation to this. To the Phædrus there
appear references sufficient in the first speeches, especially where the relation of the lover to the beloved
object is spoken of, to render it unnecessary expressly
to bring them forward. But several of these speeches
have, more especially, a peculiar reference to the Lysis,

as they respectively take up respective points of what was there laid down as the ground of friendship and love, and always found inadmissible ; and they pursue their panegyrics of love accordingly : so that that dialogue, of the over-sceptical tenor of which complaints might with justice be made, finds here its appropriate solution. Thus Phædrus lays down in the most general way the endeavour after the good as the ground, and the secure attainment of it as the effect, of love. Pausanias, though he does not expressly say it, speaks more of resemblance : whence he gets a twofold love, the one superior, the other inferior. Eryximachus further assumes that there is a sympathy between opposite principles, and Aristophanes lastly gives a comic dress to the theory which maintains that love tends to a union of counterparts. His view is, that not *all good*, as appropriating and informing, is the counterpart of being, but that the notion to be entertained, in speaking of the good as the object of love, is a supplementary completion of the sensuous unity of existence. And nearly the whole of this is criticized by Socrates, from the notion of love which he himself sets up; whence it is easy to see how far, and in what sense, he is compelled to reject the theory that love tends to the good, and to the union of counterparts, and how he would certainly have adopted that theory if it had only been a little more accurately defined. And here we can illustrate, from a particular side, and with a view to showing its correctness, the arrangement we have adopted of the dialogues up to this point. If we first consider the Lysis, it now becomes incumbent upon us to show satisfactorily that this dialogue must stand nearer to the Phædrus than to the Banquet, and why it must do so. And this is seen, as it appears to me, evidently enough from the different form under which the notion common to the two dialogues, of the neither good nor bad, is stated in both; in the Lysis, indeed, quite inartificially, as being derived from the common conversation of ordinary life, so that it can be considered only as a feeler in reference to the higher department of the investigation; as something, as it were, which might be true, if the necessary confirmation were added. And what confirmation then is there here, when Socrates expresses his surprise at the theory brought forward by the wise Diotima? The analogy of a mean precisely similar in another department, namely, the notion, treated of in the Theætetus, of true conception: and every reader will certainly be put in mind, even though it is not expressly here mentioned, of what is said in the Sophist of non-existence—namely, that it is no real opposition —as the peculiar ground of the certainty with which this theory may be enunciated. If, therefore, these confirmations had been already given in the works of Plato when the Lysis was written, why should he have enunciated the theory in that dialogue only so precariously? We have the Lysis therefore manifestly rejected to a place the other side of the Theætetus, and when once there, it becomes easy, if we would assign its place to it, to force it to retrograde a dialogue at a time, and remain in its natural position immediately next after the Phædrus; and the more, if we bear in mind the remarks there made upon the weakness of the Lysis in point of dialectic composition. For as soon as we have become fully aware that Plato's whole theory of love rested upon the Hellenic character, and

that in every thing even of higher purport which he
would contemplate under this idea, he was compelled
to proceed upon the condition given in that character
of the sexual passion and the sexes; and, consequently,
if we are not to be surprised to find here precisely
the anti-modern and anti-christian pole of his style of
thought, we must allow that in the Symposium love
is discussed in a more judicious, manly, and, that style
being supposed, more perfect manner, than in the Phædrus. And this because the philosopher is now no
longer satisfied with that youthful idea of the relation
between the lover and the individual loved, even in its
most sublime sense, as a representation of the philosophical impulse, declaring it only proportioned and
appropriate to the notions of a beginner; and because
the desire to generate is now no longer according to
him the highest object, and in itself immediately divine,
but as the child, indeed, of that immortal and eternally
supplying Poros, though, at the same time, of the needy
Penia as well, it has its origin indeed in the immortal principle, though only in so far as that principle
exists in the mortal being, in order also to produce
the immortal in this last; and therefore Diotima takes
especial pains to show that in mortal man, even knowledge herself appears as mortal; not as that which
is ever immutable and self-consistent, but only as that
which is ever renewing itself; and therefore, confined
between two periods of time, is in each several instance
only recollection going back to its eternal and permanent archetype; and she endeavours to show that love
cannot in any way generate the eternal nature and immortal essence of knowledge, but can only generate for
it its state of mortal appearance, and not only vivifies

it in the individual, but by this transference from one
to another, makes it immortal in the mortal. But
whatever pains she takes, are available only to those
who know from the Statesman, that the finite, as such,
is never the immutably permanent and self-identical,
and who, being already acquainted with the doctrine
of the suggestion of knowledge, and the relation it
bears to its eternal essence, as contained in the Menon
and elsewhere, only require some still more palpable
assistance. So that from this point also, the place we
have assigned to the Symposium acquires additional
justification. And what is more, our general arrangement receives remarkable confirmation from what Diotima says of the gradual advances in the mysteries of
love. For this gradation harmonises most accurately
with the continually developing philosophical speculation in the works of Plato, so that he here, unconsciously perhaps, as is often the case with beauties,
most elegantly exhibits a mirrored likeness of himself.
For first of all, the Phædrus with its enamoured preference for one object, is excused as a work of youth;
then the beginner rises to the contemplation of the
beautiful, in practical exertions and laws; consequently,
to investigations into the political virtues, such as we
find in the Protagoras, and the dialogues connected
with it, and in the Gorgias. Then come the modifications of knowledge, in their plurality indeed, but still
as modifications of knowledge, consequently, with the
consciousness of the peculiar character of knowledge as
exhibited from the Theætetus onwards; and thus the
mind rises at last to the conscious contemplation of the
absolutely beautiful, as it is beheld in disconnection
with any individual beauty; and, as producing all in-

dividual beauty in the world, both moral and material, will manifest itself to us in the last and later division of his works.

For the determination of the time also when the dialogue was written, we find yet further some evidence, though of an uncertain character, in the anachronism already censured elsewhere, by which, in the speech of Aristophanes, mention is made of the destruction of Mantinea, which followed four olympiads after the death of Socrates, and it is certainly true that at the time when Plato wrote, the circumstance must have been fresh in men's recollection. But are we not to suppose that this recollection must have been as vividly renewed at the time when preparations were made for the restoration of the town, and do we not therefore still continue in doubt between the ninety-eighth olympiad and the hundred and second?

The characters, with the exception of the otherwise sufficiently well-known poets, have been already introduced in other dialogues of Plato, and in Wolf's Introduction to his edition of the Symposium, enough for the satisfaction of every reader is compiled together about them. But why these persons in particular, and not others, should have these speeches put into their mouths by Plato, is a question which, as regards many of them, might be a difficult one to answer.

Only we might regard Agathon's character as founded upon historic truth, and we find Phædrus here, partly because he was described in the dialogue that bears his name, as a great friend to speeches and as a cause of many, partly to remind us still more decisively of this dialogue. As to Aristophanes, I should be inclined to regard his introduction here in the most friendly relation to Socrates, as an honourable compensation for what was said in the Apology; especially when we take into consideration the quotation from the clouds; perhaps also to show how entirely all bad feeling had vanished in him who had in earlier times written that beautiful epigram upon the poet, notwithstanding all the satire which the latter had aimed at the philosopher.

IX. PHÆDON.

It now becomes incumbent upon us to explain more accurately the proper meaning of what has already been said preliminarily in the Introduction to the Symposium, as to the relation and connection between these two dialogues. Now, if the reader would assume with us, by way of experiment, that the Symposium and the Phædon constitute the third description, that of the Philosopher, as connected with the other two already given of the Sophist and the Statesman, we would then, in order that a more accurate view of the subject may not escape him, draw his attention to the fact, that in the speech of Diotima the passion for wisdom is expressly excluded out of the idea of love, in order that this province may be assigned solely to parturition in the beautiful*, and that reference is as it were thus made to another place; which might at once, and of itself, be regarded as a prefatory indication of the Phædon. For it cannot certainly be denied, that if the good is the object of love in general,

* Τόκος ἐν καλῷ. *Symp.*

then wisdom for its own sake is to be the predominant object of the love of wisdom, so that this feeling as essentially belongs to a man's life and conduct, as the communication and engrafting of wisdom in others. And it is by the mention of these two peculiarities of the philosopher, that his relation to the sophist and the statesman is first fully defined. For the statesman as such also creates, but only as preparing in their kind the superior natures that vibrate intermediately between the furthest extremes, which are thus made most susceptible of knowledge; so that the philosopher best receives the object of his love out of the hands of the true statesman, in order then to create and perfect in that object the higher life of knowledge. And the sophist likewise is also engaged in dialectic separation and combination, but, confined as he is to the world of sense, and involved in pleasure and vanity, he adheres only to the terrestrial copies, and will thence obtain and possess for itself only the non-existent. The philosopher on the contrary struggles to acquire the self-existent, and to preserve it pure in knowledge, and, therefore, in order to exalt himself to the archetypes, in which alone it is to be found, he seeks how he may make his soul, in which they dwell, work for itself alone, and go free from the influence of sense and matter collectively. And this is that passionate desire to become pure spirit, that wish for death in the wise man which we find described here, at the beginning of this work, and out of which all the following investigations develope themselves. But, it will be said by many, even though this wish for death is the other essential inpulse of the philosopher in Plato's opinion, still, it does not form the most principal subject-matter of the Phædon, but appears only to subsist as an introduction, and an occasion subordinately giving rise to all the discussions upon the soul's immortality, which clearly constitute that to which the chief importance is attached. Now, that the subject of immortality, at least, goes equal shares with that of the wish for death, I am not going to deny, only let it not either be overlooked, that the possibility and truth of knowledge are continually, and repeatedly interwoven with the allegations of proof respecting immortality, and that as regards our author, the two are in fact most intimately combined. For the endeavour after knowledge could not exist at all under the form of a wish to die, not even in a philosopher, if it were necessarily, at the same time, a wish for annihilation. And if the soul is to apprehend the essentially existent, which is not subjected to origination and destruction, and to all the conditions of imperfect existence, it can only do so, (according to the old principle, and one, which in this argument must be always born in mind, that like is only apprehended by like,) as existing similarly, and in the same manner with that essential existence. Thus, then, the immortality of the soul is the condition of all true knowledge as regards men, and conversely, the reality of knowledge is the ground upon which the immortality of the soul is most certainly and easily understood. Hence, in the former dialogues also, in which knowledge was investigated, immortality was always presupposed and investigated simultaneously ; and one may say, that, from the Gorgias and Theætetus downwards, the two subjects are continually approximating in their progress, until they are at last in this dialogue most closely combined. Whoever then comprehends the connection of these two points in the sense in which Plato meant it, will certainly no longer hesitate to place the Phædon and the Symposium together, and to recognise the reciprocal relation of the two. For, as the love there described exhibits the endeavour to connect the immortal with the mortal, that pure contemplation here represented is the endeavour to withdraw the immortal, as such, away from the mortal; and the two are manifestly in necessary connection with one another. For, if the soul in its advances towards knowledge wishes to be continually removing further from the sphere of imperfect existence and appearance, and to be at last entirely separated from it, it is but a return fairly due from a soul in this condition, as it is, notwithstanding, incumbent upon it to interest itself continually in every thing not endowed with soul, first, to engraft knowledge in other souls destined to move longer in this sphere. And on the other hand, if the soul exerts itself to introduce the truth into others, the only proof of its love for them that can be given is, that it adhere itself to truth alone, and fly as far as possible from the semblance of it. Now, of these two essential characteristics in the conduct of a philosopher, one predominates in each of our two dialogues respectively; although their necessary connection did not admit of a complete separation, in that respect also entirely corresponding to the character of the second period of the Platonic composition. For, as the description of love in the speech of Diotima could not exist at all without reference made to pure contemplation, so also in this dialogue, where, properly speaking, that contemplation is represented, we find manifold

allusions throughout to the passionate desire always to
live with sympathetic minds, and to co-operate in cre-
ating truth within them, as a common task and profit;
only, that as regards Socrates, in order as it were to
secure him a tranquil departure, this is represented as
already essentially completed in his own peculiar circle.
And this leads us also to remark how the dramatic character in both dialogues appears so very analogous, and
indicates the same relation. For, in the Symposium,
Socrates is eminently exhibited in the joyousness and
pride of life, though it is not forgotten at the same
time how he is plunged in philosophical contemplation,
and can postpone all else to that; in the Phædon, on
the contrary, what appears most prominent is the tranquillity and cheerfulness with which he expects death,
as the liberator from every thing that interrupts contemplation; and on the other hand, he does not nevertheless interrupt his accustomed social practice, but
even with the fatal goblet will observe the sacred cere-
monies of the festive meal. It is, indeed, generally allowed that little is to be met with in the way of description more beautiful in its kind than this of the
dying Socrates; but still the mind is not completely
filled with the greatness of the subject before the two
images of the same man, that given here and in the
Symposium, are combined into one.

If then it should be asked why, if the case stands
thus, Plato has not done this himself, and in general
worked up into one piece the description of the philosopher in his two-fold character, we may reply, that
since we can no longer enquire of Plato himself, this
question on the one hand goes too far, and it cannot
be incumbent upon us to give an explanation of the

fact; and, on the other, it is easy to point generally to the progress which even at this period the philosophy itself of Plato had made towards perfection, and to the influence it had upon the form of his works; so that without total separation, there yet prevails in all of them a preponderating antithetical character, and the Symposium and Phædon are most naturally connected together, exactly in the same manner as the Gorgias and Theætetus are. One may even venture to say, that in the dialogue we are now considering, this influence is particularly reflected in the description of the opposition between soul and body, two things which, regarded from without, are quite distinct enough; but still, when the fact itself speaks, can never be completely disconnected from one another. For the rest, however, it would be a strange misunderstanding of what has been said, if any reader were to understand this so strictly and literally, as to suppose that the two dialogues constitute the third part of the trilogy which was promised in the Sophist, as if Plato, fearing the frequent repetition of the same form, had now determined to exhibit the philosopher in a different way, and because, instead of the somewhat dry ironical subdivision, he had again chosen the most elegant dramatic form, he was by that perhaps induced to divide his subject, and thus constructed the two dialogues with one another, and sketched them at the same time. For this would be too dry and mechanical a process for us to think of maintaining it. But Plato may easily have let the trilogy go unfinished, thinking that his readers might now turn a speech in the Phædrus to the construction of a philosopher after the manner of the second part of the trilogy, combining much both earlier and later in point of composition, to which he might mentally refer them. But even supposing this to have been the case, still, and this is all, properly speaking, which we maintain, in his progress or his career as an author the same problem must necessarily have returned upon him under another form. For our two dialogues form the first, as the Philebus forms the second point of transition from the dialogues that have preceded, and were characterized by the indirect process to those that follow, which belong to the immediately constructive class. And, when Plato was upon the point of adopting another method, and wished yet once for all to connect together what he had surveyed by the one already used, and what, although without every where enunciating the results with equal precision, he had also in reality taught and established, when he wished to conclude the old matter as well as prepare the way for the new, what could be a more natural result than that he should describe the process of a philosopher as a purely mental process, as he had practised it according to his own inclination and judgment; for the description of his own mode of operation would now for the first time come in his way? It must, indeed, always remain a remarkable circumstance, and one that might point to an earlier period for the composition of this dialogue, that that dramatic character, which in the dialogues immediately preceding had almost vanished, and in the Philebus again is likewise much suppressed, comes out in such strong relief in these two, as it were in its last and highest glory. But, in the first place, every reader must see that there is no other dialogue, and least of all is it the case with the earliest, as the Phædrus and Protagoras, in which the dramatic character is so completely part and parcel of the subject, or so intimately identified with it as in this dialogue, and it could therefore never display itself in its full splendour with more perfect right. And again, a variety of other circumstances may have given occasion to this display; in the Symposium, first, which we know certainly upon other grounds not to belong to the earlier works of Plato, that apologetic tendency which cannot be denied to exist in it, and for which a living representation of the Socratic mode of life must have been of great advantage; in the Phædon, probably, Plato's recollection of his own Sicilian affairs, and the wish to show how impossible it was that a cowardly fear of death should exist in the breast of a true disciple of Socrates. It is therefore by no means the close connection with the Symposium that alone determines this as the proper place for the Phædon in the works of Plato. Rather should we say, that it is that combination of all that has preceded, which is so manifest, and to which we especially refer all who would be convinced upon this point; and then, whether that particular relation presents itself in a light more or less clear, can make but little difference as regards the principal question.

And first of all, it must be evident to every one, that it is only on the transition from the previous works to those that are to come, that the account would be in its proper place, which Plato in the person of Socrates here gives us of his own advances in speculation, and of the turns in his philosophical career; how, for instance, he begun with Anaxagoras; how, from the study of that philosopher, the idea of the good, and the supremacy of reason as the highest *norma* of

all cosmical contemplation, first shot upon him; how
by the dialectic method he convinced himself of the
unsoundness of the Empedoclean doctrine of physics, and
therefore, so long as his own ideas were not sufficiently
clear and distinct to follow them out consistently and
plenarily as principles, he could not proceed otherwise
than critically and hypothetically; and this applies particularly to his speculations upon the Eleatic and
Heraclitic philosophy, and to the result of those speculations, which taught him that in the eternal forms
alone is found the constant as connected with the
changeable, and real unities as connected with plurali-
ties, and that it is only upon them, and the relation
of things to them, that knowledge or science of anything whatever can be constructed. And this principle
is here for the first time established so totally without
restraint, and with so much reference made to the
construction of science, that every reader who is familiar
with the Platonic turns, and the value of Platonic expressions, must very easily see that when Plato wrote
this, the idea of the good had ceased to be too strange
to him, or too obscure to prevent him any longer from
constructing in connection with that principle the two
sciences which are here alluded to. But every really
attentive reader must feel in this place the most decided inclination to pass at once from the Phædon to
the Timæus, until he reflects that in Plato's speculations the ethical generally precede the physical, and
on the other hand, that the idea of the good itself
was still susceptible of more accurate explanation, and
indeed, more especially on account of disputed questions, at that time still unsettled, even required it; and
we have, therefore, yet to pass through the Philebus

and the Republic, of both of which the germs manifestly appear in this place in the Phædon. And again,
it can hardly escape any one of sound and unprejudiced mind, that the doctrine of the soul is in our
dialogue still imperfect, though in its last stage of
developement, no longer in a mythological chrysalis'
sheath, as in the Phædrus, but like the just emergent
butterfly, whose wings only want to grow to maturity,
a process which a few moments may complete. And
this circumstance in the case of the Phædrus, points
very nearly to the Timæus. For the manner in which
the soul is here described as producing life generally,
and as related to immutable essence, does indeed approximate to strict definition, but still is not definition
itself; and we observe here exactly the appearance of
an author's only producing so much of one subject,
to which a particular investigation is to be devoted,
to bear upon another, as every reader must grant
without more ado.

As then all these allusions to what is still to come,
assign the Phædon its place before the last great works
of Plato, though in such a manner as to bring it near
to them, so also, all references to the dialogues already
given determine its place after them. For, if we look
to the dialogues forming the second part, in the order
in which they are here published, we find that in
that arrangement the connection which obtains between
the Platonic doctrine of knowledge and that of immortality has not as yet been indicated by decisive
strokes, but only in a vague and sketchy manner,
inasmuch as, wherever perfect and immutable existence
is spoken of, in opposition to that which is imperfect
and mutable, mention is also made in some way or

other of immortality. It is first brought nearer, by
the way in which in the Menon the doctrine, that
knowledge is recollection, is expounded and put into
tangible form, and to this Plato himself appeals here
in the Phædon, perhaps more definitely and expressly
than he anywhere else alludes to an earlier work. For
a denial of this appeal would scarcely leave us anything remaining, but to suppose that the speech of
the Socratic Cebes refers only to colloquial discussions,
whether of Socrates or of Plato, and that the Menon
was composed after this had been said by Cebes, though
not indeed then by Plato, but by some one else, a
supposition, however, which it would be difficult to
make appear probable to any one who understood the
practice of sound criticism. But the connection of which
we speak could not be well represented quite clearly
until the investigations contained in the Sophist had
preceded; and the ease with which Socrates admits all
principles relating to this point to be taken for granted
as long since dispatched, would be, without such a reference, inexplicable. The exposition, therefore, of this
theory follows in this place, being the first in which
it is found; but here it is quite complete, and that
part of the dialogue in which it appears is indisputably
the kernel of the whole. And agreeably with this supposition, the Platonic Socrates himself clearly lays most
weight upon the theory, that the ideas and the soul
exist by a similar necessity even before we are born;
and moreover, that there is a similar mode of the existence of ideas and of the soul, without the sphere of
that imperfect existence in which it appears in life. To
Socrates and his disciples this is the immediately certain principle to which they firmly adhere, simply,

because it is immediately one and the same with that
of the reality of knowledge, and they who understand
Plato otherwise, or at least foist upon him any other
conception of immortality, as if *it* were that of which
he is immediately certain, and the result of his demonstration, might learn to be cautious from this passage,
not to associate themselves without intending it with
those who dream, erroneously enough, that, according
to Plato, the ideas had a kind of sensible existence, or,
somehow and somewhere, a special and external being,
or I know not what, out of nature and out of the mind.
For, with the exception of what is necessarily connected
with that higher and truly immortal existence of the
soul, and is here also followed out as a regular theory,
that, namely, the repeated appearances of the soul in
the body always proceed out of the abundance of that
immortality, and are real repetitions, and not new creations; with the exception of this, Plato arranges all
other conceptions and minor points subordinate to that
doctrine, as something not homogeneous with it, nor of
an equal degree of certainty, considering them partly
in the light of amusing conversation, and exorcisement
of the baby within us which foolishly fears death, while
they have in part quite a different bearing. Thus,
for instance, the repeated and always perfected appearances of the soul in the life of the body are quite
homogeneous with, and correspondent to its different
places upon the earth, in one of which it may see more
clearly, and be less exposed to disturbing influences
than in another; but what it sees must still be only
material things, and it is not in a more distinct conception of clearer impressions of ideas that every glimpse
of higher and really immortal existence is vouchsafed to

it, but only in knowledge itself. Hence, both do indeed serve more to specify the whole province of the soul in the kingdom of imperfect being and of corporeal life, than to exhibit or define more closely immortality itself. Nay, who can say that the whole of Cebes' objection, that the fact of souls lingering among many bodies does not nevertheless prove their immortality, an objection which is somewhat harshly and unexpectedly directed against Simmias the disciple of Philolaus, is not covertly meant against the Pythagoreans, who thought that they had in the doctrine of Metempsychosis demonstrated the immortality of souls, and therefore, produced no more accurate information upon this point; a deficiency upon which some regret is expressed in an earlier part of the dialogue. Only, let no reader be misled by this, and by the mention of the harmony, to suppose that Simmias probably brings forward his argument, that the soul may be after all but a *disposition* of what is given in the body, in the name of the Pythagoreans. On the contrary, these philosophers were perfectly agreed with Plato, that only virtue and vice could be regarded as arising from a disposition of the soul itself; and the argument may be rather considered as exclusively in the spirit of the strictly atomical system, to which indeed Empedocles, in this point of view, in no small degree approximates; so that it might scarcely be possible to decide, from whom in particular the dress into which the thought is put is either borrowed or adapted. And if there are any to whom the answer appears, partially at least, obscure and unsatisfactory, let them not overlook that it refers to the distinction already started in several places between the ideas subjected to the conditions of more and less, and those which, as expressing independent existence, have also their own measure in themselves; for from this it may be discovered, although it is not quite after our manner of viewing the subject, how far the theory of the disposition may be placed among the former, and the soul only among the latter.

Now without taking into consideration this general reference to the previous dialogues up to this point, by means of the connection between the doctrine of knowledge and that of immortality, further allusions to other earlier matter more or less connected with that pervading and principal point, are not wanting. Thus, for example, besides the quotation already alluded to, we are also further put in mind of a passage in the Menon, by what is here said of public and civil virtue; and it would seem as if Plato here wished to show that this inferior kind of virtue, properly speaking only a shadow of the true, may even exist without being based upon any independent or true principle; and that view in the Statesman, of the natural qualifications which lead some to this and others to that species of virtue, forms as it were, the transition between the two. So also, when the true virtue is spoken of, and it is described to be rationality, the way in which the Protagoras is referred to, and every possible misunderstanding of the dialectics there employed is once for all now removed, necessarily supposes the existence of all the intervening dialogues between that and the Phædon. For we are now first enabled to learn, what nevertheless necessarily belongs to the subject of that dialogue, that the comparative estimation of different degrees of pleasure against one another, cannot constitute any kind of knowledge. Moreover, the derivation from the dead, of those who are in the natal state, which is here taken generally from a natural law affecting every created being, has been already given in the Statesman in a mythical description, which every one will easily recognize as the earlier of the two. So also, in the very same place, the first foundation is laid of the most sublime expansion of, and most general speculation upon, the idea of the soul, as it is said that even heaven and earth are participative of the nature of the body, which must thus necessarily possess a soul, so that, viewed on this side also, the Phædon comes between that work and the Timæus, as preparing the way for the latter by more minute explanations and accurate definitions. In like manner, when we consider closely what is here said of pleasure, we can scarcely suppose that it is of an earlier date than the discussion in the Gorgias, so much more dispassionately is it introduced, and drawn from views so much more profound: while we must at once recognize it as earlier than the Philebus, which first contains the full discussion of the pleasant in this point of view, nay, it seems almost as if Plato here wished to prepare the way for a still necessary discussion of this subject, which was to be more mature, more tranquil, and with more regard for nature. But for all who from the Phædon as their point of view, take a survey of the works hitherto communicated, the comparison of this dialogue with the Phædrus will have most attraction from the manifold points of contact between the two. And, it will probably be the case with most, that if they put aside the Phædon for a short time, and then fix their attention upon the Phædrus, they will find in it particular points which appear

to them too similar to allow of a great interval between
the two; and even many in which they discover a
foretaste of the Timæus, and they might on that account consider the Phædrus as later than the Phædon;
whence I explain to myself the fact, that this opinion also has not been without its followers. Whoever,
on the other hand, places both works at an equal distance from the Timæus, and is consequently in a condition to survey the whole system uniformly from the
two, can hardly, I think, fail to feel surprise when
he sees how much more perfect the Phædon appears;
wiser, and worthy of more mature age; so that it
stands to the Phædrus precisely in the relation of the
dying Socrates to him who still hopes to learn much
from the people in the market-place. For even the
mythical part, to go no further, how much more
sober and judicious is it! In this dialogue we hear no
more of a supercelestial region, and of a dazzling gaze
at ideas, and no necessity arises to assist the dry uncertainty of them by an indistinct image; but it is
sufficient, in order to demonstrate the revolution of the
soul, to give a theory of the earth, which, though constructed indeed upon lore of poets and wise men, is
taken from later sources, and such as contain more of
a presentiment of science. Nay, though a special meaning is not to be looked for in every particular, we
should, nevertheless, scarcely be disposed to disagree
with any one who might suppose that what is said of
Socrates' treatment of the Esopic fables, is a justification of the fact, that in the majority of the Platonic myths so little original invention is contained.
And how much more finished is the philosophic talent
in the Phædon, how much more definite the connection

of the author's own views, how differently, compared
with that youthful joy in the first elements, is the
philosophical method spoken of, after long practice and
complex knowledge; so that certainly in the Phædrus,
the young Plato might more easily make Socrates speak
so like a youth, than in the Phædon so like a sage.
Nay, even if it is to be supposed that Plato, when he
wrote the Phædrus, already professed an acquaintance
with the Pythagorean writings, which does however to
us never seem necessary, how very differently is this
school treated of, when it appears in the light of distant
mythical wisdom, and here, where Plato sets to work to
complete what is insufficient in their doctrines. And
then, as to the proof given in the Phædrus, of the
immortality of the soul; will any one bring himself
to believe that this would be an acceptable supplement,
after all the discussion in our dialogue upon that point?
Or, must not every one see, on the contrary, that Plato
set aside this proof, and as it were disowned it, because he now shrank from calling the soul, as he there
does, the original principle; or God, who is the real
original principle, soul?

Those, therefore, who believe the Phædon to have
been written immediately after the death of Socrates,
and the Phædrus not before his Egyptian travels, what
proof can they bring forward but that already anticipated in the Introduction to the Phædrus, except
perhaps, on the one side, the grand discovery, if we
are not the first to make them a present of it, that
in the Phædrus Simmias is ranked above Phædrus as
an occasion of arguments, because he occasioned those
in the Phædon; and on the other side, those particular
passages in the Phædrus in which doctrinal points are

enunciated with greater precision than appears suitable to a first piece, and in which words occur, which suppose the existence of investigations not to be found except in subsequent dialogues? But any one must see at once how little that circumstance will avail against all that we have established; and thus, it may be left for every reader to explain for himself, how these few passages in the Phædrus arose from the dialectic tendency of the dialogue, even when the Platonic philosophy was yet in an entirely undeveloped state, so that there may be no occasion for the subterfuge, that they were first introduced on a subsequent elaboration of the work, although they look sufficiently as if they had been so introduced. Finally, without any reference to the Phædrus, there would be nothing to say in favour of so early a position of the Phædon, except that so elaborate a description of Socrates would have been in its place only a short time after his death, and that the passage in the Theætetus about the flight from this world, is intended to be an elucidation of the wish for death in the Phædon; and the allegation of such arguments is sufficiently tantamount to bringing to light the weakness of the cause.

This analysis, into which all that there was to say by way of preface upon the subject of the dialogue, has at the same time spontaneously worked itself, will, it is hoped, secure to the Phædon its place between the Symposium and the Philebus. Beyond this, we find no immediate chronological traces, though several indications do indeed point to a somewhat advanced period. We will draw attention to two only. In the first place, the way in which Socrates not only in the myth describes the locality of the Hellenic education as the

worst district upon earth, but also expressly advises
his disciples to seek for wisdom even without Hellas,
among the races of barbarians, bears throughout the
dress of a late period, where from an acquaintance
probably with the Pythagoreans in particular, the passion for the wisdom of the East was excited, and has
an entirely different bearing from particular commen-
dations elsewhere bestowed upon the Egyptians, or
Locrians, or Getæ. And in the next place, an acquaintance with the writings of Philolaus is manifestly
here supposed, and the dialogue itself sufficiently teaches
that these had not yet at that time become naturalized
in Athens itself, because it is only to his Theban
friends that a knowledge of the doctrines of the philosopher, who had lived there, is attributed; and a different style is usually observable in enquiries made after
writings already known at Athens; so that the legend
certainly acquires a degree of probability, that Plato
brought these books home with him from his travels
as a present from his friend.

X. PHILEBUS.

From the earliest times to the present, the Philebus
has been regarded as one of the most important of the
works of Plato, and also, as one of the most difficult.
Even those who, strangely enough, consider the great
majority of his works only as play and pastime, do
yet think that he is at last in this dialogue serious for
once, and intends to say something that has a meaning. Pity only that this correct sentiment has never

grown into a clearer insight into the work, for those on the one hand, who have in general taken a right view of its most universal bearing, have not been so fortunate in their endeavours to penetrate into the details, and superadd, therefore, to the difficulty of the subject a perplexed style of expression, and confusion of language upon these points; while they who speak easily and intelligibly of the same, display little else than the narrowness of their own capacity to see the meaning of such works, and consequently a very deficient criticism.

Now in this result of the pains we have bestowed upon the dialogue, the place which it occupies, and its connection with the earlier, will contribute much to facilitate the understanding of it, with those who adhere to the indications already given. And, next to these, every reader who pays sufficient regard to the structure of the whole, and the way in which the connection is interrupted and again taken up, may get a clear conception of what is meant beyond what is actually said; following exactly the recommendations we were obliged to give in the case of the Sophist, to which dialogue the present bears an especial resemblance in its principal features. For here also we have a question, and that not an unimportant one, to which of the two, namely, in the life of man, the prize is due, pleasure or knowledge, proposed for decision just at the beginning of the work, and as soon as the question is satisfactorily answered the dialogue concludes, as if in this it had entirely exhausted its subject. But on closer consideration, we see that much that is of weight and importance is intermediately introduced, not essentially connected with the solution of that problem, or of which, at least, as much as was necessary might have been incidentally brought in, as is here the case with much besides. And this circumstance excites at the same time a suspicion, that the question started just at the commencement is by no means the only one, nay, may not perhaps contain even the main purport of the dialogue. For, after the dialectic foundation, which proves that we are not at the outset to consider pleasure and good as two names of one thing, and consequently as identical, and after the allegation of proof, that neither pleasure nor knowledge are in themselves sufficient, nay more, that accurately speaking, for this is certainly implied in what is said, neither of the two ever appears in reality unmixed with the other, Socrates might have advanced at once to that masterly explanation of pleasure according to its inward essence, and of desire, and of the intermediate state between pleasure and pain, and might have shown how false pleasure, of which several kinds spontaneously present themselves to his notice solely from these explanations, cannot partake of that admixture with knowledge necessary in the life of man. And if he had there further shown in conclusion, how, on the other hand, the latter is harmless in all its degrees even to the lowest, and how every species of it is capable of being combined, and is already naturally combined with pure pleasure, the question started would have been thus satisfactorily answered. Such matter as would have entirely dropped out, supposing this uninterrupted progress to have been adopted, consists chiefly of the second dialectic piece, in which those two pairs of ideas, that of the indefinite, the defining, the compounded and compounding cause, are established. These ideas do indeed come into application, in so far as it is shown of impure pleasure that it belongs to the indefinite, but no one will be disposed to maintain that they are set up here only for that purpose. Rather should we say, that the passage connects itself with that in the Sophist, which in a similar manner there forms the kernel of the whole. For in the Sophist also, he begins with speculations upon the nature of our notions of things (δόξαι), and thus shows the necessary union, in knowledge, of the fluent and constant, and, correspondingly, the necessary union of existence and knowledge in that principle which is supreme and original. And in like manner in this dialogue, starting from the same point, he investigates more closely the mode and manner of created existence, and of the origin of the fluent and constant elements in it. For, if we take away everything connected with form in our notions of things, under which we must reckon all that can in any way be called measure or definite magnitude, there remains nothing to constitute the abstract essence of matter but the indefinite, entirely dependent upon conditions of comparison as apprehended in fallible perception; and which is precisely the same with the absolutely manifold, never self-identical, and consequently, not essentially existent. Now the fact that Plato here avoids this definition of the non-existent, current in the Sophist and elsewhere, and thereby, although certainly unintentionally, increases the difficulty of connecting the two passages, is in part the result of the same subject being in fact here viewed from a different side, and consequently needing different forms of expression; and moreover, Plato wished to avail himself of the language of the Pythagoreans, and that the more, because he is here already upon his way towards the Timæus, in order to show, by so doing, the coincidence between his own mode of thinking and theirs. This indefinite, therefore, and the principle of *definiteness*, here expressed particularly under the schema of number, because this expresses the mean between the infinitely great and unity, are the two sources of created existence; while the real cause of it is that which connects and compounds these two, the eternal nature of Zeus, expressed also under the name of Reason, in which the Sophist had already pointed out the necessary union of existence and knowledge as taking place. This doctrine is certainly expounded very briefly and imperfectly, both as regards the necessities of the reader, and also as compared with that to which it is to serve as a supplement, although the exposition here has the advantage of not being given in so indirect a form, but more positively. And this part of our dialogue might be added to anything in the others that have preceded, if anything can be found tending to justify the opinion, that a full understanding of the philosophy of Plato from his works was only in the power of his disciples, who, on the perusal of them, could call to mind his other instructions, while, from others, the best part remain concealed. But we have not been so badly dealt with; attentive readers who have followed hitherto the developments of the doctrine of forms and original existence, and that which is derived from it, will follow also here. But even to such it must ever be matter of surprise, that Plato, when he denotes the universal causative as reason or mind, appeals only to the general feeling of mankind, and when he establishes that principle of indefiniteness as an original principle, not produced from the eternal

nature of Zeus, but only bound up with it, in so far
as the monarch mind dwells in it, this is a point
upon which, as the subject lies close upon the border
of the properly philosophic speculation of Plato, and
approximates to that which he believed it possible to
explain mythically only, not even the immediate scholars of the philosopher were more scientifically instructed
than we ourselves are from the Phædon, where Socrates
equally contents himself with the arranging mind, and
where the method of discussing the opposition between
body and soul favours the view of the originality of the
indefinite.

Again, what is here said incidentally only of the
soul of the universe, intimating rather than explaining
the mode of connection between created being and original existence, stands in the closest reference to this
speculation upon the former, and has, on the contrary,
little or nothing to do with the question of the precedence of pleasure or knowledge. This also depends
upon the Phædon, and will only be understood to the
whole extent of its meaning by those who bear in
mind how, in that dialogue, the immortality of the
soul is demonstrated from the nature of consciousness,
and the law to which all opposites are subjected in
the sphere of apparent existence, and an alternation, as
it were, established between a personal existence of the
soul, and one not personal. With these hints also is
connected the extremely remarkable enlargement which
is here given to the doctrine of recollection; for every,
even bestial, desire is in this place considered in the
same way as, in the Menon and Phædon, this doctrine
is demonstrated with regard to ideas, as if those desires also, when they appear for the first time, must

be based upon a recollection of that state which is now the object of them. And the purport of this clearly is to intimate that brute instinct also is to be taken into the nature of the universal soul.

Now if we collect together all that concerns the immediate object of the dialogue, the comparison, that is, of pleasure and knowledge, and then ask for the connecting link whereby those hints and this discussion are combined together into one whole, we shall find the answer immediately in that passage in which Socrates says, that if pleasure were the good, it could be so only in the mind, and that then there would be none whatever in bodies, and all other beautiful and good things. He therefore cherished the idea of not confining the good to the life of man alone, but of extending it at the same time over the whole sphere of created existence, and it must also have been a great object to do this, with one who had made the idea of the good the principle of the knowledge, not only of man himself, but also of that of all other things. And he wished at the same time to establish this common basis for the books of the Republic, as well as for the Timæus, and this is the object of the investigations here given of created existence as a mixed compound, these investigations being only intended to show the relation in which the good stands to it. For after having thus discovered the nature of the good, and satisfied himself, first of all, as is likewise here done, that material things as they actually occur to experience cannot form the object of knowledge, but only the idea of them, as that which the former try to resemble, though they must ever fall short of perfect similarity,—then, and not till then, could he pass to the speculation upon man as well as nature, and the Philebus is eminently, in this respect, the immediate introduction to those two great works.

From this point of view then, much that was difficult to be understood or overlooked by the majority of persons may be pretty easily explained. How, for instance, knowledge and pleasure descend to the fourth and fifth places instead of taking the second and third. For at the end the two opposite theories are united, and therefore the formal elements of the good, upon which the perfection of the compound mixture, as such, depends, and which are also common to material things, are ranked first, and that which exists in men in particular, forms the conclusion. Again, why the mind, which as the cause, as the source of universal order, and as the compounding power, is admitted to be absolutely good and worthy of the first place, obtains here only the third. And the reason is this, it is not here the divine and most supreme mind that is spoken of, for the true and divine Reason is exalted above all struggle for the precedence, and is presumed to be recognized and acknowledged as the good in the highest sense, but of that which has itself entered into the compound as such. Although here, a degree of obscurity not to be disguised, must ever remain. For truth, which Socrates first recognises as the condition of every compound, and without which none whatever can exist, is now according to what is here said, made convertible with mind. We must, therefore, say in explanation, that mind, as the sole locus of truth, does certainly first give reality to material things, and therefore also, as the mediating power, rightly stands between the general elements of the created good and those which are peculiar to man. Another point too, in appearance not less obscure, can only be understood upon a similar view of it. It is, why Socrates first explains proportion and beauty as to a certain degree identical, and then again separates the two in the most decided manner. And the explanation is, that it is by the presence of definite measure generally that a thing first attains individuality and becomes a *thing;* while beauty, although limited by definite measure, is the superadded perfection to that essential condition.

From what has been hitherto said, it must now be clear in what sense our dialogue intervenes immediately and next between the Phædon as its immediate antecedent, and the two constructive works, the Republic and Timæus; and that in its particular relation to the last, if we would go back to the farthest possible point, it is grounded upon the Parmenides, but next and immediately upon the Sophist, to the dialectic profundity of which it is supplementary by sensible and palpable clearness. And partly on this account, and in part because the reference to the Republic, and, consequently, the ethical character, is predominant in it, this dialogue has not, like the Sophist and Timæus, any other leader than Socrates himself. For the expressly enunciated, though less general subject, the claims of pleasure in the definition of the good for mankind, is the especial foundation of the books upon the Republic, because it is only after a decisive subordination of pleasure that the idea of a really common life can be established—otherwise it merely remains to mediate the antagonist claims of self-interest. Hence, therefore, the books upon the Republic very naturally recommence with this point.

Of the principal matter now of the dialogue, which concerns the comparison of pleasure and knowledge, it may be said that it again takes up and perfects the Theætetus and Gorgias together, so that we have at the same time in the Philebus a justification of the juxta-position in which we place these two dialogues. For what is here said of false conception is exactly the same with what has been already set up in the Theætetus, though in that dialogue it may have been lost to the many under its sceptical disguise; and generally, the whole relation of perception to that conception which contains at once the assertion and the judgment in itself, supposes the Theætetus and is supplementary to it. And the disquisition upon pleasure, manifestly an excellent and finished physiological view, is in like manner partly a repetition of, and partly supplementary to, what is said in the Gorgias, and certainly penetrates far deeper into the nature of the subject. And the present dialogue, in proportion as it is more mature and judicious than that, is also more charitable. Plato here justifies as necessary the harsh treatment which the advocates of pleasure there receive, if, without thinking of the persons, the theory is to be exhibited in its true light—yet how slightly he touches upon the subject. Nay, even with regard to the art of speaking, there degraded so low, we here find an extenuating sentiment. Even tragedy and comedy are spoken of in a different feeling, although the ingenious manner in which he explains what we find upon that point, certainly refers to his repugnance, at that time certainly of general notoriety, to this class of composition. Not that it is the case, however, as has lately been maintained, that the books upon the Republic had at that time been actually written, and the sentiments we meet with in them are here to be defended.

Thus much may be said by way of preface as regards the subject-matter. As to the form, it is indeed true that the Philebus, in its inward construction, nearly enough resembles the main dialogues of this indirect series. But in its outward dress, it may with justice be accused of a degree of negligence, and it will probably be an universal opinion, that in this respect it does not furnish any such pure enjoyment as the majority of the Platonic works up to this point. That peculiar dialogic character which we are accustomed to find in Plato, does not come out into proper relief, the dialogue does not form itself spontaneously, as the origination of the subject is put behind the scene, for which the dramatic position which Philebus thereby obtains is no compensation whatever. I should rather say, that Plato disdained making preparations for introducing a subject which at that time afforded matter of general discussion and dispute. In like manner the transitions are the result neither of the incidental occasions of the dialogue, nor of the opinions and objections of the interlocutor and his particular disposition, but the whole lies ready in the head of Socrates, and comes out with all the personality and arbitrary character of a connected speech. In short we may clearly see, that here in the transition to the properly constructive works, the dialogic character begins to be only an external form, from which Plato cannot escape, partly from habit, partly because he will not dispense with Socrates. Perhaps it is because he feels the inconvenience of this position that he applies various artificial means of animating the dialogue, which do not indeed produce any very particular effect: the conversation sometimes becomes meaningless, and somewhat pedantically twisted in order to introduce something more than the ordinary formulæ of answers. So that one might say, that there is a certain unpleasant character spread over these conversations upon pleasure, that we observe that the author is surfeited with the indirect method of proceeding hitherto used, and that nothing is kept up more dramatically than the manner in which we may perceive, especially towards the end of all his speeches, not perhaps without disadvantage to the subject, that Socrates is hastening and ardently wishing to be rid of the young men.

APPENDIX.

I. THEAGES.

THE spuriousness of the Theages has been already
in recent times so often pointed out, and from such a
variety of sources, that a particular allegation of proof
in support of that opinion is now no longer necessary.
For, such readers of Plato as can pride themselves
upon any degree of critical perception or skill, will
have ere this discovered the grounds of it themselves,
and as regards those of a different description, such a
judgment is in their eyes only verified by a sufficient
frequent repetition of it, and such a repetition, in the
present instance, they may find.

The fable, if we may be allowed the expression,
of this little dialogue, consists in Socrates' adoption of
a pupil, and the person chosen is one of those who
are mentioned in the Apology of Socrates as already
dead before the final sentence was passed upon that
philosopher. As far as we know, Theages is not otherwise known than from two notices of him in Plato
himself, and has no opportunity of showing whether
he received much or little benefit from having made
the acquaintance of Socrates, late enough certainly, after
the Sicilian overthrow. In the dialogues of Plato, indeed, the adoption of a pupil is never brought so
forward or made so immediate an object; our author,
however, has had in his mind, as a model to work
upon, a passage in a parenthetic digression of Socrates

in the Theætetus, though without understanding how to interweave the more profound meaning of it into his composition. For Plato's principal object in that passage, which is to show how Socrates exercised an influence upon his disciples, not so much by teaching as by developing truth out of their own minds, is left entirely untouched by our composer, who adheres only to the consequence which follows from this; that according to a method of proceeding, exactly similar, Socrates succeeds with some pupils and not with others, by virtue of a divine ordinance or predetermination; and in illustrating this point he has fallen into a strange confusion and most perversely distorted amalgamation of this divine ordinance, and that personal presentiment which, with Socrates, becomes a heavenly voice; whence the passage in the Apology, where Socrates mentions this voice, is the second hinge upon which the whole of the little dialogue turns. It is very remarkable that in that passage in the Theætetus Plato does not make Socrates say that that dæmonic sign has ever prevented him admitting any one whomsoever to his society; intimating as it were by this, that he owed this privilege to all, and could not allow himself to feel a decided presentiment; hence there might easily be for a time among his hearers those who were incapable of drawing advantage from his philosophy. But he makes the voice come in then, and not before, when an unworthy disciple would attach himself, because, then certainly the inward feeling must have a voice to decide, whether the unworthiness is to be regarded as the effect of seduction from without, and the return of a genuine love for the true and good, or, conversely, the unworthiness arises from the victory of the internal nature, and the return on the contrary is ungenuine. That Plato in that passage alludes to particular cases besides the Aristides whom he names, whether of the disciples of Socrates or his own, will be clear to every one, but even this particular allusion does not seduce him into going beyond the character which in the Apology Socrates attributes to that dæmonic sign, I mean, that it was merely a *warning* sign. Our author on the contrary, while he enunciates this in almost literal conformity with what we find in the Apology, does, in the description itself, carelessly exceed this principle, for with him this sign appears as a power which comes regularly to the assistance of some persons and works influentially for them. This is indeed immediately attributable to his superficial and confused views of that passage in the Theætetus, and more remotely, I doubt not, to the fact, that he foists upon the dæmonic voice a particular and personal existence, and changes the dæmonic feeling into a little dæmon, a conception agreeable to no genuine Platonic passage, and which must be recognised as quite unsupportable, from the manner especially in which Socrates in the Apology contradicts the accusation brought against him of infidelity, as was there, we hope, satisfactorily shown.

And as in other dialogues foisted upon Plato, it is found necessary for the most part to resort to little stories taken from antiquity or foreign parts, in order to disguise the poverty of the subject-matter, so in this, two stories are introduced about the power of this little dæmon to foretell such results as must have depended entirely upon accidental circumstances; a power of which Plato never knew anything, and

which is not even justified by the expressions of Xenophon. Probably, the composer suffered himself to be
misled by a passage in the Euthyphro, in which that
person connects with the voice of Socrates his own
individual impulse, by virtue of which he predicts, in
the Ecclesia, some accidental event or other. The two
stories moreover present, in themselves, a sufficiently
strange appearance. For one of them, which concerns
a well-known Platonic personage, is not brought to an
end, and we are left uncertain as to whether the author
is to suppose it generally known, or whether he found
it elsewhere in the same form, or whether he did not
know how to extricate himself out of his talk when he
had begun it. In the other, the voice cautions against
an undertaking, the nature of which is utterly unknown
to Socrates ; not to mention that we have, it would
seem, the wise man brought into company with very
inferior people, and of a class which we do not find
in Plato.

In other respects also, the bad imitator appears
only too manifestly from under the mask he has put
on. How badly the proposition is stated, or fails to
be stated, out of the Euthydemus, that the art of
politics rules over the works of all other arts! How
this Socrates accumulates in the most tedious manner,
clumsily and at random aping the Socratic induc-
tion, examples which are no examples as they illustrate
nothing, and is still never satisfied, but begins yet once
again in just as tedious a form, only to display a
common knowledge of common things! How Theages,
only that an opportunity may be given for harping
upon a sentiment of Euripides, is obliged to delay be-
thinking himself that he does not really want to be a

tyrant, although he had previously admitted an inclination towards it, as if the innocent boy were a second
Alcibiades or a Callicles, to whom, however, he bears
otherwise no resemblance at all. And how Socrates
twists the proposition for him under his own hands,
as if he had now ceased to wish to be a statesman,
and only desired to be a good citizen, without having
instructed him in the slightest degree as to how far
the two characters are identical or distinct! But to
enumerate all that is ill done, would be, as far as the
subject-matter is concerned—for in much of the language there is Platonic colouring enough—to copy off
the whole dialogue, and we would rather conclude with
its character for brevity, and imitate it in this respect.

II. ERASTÆ.

THE spuriousness of this little dialogue is proved
with equal force by every thing we meet with in it
from beginning to end, by its most outward dress, as
well as by its most inward matter, in so far as it
contains enough of the latter description. To go no
further, it is evinced by the namelessness of the persons, the abrupt manner of Socrates in his opening
questions, and the way in which, being himself the
narrator, he concludes with the announcement of the
general assent which was awarded to him. Still more,
undoubtedly, every reader will discover upon a nearer
view a general and utter absence of Platonic urbanity

and irony, to which, however, the dialogue in its external form throughout makes immediately the most decided pretensions. The opposition between polite literature and gymnastics, never before laid down in such marked distinction, is here represented to the life in the persons of two uneducated fellows, who can scarcely be conceived to be lovers of Athenian boys of noble family, the one a kind of athlete, the other professedly a master of polite literature, though not a single polished word, nay, not even an harmonious sentence, though music is one of his accomplishments, is ever heard from him. If it is asked what is the proper subject-matter, we must look for it in the proposition that philosophy is not multiscience, for with this the dialogue begins, and concludes again with it, a distinction to which indeed the Platonic Socrates may refer occasionally, or treat of it ironically, when he has to deal with sophists who boast of their multiscience, but which Plato, after having written a single work, could hardly make the subject of a regular dialogue, unless he wished to work out some other matter under this disguise, or inculcate some further doctrine, and we look in vain for anything of this kind in the present instance. But even for Plato's first exercise, this dialogue, so awkward and unmeaning as it is, would be far too bad. For after Socrates has already allowed himself to admit, that only moderation in everything, and not excess, produces advantage, he does not at once draw the immediate consequence from this, that philosophy must therefore be a bad thing when it is multiscience, but passes first to a question which is here perfectly idle, and which again he lets drop at once in a manner which to a reader of Plato must appear utterly strange;

and then again takes up the preceding one in a different manner quite from the beginning, and this, in order to deduce from it less than he had already obtained, amounting only to the proposition, that the philosopher is a useless and superfluous character as long as there are masters in the several arts; just as if he had before gone too far without intending it. This discussion is followed lastly, by yet a third, whose object is to show that there are kinds of knowledge in which it is disgraceful for a man, such as a philosopher must be, to hold only that second rank beyond which multiscience cannot rise. But how much that is in no way connected with the subject, and which is serviceable to no end whatever, is mixed up with this last part! That about the identity of justice with the administration of it, appears to have a tendency to justify a remarkable use of language which occurs a few times in Plato's writings; but the way in which the doctrine of the identity of the four cardinal virtues is here harped upon in the most trivial manner, is only to be explained from the fact that this doctrine was one of the commonest mountebank stages; and moreover from the most superficial recollection, something upon this subject might be patched up. On the other hand, several opportunities, which however unsought for, necessarily present themselves for saying or hinting something affirmative beyond that negative explanation, or at least for pointing out by a different method where such an explanation is to be found, are left without any use whatever being made of them. For one who had understood even in any degree this art of Plato, it would have been in fact a not unworthy problem, taking this notion of multiscience as

a ground-work, and following somehow the analogy of
what is said in the Euthydemus upon the subject of
the kingly art, to lead to the true view of philosophy,
and even now an adroit imitator who should skilfully
adjust the members of the dialogue as we now have
it, and finish it further in this point of view, might
make an attempt to accomplish this. Hence, it might
even be supposed that the first idea and ground-plans
of the dialogue, which do indeed betray some such
purpose, may perhaps be mediately or immediately the
work of a more skilful hand, or that some traditionary
notices of Platonic conversations may be at the bottom
of it. But to imagine the performance itself as it lies
here before us to be Platonic, or still more decisively
as the third part of the trilogy still owing, and consequently as the representation of the Philosopher in
addition to that of the Statesman and Sophist——this is
the strangest notion that can possibly be entertained.

III. ALCIBIADES I.

IT is well known that old commentators upon Plato
celebrate this dialogue as the best introduction to the
wisdom of the philosopher, and recommend beginners
to give the preference to it in commencing the study
of Plato's writings. And it is certainly undeniable that
in the first Alcibiades, a variety of matter is touched
upon, and a number of questions started, upon which
other writings of Plato afford more accurate conclu-

sions, and that, notwithstanding, there is nothing in it too difficult or too profound and obscure even for the least prepared tyro. But we know that both in ancient and modern times many authors, themselves unable to invent anything original, have, not without success, elaborated introductions to the wisdom of others, and thus this opinion of learned men might continue to stand in full possession of all its honour and dignity, with reference to the present dialogue, even though before the judgment-seat of a quick-sighted and accurate criticism the work should be discovered not be one of Plato's. It is, indeed, but little profitable to be the first to communicate doubts of this kind, and to explain the grounds of them; for the faculty of critical perception is but sparingly distributed, and among those, perhaps, who are not deficient in this respect, an accurate knowledge of the author, without which, however, a judgment cannot be formed, is still more rare. And then come at once the great multitude of those who, incapable of investigations of this kind, proceed in defence of what is traditional in such a manner as neither to instruct or satisfy us. And yet these are the men to whom, after those afore-mentioned, he who suggests such doubts as those of which we speak has to look. In the present instance, however, it is imperative upon us not to shrink from declaring our opinion upon the dialogue in question. And therefore, let us once for all undertake to say, that this little work, which, with those who are accustomed to admire in the gross, has been ever a subject of most especial commendation, appears to us but very insignificant and poor, and that to such a degree, that we cannot ascribe it to Plato, even though any number of those who think they can swear to his spirit, profess most vividly to apprehend it in this dialogue. We will, however, only declare our opinion, without making any very great exertions to gain over others to coincide with it; and we intend now, only to establish generally the main points upon which it depends, and in the annotations, occasionally to point to the particular instances tending to confirm it. Every reader may then take it as he will, and others to whom it may seem worth the trouble, can turn the subject over and over, and bring the conclusion more home to the apprehension and judgment of readers in general.

First of all then, we venture to prophesy that one thing in particular, if we can trust to our own feelings in any respect, must strike an attentive reader already acquainted with the spirit of Plato; that the dialogue upon a first perusal of it, will leave upon his mind an impression of singular want of uniformity to which he is totally unaccustomed. Particular passages, very beautiful and genuinely Platonic, may be found sparingly dispersed, and floating in a mass of worthless matter, consisting partly of little broken dialogues busied about nothing, partly of long speeches. Of these, the first is so tedious that the god, when, as it seems, he resolved especially to defer the colloquial meeting of Socrates and Alcibiades until an opportunity had arrived for delivering these speeches, did neither of them any very great service. The second, with a display of strange statistical notices, celebrates Persian and Lacedæmonian virtues and riches; the virtues more in the manner of Xenophon than Plato; the riches and luxurious pomp, for the reason that no irony can be discovered in these laudatory descriptions, in a style throughout unsocratic. Accordingly, the reader will also feel himself utterly unsatisfied, and regret that he has been compelled to wade through useless digressions raised upon the most trifling subjects, and that on the contrary, most important matter is superficially passed over, or, so to speak, the cup is broken before it is tasted. If then, after this first impression has been overcome, he thinks to inquire more closely into the real meaning of the dialogue, if such there be, he will feel at a loss where to turn, and will certainly allow first of all, that the work contains extremely little upon the subject which the second title of it professes, I mean that it is to treat of the nature of man. Viewed from without, the whole bears in its construction a kind of false resemblance to certain dialogues contained in our second part. For these, so to speak, have first of all an external thema, expressly enunciated, and yet forming to a certain degree only the shell of the whole, and then another concealed one, connected with the former, and containing more profound results. And thus, in the present case, it might be considered as the external thema, that Socrates is to prove to Alcibiades that he must acquire from him other kinds of knowledge previously to devoting himself to the conduct of public affairs, and, on the other hand, all that Socrates brings into the argument with a view to establishing this proof, might be taken to be the proper core of the dialogue. But even the first point is not brought out pure and distinct; for in the first place, Socrates does not show that he alone has the power of teaching Alcibiades what he stands in need of, and in the next, again, he goes beyond this thema, and by way of conclusion, is induced to make some remarks upon education in general. And still less does the matter intermediately introduced constitute of itself a complete and regular core. For that Alcibiades has neither discovered nor learnt what is just, that what is just and useful is the same, and then again that Pericles, though an excellent statesman, and here more than ever in any other Platonic dialogue, extolled without a trace of irony, has, notwithstanding, imparted his sagacity to no one, all these points have no connection whatever with one another, and each stands where it is, only in its loose external relation to Alcibiades' imperfect state of mind. Finally, we must not imagine for a moment, that in these speeches some philosophical secrets or other are intended to be contained. On the contrary, though many genuine Platonic doctrines are very closely connected with what is here said, not even the slightest trace of them is to be met with. Thus, Alcibiades might have extricated himself out of a very inconvenient dilemma by the slightest mention of the doctrine of recollection; again, other matter is connected with the distinction between knowledge and conception; but in both instances these references are left totally untouched, and we are only reminded in the most external manner by one passage of the Laches, of the Gorgias by another, and of the Protagoras again by a third.

It must, however, be allowed that the majority of readers have not looked for the secret treasure and proper end of the dialogue in these speeches, but rather in the little that is here said at the end, upon the necessity of self-knowledge. Now, this does certainly come forward at first with many pretensions to profundity, but presently turns to the most superficial

matter, and we are obliged to put up with a few perfectly vulgar sentiments, which we find elsewhere expressed with much more elegance. Accordingly, if we
are to name something as the proper subject-matter of
the dialogue, scarcely anything else remains but the
insight into the nature of the god-head, which is recommended as a means for the knowledge of man, but
our dialogue is incapable of discussing this subject
except in the most meager style ; so that the morsel
seems in fact not worth the whole apparatus, independent of the fact, that the particular members of this
apparatus are not in any way connected with it. Neither
in the composition, generally, does any trace appear of
such an inward relation of every detail to one single
point as we find elsewhere in Plato. It is equally in
vain to look here for the strict dogmatic connection
which we find in the Sophist and Philebus, or even for
that apparent passiveness of Socrates in the conduct
of the dialogue, under which every thing seems so much
the more to grow purely out of the subject itself. On
the contrary, Socrates intrudes in mere caprice, and
drags out one thing after another, generally, though
he makes many words, breaking off the subject shorter
than is his custom, and only applying, in fact, every
point to shame his interlocutor, so that the whole acquires an eristic character, which no other Platonic
dialogue bears with it in a similar manner. And when
we reflect that the interlocutor so rudely treated is not
a sophist, who is to be exposed in his worthlessness, nor
even a boy who must be content to be the object of a
little bantering for the profit and advantage of others,
nay, not only a noble Athenian, but that Alcibiades,
who is universally celebrated by Plato as the richly

endowed minion of his instructor, we might be inclined to maintain that the treatment of the relation between these two, and the keeping, or rather the want of keeping, in their characters is still more unplatonic than anything else in the present dialogue. For instance, this Socrates, with the mute character which he boasts of having so long played with his minion, and this careful watching which could be neither agreeable to him nor worthy of him, now introducing himself with a long speech, the like of which he hates as he says elsewhere, and with an arrogance which he hates still more, professing himself the only teacher capable of instructing in the art of politics—this character is indeed manifestly the direct opposite of the Platonic Socrates. In the representation of his relation to Alcibiades, moreover, all appearance of the love of the boy is avoided as pedantically as possible, and due merit assigned to the fact, that Socrates has not even once addressed Alcibiades until the time of his youthful bloom was as good as entirely passed. But how are we to reconcile this with the manner in which the same relation is treated of in the Protagoras and Symposium? In the Protagoras Pericles is still alive, and yet Socrates and Alcibiades appear as old acquaintances, who must already have conversed much with one another; and what Alcibiades tells us in the Symposium, must also be taken from the time of his bloom; for he can hardly intend to say that he wished to force himself as a minion upon Socrates when his bloom was passed.

And then how completely Alcibiades himself appears without any resemblance to him whom we find elsewhere represented! At first, one might suppose him here cut out after the pattern of Callicles or Ctesippus, but he soon changes and shows himself prodigiously shamefaced and shy, so that he cannot ever be put into harness, although Socrates is constantly bringing him up anew, and frequently without necessity and without justice, and leading him off again dissatisfied with his answers. In short, however we may consider it, our present dialogue is in this respect either a contradiction of all other Platonic dialogues, or else Plato's own dialogues are so with reference to the rest. And whoever does not feel this, we cannot indeed afford him any advice, but only congratulate him that his notions of Plato can be so cheaply satisfied. We would, however, yet further draw the attention of others to one or two points from which perhaps in the sequel—for we are not in any way inclined ourselves even to start the subject here,—more accurate conclusions might result as to the particular mode in which the present dialogue originated, and has come down to us. For what is most Platonic in it may be indeed in part imitation, sometimes more close and sometimes more remote, of other passages, and as regards the subject-matter may be drawn from reminiscences of other works; in fact, it is of such a description, that though we cannot believe Plato to have literally written it thus, it may be perhaps based upon hints taken from his own instructions; as for example, the discussion upon the relation of justice to profit, which was a very available example in illustration of his doctrine of the community of ideas. Moreover, some particular passages are in fact of such a nature, that we might not be very loath to suppose that they came from Plato's pen exactly as they stand here. And if we consider further the way in which the greatest part is here not

worked out, but only laid down as a thema, the ab-
ruptness or awkwardness of the transitions from one
part to another, especially when a piece of worthless
and empty dialectics ends or a new one begins, and
how the superior matter which is torn asunder and
deformed by these foreign additions might stand in far
more accurate connection, we might almost be tempted
to think that an immediate disciple of Plato somehow
or other got hold of a sketch of a dialogue of his
master which had probably come down from earlier
times, and which the latter did not finish but reject,
and distributed into other dialogues, as the Gorgias
and Meno, and some still later, what he intended to
teach in it. But this dialogue, at least if Plato had
really finished it himself, would scarcely have been
called Alcibiades. This appellation was certainly but
little appropriate to such a colloquy with Socrates.
For his boiling vivacity would not have borne to have
attributed to it the character of a passive interlocutor,
though of the best kind, like Theætetus for instance,
and Plato could scarcely have thought of engaging him
in violent polemics against Socrates, as he does Callicles; so that it may certainly be fairly maintained that
instead of two Alcibiades', which up to the present
day have been attributed to Plato, he did not even
write one.

IV. MENEXENUS.

No reader of Plato, it is presumed, will feel any surprise at finding this little work not brought forward in the series of his properly philosophical writings, to which, inasmuch as no philosophical subject is treated of in any part of it, the Menexenus has as little claim to belong as the Apology of Socrates. The occasion of the latter, however, is clear and manifest; but what can have induced Plato to venture at a late period into the province, to him entirely strange, of regular state speeches, may reasonably be expected to be not very possible for us now to decide; at least, nothing appears in the work itself which could give a determinate direction to the conjectures of ingenuity. That the speech is placed in some relation to the funeral oration of Pericles, which Thucydides has preserved to us, is certainly manifest, but when Socrates refers both to one authoress, and that authoress Aspasia, this is a jest, out of which it will not be easy for any one to extract any serious meaning; nor, when he says that the later oration contains much that was omitted in the earlier, is this a much more available indication, inasmuch as the aim of the two speeches is so completely different in each, that we do not see why the second should have in any way contained what we find in the first, and we might feel more satisfied with this opinion, if it was pronounced by a later author who had laid it down as a law at starting, that such a speech must begin from the beginning with a panegyric upon all the exploits of the Athenian people.

Another thing which may easily strike any one is, that Plato probably intended in this speech to set up a counterpart to one of Lysias, and in fact, when we compare the funeral oration of this rhetorician on the same occasion with that which we are considering, it is not possible to overlook a great similarity in point of arrangement, and an equally great diversity in point of character and execution. What is loosely connected together in Lysias is here combined into a whole, by means of distinctly enunciated ideas, the connection of which is impressed upon the hearer by means of words, whose sound is an echo of their sense, brought into strong and prominent relief; the tender element in the sorrow is compensated by manly advice, and the whole speech is at the same time pervaded by a more exalted aim. But had this contrast been the actual object in view, must we not suppose that Plato, who so well understands how to give a hint, would have found some means of intimating the same in the dialogue which comprehends the speech?

If then this explanation also leaves us where we were, might we not venture to say, that Plato intended by such a speech as this to give a practical answer to the objection occasionally brought up against him, that his dislike to the art of speaking was the result of his own incapacity to prepare speeches, which Socrates in his dialogue is so often obliged jestingly to acknowledge? and that he chose in particular this opportunity for doing so, because in the Corinthian war one of his own friends had met his death? Nay, that from his partiality to this exhibition, he has himself practised the severely censured and hypocritical department of the corrupting art, inasmuch as in the historical narrative here given, none but the fair side is ever presented, and all faults in the state are withdrawn into the dimmest obscurity, while in particular, the later relations with the national enemy of the Hellenes, the Persian king, are embellished and represented in a manner which may scarcely be justified upon historical grounds. And therefore it is, we might suppose, that Socrates treats it as such an easy matter to flatter the people before the people, and hence too, that the speech is ascribed to Aspasia, who must have been pretty well versed in the art of seductive embellishment. And in like manner another person might say, that as Plato in the Philebus relaxes his overstrained polemics against the art of speaking, so likewise he did the same at an earlier period in the present dialogue in act and deed. For that the Menexenus is in fact nothing but an attempt to improve, by giving them a better direction, all these speeches in which the people were ordinarily only flattered; and that the appearance of this flattery is all that is preserved in the present case, and that there is manifest throughout, an endeavour to bring into right vivid consciousness the true idea of the Athenian people and state, in order by this means to give a more exalted turn to the national mind. And a third, again, might make an attempt to connect the present dialogue with the Symposium, in a sense different from that in which the former connected it with the Philebus. For appealing to the great difficulty which exists of explaining the whole, if we take it in a serious point of view, and to the way in which even what Plato must have been most in earnest with, I mean the recommendations to virtue, is itself pushed beyond the line of all that is serious, by repetition and bantering, he might attempt to represent it as in the main a playful imitation of the rhetorical styles. And who can tell how much a skilful critic, having once given a hint of this view, furnished with great reading in the orators, and the commentaries upon them, might not bring forward in support of the same; something certainly more profound and various than what Dionysius says, who only reminds us of Gorgias, Licymnus, and Polus, and once, in passing, of Agathon.

But as far as we are concerned every reader may find in the speech as must jest or earnest as he will, and conjecture according to his own notions what Plato meant by it; much, however, will be gained at once, if we could but persuade our readers not to attribute to the dialogue which contains the speech, a similar value with the speech itself, nor pay it the same regard, for then, at all events, the difficulty vanishes, which arises from the circumstance that none of the different views will meet with any confirmation in the dialogue. We are indeed fully aware that by many persons even the introduction has been discovered to be beautiful, and has been much admired by them. But with how much that is unplatonic has this been the case when it has once come forward under the name of Plato. Certainly, at least, even supposing Plato to have written this introduction, it is not particularly worthy of him. To go no further, for the omission already censured, that it does not assist us in the slightest degree to a trace with regard to the particular meaning of the whole, this dialogic setting deserves some blame, and moreover no discriminating reader, we presume, will receive much pleasure from the awkward deference of Menexenus, who will only take in hand public affairs when Socrates

permits it, nor from the pointless way in which Socrates
expresses his opinion, that he must certainly be a great
orator by reason of Aspasia's instructions, nor from
the coarse jest, that he nearly got a beating on account
of his slowness at learning, and that he would even
dance naked for love of Menexenus. It is certainly a
very pardonable suspicion, that this setting is probably
the work of another author, who gladly set himself to
construct a dialogue out of the speech, and thought it
impossible that a Platonic creation should come into the
world without Socrates. Such a person may then have
easily given in Aspasia an awkward imitation of Diotima, and thus have fallen unsuspectingly into an anachronism with which none of the others of Plato are
at all comparable : I mean, that Socrates delivers a
speech referring completely and entirely to something
that did not ensue until long after his death, and that
he professes to have this speech from Aspasia, who
must have been already dead long before him. And
thus it would be in vain to look for any serious meaning in the promise given by Socrates to produce yet
more such state speeches from the mouth of his mis-
tress.

V. THE LARGER HIPPIAS.

THE object of this dialogue is certainly purely philosophical. For the explanation of the idea of the
beautiful in its full extent, as it embraces material things
as well as immaterial, would certainly be worth the
trouble, and quite as important as regards the philosophy of Plato, as the object of many of the smaller

dialogues to which we have assigned a place in the larger series. But the reader, if he looks to the mode in which this subject is treated, will certainly not be surprised to find the Hippias Major only in this place in the Appendix. For it is throughout sceptical to a degree which characterises none of the others; a multitude of different explanations of the beautiful are taken up and all of them refuted. And even, when the upshot is taken of all to which the reader is conducted or referred in this process of refutation, we find it to consist only in a couple of perfectly familiar positions, which teach that the origin of the bad is not in power but in impotence! and that the beautiful and good should not be separated; and this last, indeed, is the only point upon which Socrates expresses himself with clearness and precision. In consequence of this absence of scientific tone, we cannot number the dialogue among those properly called philosophical. Thus, it does not stand in any visible connection of progressive development with any other whatever. In the persual of it, certainly, every reader is immediately reminded of the Philebus, and it is only on account of this connection, and not with a view of indicating, even in the most remote degree, a period at which the Hippias might have been written, that we assign it its present position. For in the Philebus, Plato expresses himself with the greatest precision as well upon the subject of the connection of the beautiful with the good, as upon that of the nature of the beautiful itself, and considers it not only in its moral bearing, but also according to the first elements of that which we call beautiful in material things. But no one will there find even the most distant reference to the in-

vestigations here pursued, nor again in any part of
the Hippias is any proximate preparation discoverable
to what is discussed in the Philebus.

In short, it must be at once manifest to every one,
that a scientific treatment of the subject, the beautiful
that is, in speaking of the present dialogue is almost
entirely out of the question, so completely is all such
kept out of sight; and quite as certain is it, that the
impression which every reader must receive from the
whole is, that a polemical purpose is the predominant
in it. And under this purpose the dialogue has in
view two remarkable explanations of the beautiful. In
one of them, that the beautiful is the *fitting*, we easily
recognise the spirit of the Hedonic schools, in so far,
that is, as according to them the good is only something capriciously established, consequently agreeable
and fitting. Only it may excite our surprise, that in
discussing this point Socrates adheres so exclusively to a
kind of almost verbal dialectics, without following his
usual practice of exposing somewhat severely the notion
which is the basis of the theory. With regard to the
other explanation, that the beautiful is the pleasant
as apprehended by sight and hearing, pointing as it
certainly does to the same principles as Plato lays down
in the Philebus, it would be very interesting to know
who it was that brought forward this explanation in
Plato's time, or whether it was invented by himself in
order to indicate that property of the beautiful which
he mentions in the Philebus as the essential element
in it. But, though· this explanation is certainly given
as lying very close at hand, notwithstanding that we
cannot now point out the author of it, it is impossible
to believe that the substance of these explanations which

Plato puts into the mouth of Hippias about gold, and
the pretty girl, was derived from any other authors.
And thus it is impossible for any one to avoid asking
himself, how it happens that Plato exhibits the not
undistinguished sophist as guilty of such an unheard
degree of stupidity, as not to be even in a condition
to understand a question as to how a word is to be
explained? The personal ridicule indisputably appears
here under a far coarser form than anywhere else, not
excepting even the Euthydemus, where the persons are
probably in no instance strictly historical, and it would,
exaggerated as it is, have certainly destroyed its own
effect.

This manner, or rather absence of anything deserving the name, scarcely reconcileable as it is with the
propriety and polish of Plato, may perhaps excite a
suspicion in the minds of many as to the genuineness
of the dialogue, because we might certainly meet with
it very naturally in a less experienced imitator, who felt
that it was necessary for him to give himself an easy
task if he was to succeed in any degree in the irony
and dialectics of his prototype. And the suspicion once
excited, much certainly will be found apparently con-
firming it. Thus, at the very beginning Socrates indulges in a piece of sophistical dialectics, which might
induce us to believe, that not anything, being what
it is, can be useless, a piece of art which would not be
unworthy of any of the persons in the Euthydemus.
Were this a parody of anything of the kind resembling
it, one should think that Plato would rather have put
it into the mouth of the sophist than of Socrates. On
the contrary, Hippias meantime exhibits in his beha-
viour a plain common sense which he is not quite able

subsequently to keep up, and with a moderation which is not very carefully returned on the side of Socrates. Then, in the arrangement of the whole, it certainly strikes us as something strange, that in the first half of the dialogue all explanations of the beautiful come from Hippias, and in the latter all from Socrates, who there contradicts himself, and that for the most part in an unnatural and precipitate manner, without being in any way compelled as it were to do so by the course of the dialogue, but, in fact, going out of his way for the purpose. Lastly, the play with the man in the back-ground, to whom Socrates is always obliged to render an account, is brought out into almost too coarse relief to have come from the hand of Plato—for the man threatens to beat him, like Aspasia in the Menexenus, and Socrates afterwards puts himself by name in the place of the man, without, however, its being made clear that he meant only himself from the first, and in such a manner that no particular effect whatever is produced by his doing so, and the resort to this expedient again is altogether contrary to good taste. But it might, notwithstanding, be rather precipitate to entertain the notion of making these grounds very importantly valid, and we could not justify the placing of this dialogue in the same class with those which we have strictly and unconditionally rejected. There is an abundance of pleasantry dispersed over the whole, and when we have made due allowances and considered further that this was the principal object in view, and that in the second part a variety of contemporaneous matter is criticised under the name of Hippias as well as of Socrates, we shall be readily disposed to pardon the exaggerations as well as the extravagancies of the humour which prevails in the dialogue. We may, moreover, easily see how much of the polemics generally is grounded upon self-defence. The earthenware, kitchen-furniture, and the golden mill, are purposely introduced in defiance of those who were pleased to ridicule examples taken from trifling things; and that superintending listener is to be regarded as exemplifying in the highest degree the practice which sometimes occurs when Socrates asks his interlocutor how he must answer a third person making this or that objection. And who then can say how many other personal allusions may be here concealed in consequence of which much that remains is even more beautiful than it appears to us. Even the senseless answers of Hippias may be parodies of others like them, or of the superficial manner in which the good and the beautiful were by many made to consist in this or that particular thing without penetrating into the real essence of them. But why Hippias in particular is the person to give his name to these, is a point upon which no one will look for information. Only, it is not very probable that Plato should have chosen him twice, and each time for the unfortunate hero of a private colloquy with Socrates, especially as the two dialogues have no internal relation whatever to one another. If then one of them is to be considered Platonic, and the other not, the victory will be with the larger of the two. For many traces exist that the author in the composition of the smaller dialogue had the larger before him. Particular expressions of ridicule directed against the man, which the larger dispatches in a few words, are spun out in the former with disproportionate prolixity, and the banquet of speeches to which in the larger dialogue the Sophist invites Socrates, is exactly concluded in the smaller.

VI. CLITOPHON.

In the old catalogues of the writings of Plato, the Clitophon stands, not among those condemned as spurious, but in the middle of the genuine list, and has been in like manner adopted into all the editions up to that of Stephanus, who, like other later editors, has followed Serranus. And thus it finds a place here, with the same right as all the other dialogues of that collection.

The defence of its legitimacy, however, is a task which we could not pledge ourselves to undertake with success. The very commencement, where Socrates addresses Clitophon, who is moreover represented as the only person present, in the third person, and laments his depreciation in such a manner that Clitophon can say to him that he is manifestly sensitive—this, to go no further, is completely unplatonic. Then it cannot in any way be conceived that Plato should allow his Socrates to be put down in such a manner. But even if we would assume that the dialogue is only a fragment, and that the refutation would have followed immediately, still it is far from easy to see for what purpose Plato should have introduced generally such an attack upon Socrates—an attack which, in all his writings, is fully repelled, both immediately and by the ironical matter contained in them.

If then we are once agreed that this little piece is not from the hand of Plato, there is yet room for great variety of opinion as to its tendency and object. There is, indeed, no question that in the works of several of the lesser Socraticians the wisdom of Socrates especially presented itself in its negative character only, as a confutation of the errors and exposure of the insufficiencies of other methods. Now, if this method is itself intended to be here censured as insufficient, the piece might be regarded as complete. This Socrates is then to be represented as actually reduced to silence, and this method might thus be intended to convey a justification against the objection made against Plato from various sides, of far exceeding the real Socrates. And perhaps it was under this supposition that the ancients assigned the Clitophon its place before the Republic, to stand, as it were, in the place of an exculpatory introduction, because this dialogue appeared to them to be the first place in which much that extended far beyond Socrates was particularly and manifestly taught. But then, in the first place, the insufficiency ought to have been represented more fundamentally on the side of doctrine and knowledge, than on that only of admonition and excitement, for which wisdom can only furnish a mean. And then again, it would be strange that the dissatisfied person applies directly to a sophist like Thrasymachus. It is certainly, therefore, more probable that the dialogue comes down from one of the best oratorical schools, and is directed against Socrates and the Socraticians in general, Plato not excepted. And we must be much confirmed in this view when we see how the whole is actually a running parody and caricature of the Platonic manner, especially of all that appears against the sophists as teachers of the art of politics, and which must have so naturally found an application to the teachers of the art of speaking, who were Plato's contemporaries. We

are most vividly reminded of what occurs to this purpose in the Protagoras, the Gorgias, the Euthydemus,
and even the first Alcibiades; and the elegant negligence of certain Platonic periods is here imitated with
a richness which cannot well fail to make a lively impression. If, on the other hand, this dialogue is to
be ascribed to the Platonic school, and to be looked
upon as conceived in Plato's spirit, then we need certainly consider what we have here to be only an introduction, and must suppose that Clitophon's triumph
was to be converted to a serious defeat, and that a
satisfactory and brilliant justification of Socrates was
yet to follow. But still this can hardly have been the
original design, as, in the first place, the return of the
conclusion to the commencement is too decided, and,
in the second, Socrates would certainly have begun his
attack at an earlier period in the dialogue.

PART III.

REPUBLIC.

WHEN we compare the compass of this work with even the largest of those which have preceded it in our arrangement, and consider that it is a second repetition of a continuous dialogue advancing without interruption, and, moreover, one that began first, in the evening, we must have been already very vividly convinced by what is said in the Symposium, that he whom Socrates once gets into conversation must hold out the whole night, and even to the morning dawn, though others may have all made off or surrendered themselves to sleep, and that he is as little wearied by repeating his own or other persons arguments, as of investigating and developing truth from the first in common with others. In this character he here appears, inasmuch as he repeats again the whole dialogue on the day immediately succeeding this, and such also was the case the day before, when it was first held. For of the large party, the individuals composing which are at first mentioned by name, partly as accompanying Socrates and Polemarchus, and partly as already present in the dwelling of the latter, the majority disperses one knows not how; at least, they do not say that they prefer the spectacle which is in reserve, of the newly introduced holiday torch-dance, to the continuous and self-evolving argument of Socrates concerning justice and the republic. Only the two sons of Ariston, who, after

Polemarchus and Thrasymachus had first disputed with Socrates about the idea of justice, testified by stout objections an especial call to the task, stoutly continue to stand to the argument in alternation with Socrates, without its appearing however to be of any particular importance whether Glaucon or Adimantus sustain the conversation.

Now if the author appears by this dress to convey a wish that his readers should in like manner conceive and enjoy the work as one undivided whole in itself, as the arguments themselves are to be supposed delivered without interruption, and again related without a pause, the division, on the other hand, into ten books is an obstacle to the accomplishment of that wish. This division, although Aristotle does not notice it, is certainly of great antiquity, and since from the time of the commentators upon the Stagyrite until now the work is always quoted according to it, this division must be always kept, but it is not so easy to make it probable that it comes from Plato himself. I, at least, cannot prevail upon myself to suppose that if Plato had found it necessary to divide his work, he would have been likely to project a dismemberment of it so perfectly mechanical, and bearing no relation whatever to the subject-matter— one which every reader who would search into the internal connection of the whole must entirely set aside, if he would avoid falling into confusion. For it is only with the end of the first book that the first part also of the work concludes, and in like manner, the conclusion of the whole commences with the beginning of the last book, but beyond this, only the end of the fourth book and of the seventh coincide with an important division in reference to the subject-matter. All the remaining books break off in the middle of a discussion in such a manner that not even any phrases in them could be turned to denote conclusion or commencement. Since then, the books pretty much resemble one another in extent, it may easily be the case, that the first important break was adopted as the standard, and as many compartments formed as would come out sufficiently similar in length to this, a proceeding in which, clearly, the transcribers and the libraries must have been all that was had in view.

Accordingly, if we totally reject the notion that this is an original subdivision, or one connected with the internal arrangement of the whole, and go to find the latter according to the indications in the work itself, we must give the composer credit for having attempted by every method to recompense the reader for the want of regular external divisions, and to facilitate as much as possible the apprehension of the connexion. For with exemplary accuracy the point of commencement of every important digression whatever is distinctly marked, and at the end, again, reference is made to the point from which the thread must be taken up anew. In like manner, it is generally made very observable where a new section begins, and comprehensive summaries of all that has gone before are so little spared, that it must be extremely easy for every reader with any degree of attention to keep the thread—nay, that it seems almost impossible to fall into any uncertainty as to the real object of the work, and the relation of particular parts to the unity of the whole.

Now, the course of the entire work is as follows: In the confidential, introductory dialogue between Socrates and Cephalus upon the subject, especially, of old age, the latter mentions the legends respecting the infernal world which at this period of life particularly present themselves to the mind, and extols it as the most important advantage of wealth, that the rich man can meet what awaits him with a more confident spirit, as he has been less tempted than the needy one to commit injustice. To this Socrates tacks the question as to the nature of justice, while he immediately rejects as insufficient, by the application of familiar instances, a very current explanation of it, that it is truth in speaking and honesty in restoring. And here Cephalus, who, independently of any thing else, is already too far advanced in years for such dialogues, resigns his place to his son Polemarchus in order to attend to the sacrifice out of doors. And Polemarchus then entrenches himself behind an explanation of justice given by Simonides, which Socrates, however, destroys in like manner by the application of his frequently tried method. Upon this the Chalcedonian Thrasymachus comes forward with the big swagger of a sophist, here and there reminding us of the rough jests in the Euthydemus, and occupies the place of Callicles in the Gorgias of Plato, setting up the proposition that justice is only the ordinance made by the stronger for his own advantage; and hence that it tends to the hurt of the weaker party to be just, while injustice is wisdom, and the unjust life the only one desirable. Socrates defends himself by the analogy of all the arts of governing powers, which universally provide for what is best for others, and indeed for the weakest, and by no means for themselves. And because the wise do in no case cherish exorbitant notions beyond the due proportion observed among their fellows, and inherent in the thing itself, while the unjust, recognising no proportion whatever, do not follow this rule, injustice, it is argued, can scarcely be called a part of wisdom. To this is at last annexed a proof of the position, that injustice, so far from giving strength, and by that means conducing to advantage, is, on the contrary, since it naturally excites discord, of a weakening tendency; consequently, that a just life is alone a happy one, because, moreover, the soul can perfectly execute its office, comprising the duties of deliberation*, governing, and superintendance, only by means of its own proper perfection, and that is confessedly by justice, and not injustice. Thus the first book does indeed conclude with the victory of Socrates over the sophists, but also with the lamentation of the conquerer himself, that the nature of justice has still not been yet discovered, consequently, that the question started remains where it was, perfectly untouched. And by this conclusion the book is clearly enough marked as an introduction, so that the arguments up to this point can only have any value as preparatory to what is to follow.

And by this conclusion the same also is virtually maintained of all the Socratic dialogues previously given in this translation, as many of them at least as discussed any virtue whatever, inasmuch as they all failed to discover the correct explanation. Thus the Protagoras treated the question of the unity and communicability of virtue, but without defining the idea of virtue itself; thus in the Laches courage is discussed, and in the Charmides, discretion. And since, in the question of justice, the opposition between friend and enemy forms an important element, even the Lysis might occur

* ἐπιμελεῖσθαι καὶ ἄρχειν καὶ βουλεύεσθαι.

to the mind on the present occasion. Hence it is certainly not without any object, but rather with one very
definitely in view and very judiciously attained, that
this first book of the work before us recalls those earlier
ethical pieces to the memory of the reader, whether we
look to the method of the investigation, or to the
general outline of the composition, or to the language
and the style. Throughout, indeed, the tone here given
is an echo of that in the Protagoras more than in the
others, and that dialogue likewise treats the ethical question more generally than any of those works. We are
reminded of it by the pomp of the appointments and
introduction, by the number of persons all possessing
some celebrity, by the preference of the sophist for
long speeches furnishing no proof, by the appeal to the
lyric poet in ethical matters, in a word, by almost every
thing. And if, as is certainly the case, the Thema of
Thrasymachus reminds us very definitely of the Gorgias,
this does not agree ill with the place which we have
assigned to that dialogue, as a transition, that is, from
the first main division of the Platonic works to the
second. This method of recalling to recollection by
resemblance what is gone before is indeed most eminently suitable to a writer not permitted by the form
of his works to appeal in the later immediately to the
earlier; but still the entire phenomenon is not to be
explained from this circumstance alone, as this object
might have been more easily reached by particular
allusions. On the contrary, if we would completely
understand Plato's meaning, we must not overlook the
fact that all this resemblance between the work before
us and the other ethical dialogues completely vanishes
as the work advances. The crowd of persons disperses,

and no one takes part any longer in the dialogue except Glaucon and Adimantus, although at a more advanced period all are once more represented as present and summoned to the scene of action. Thrasymachus only stirs on one single occasion more, and then quite appeased and pacified, as it were to shew that all enmity with the sophists is at an end. Even the method is completely changed—Socrates no longer comes forward with questions in the character of a man who is ignorant, and only looking for greater ignorance in the service of the god, but as one who has already found what he seeks, he advances onwards, bearing along with him in strict connection the insights he has acquired. Nay, even in point of style, it is only the immediately succeeding speeches of the two brothers, as constituting the transition, that bear any resemblance to what has gone before, no dialogic embellishment or attractive irony is hereafter to gain the prize, but solid strictness of argument alone. The whole store of the youthful virtuoso glitters here once for all in the introduction, and is then extinguished for ever, in order to make it as well as possible understood, that all that is beautiful and pleasing of this kind occupies a place in the province of philosophy only in preparatory investigations, the object of which is more to stimulate and excite than to advance and come to satisfactory conclusions; and that when a connected exposition of the results of philosophical investigations is to be given, such embellishment would contribute more to distract the mind than assist the perfect comprehension of the subject. And in these preparatory arguments some points are established to which it may be useful shortly to call attention, as they prove of importance in the sequel, without being here made particularly prominent. The first is that in the comparison of the different arts that exercise any authority, the profit thence arising is entirely separated from the proper object of the exercise of the art, and aptitude in the acquisition of profit is rather set up as a particular art which one and the same man possesses in conjunction with others. This yields a conclusion, the first we have, upon what was said in the earlier dialogues, and especially the Gorgias and the Sophist, of the art of counterfeit in all its manifold ramifications. For every art may become a counterfeit art when it comes to be treated only as a way and a means calculated for the acquisition of gain. And we have also from this a further result, which is made the basis of many of the subsequent propositions, that every art, especially such as exercise authority, the higher it rises and the more purely it is practised must be so much the more free from all admixture of desire for profit. The second point is that position, so very easily, and we may even say, notwithstanding many circumstances at that time favourable to the case, too easily granted by the interlocutors, that those who are most adapted for governing do yet only engage in it because there is a punishment for refusing, which is, even if there be no other, that instead of governing themselves they are governed by others worse. Meanwhile we should not consider as a fault in Plato the facility with which this position, so important as regards his Republic, here passes for true in its general form, since the particular way in which it is afterwards brought into application justifies itself by an extremely brilliant illustration. In the third place, further, it is to be observed that Socrates' last discussion with Thrasymachus begins to take a turn, representing justice not only as something existing between two persons separate from one another, but also as something internal, and so likewise injustice as something causing discord and distraction when it inhabits different parts of one and the same whole. And it is by this consideration that the way is prepared for the form and method in which the question of justice is treated of in what follows.

The description of this form and method, and the preparations for the line of proceeding resolved upon, occupy *the second part of the work*, comprising the second and third, and the beginning of the fourth book. And the continuation thus proceeds.

On Socrates expressing his regret that the notion of justice has not been yet discovered, Glaucon subjoins a fresh set of arguments in favour of Thrasymachus, as conceiving him to have given up his cause too soon, inasmuch as it has by no means been yet proved that justice is more advantageous than injustice. For, that only the appearance of justice has been shown to be useful. But that in order to put justice to the proper test, it is necessary rather to conceive the just man bearing all the appearance of injustice, while to the unjust man, on the other hand, concealment must be conceded, and he must be furnished with all the appearance of justice. And after Glaucon has estimated injustice in this manner, Adimantus also comes forward and further states, that it is imperative upon the praise of justice to say nothing of the friendship of the gods, and that nothing partaking of the nature of a reward should come under consideration, but, that the only question is, what effect they each have on man in and for themselves. If then, by this postulate, Plato does as it were supersede himself, and declare the demonstrations in the Gorgias and Phædon insufficient in what relates to this point, a purely ethical ground is now for the first time gained thereby, and the same Socrates undertakes the more subtle and laborious problem, and lays down his plan of proceeding, which is to be, first to search for justice in the state, where it must be in larger characters, and, consequently, more visible to the eye, and then to return to the individual mind, in order to see whether and how far it is the same in the one as in the other. And this plan is executed exactly in the same manner and in the same order as is here projected in the next third main division of the work, while this second part describes the Republic itself with a view to that, its origin and the way in which men are educated in it and for it.

And here it is remarkable, first of all, how Socrates makes the state originate in the necessities, the basis of which is the original difference of men, since all are not equally adapted by nature for every thing which life requires, and consequently cannot, by practice, be equally accustomed to every thing, without, however, hinting even by a single word how they who are thus to compensate their mutual deficiencies, are to be found. But, though he looks upon a state as the work of necessity, his opinion certainly was not that it must originate from a random search or accidental meeting of individuals, but the general Hellenic hypothesis is the basis of his theory, that every united body, however small its compass*, produces such

* Schleiermacher adds—and the German reader cannot be sufficiently reminded that in Greek *Stadt* and *Staat* (urbs and civitas) the city and the state political, are one and the same.

a perfective compensation of natures, and that necessity is only set up as representing the social nature of man, and the business of the state consists in converting local proximity among men into a regular condition of mutal aid and support, in order thus to keep men in a peculiar manner united in a fixed proportion. And even this on the other side, is not without a definite reference to the mind, in so far as not only here but elsewhere also in Plato it is represented as a compound, and that of such a nature that it is impossible human life should exist if any one of the component parts be wanting. We feel at once that more doubt attaches to that hypothesis which supposes that attention to war and defence, with which the whole organisation of the Platonic state is most closely connected, arises only from an endeavour after prosperity—an endeavour, of which Socrates himself particularly disapproves, declaring the only properly healthy society to be that most simply constituted union which confines itself to the production of the most indispensable necessaries. But according to this, so long as the state is in the enjoyment of that health, no other species of legislation could consistently appear in it, except just that which Socrates at the end of this part passes over as insignificant, that, namely, regarding barter and affairs of contract. Now, then, if we apply this theory to the organisation of a well-ordered condition in the mind itself, all the virtues would thus rest upon a morbid state. Perhaps, however, the praise bestowed upon an entirely undeveloped social state as being the only one consistent with real health, is not to be taken so seriously as it has been echoed by many in modern times. For, although at the urgent demand of the others Socrates particularly names sensual enjoyments, luxuries and arts, which are in the sequel for the most part rejected, as what may be according to his theory admitted, yet still there are wanting in that description of the original simple society, not without full consideration, I am tempted to suspect, all the spiritual elements without which it is impossible to live. The proper bearing of this too is therefore, probably, upon the reference to the mind, in which not before it is susceptible of a great multiplicity of sensual attractions, and manifold activity in itself, can virtue appear in a definite form, or the opposition between good and evil develope itself. Only the theoretical representation of the state itself does indeed seem to be too much sacrificed to that relation, when it is intimated that, because in the mind the separation of the functions is the ground upon which the whole doctrine of virtue that follows rests, that, therefore, also the operations of war and defence, because they correspond to a peculiar function in the mind, do, notwithstanding the fact that war occurs in the state only at intervals, form a particular profession distinct from all others; so that Plato here appears as a sworn advocate, the oldest philosophical one probably, of standing armies. And not even, upon his own theory, with perfect fairness; since it can only be said of the leaders of the army that their work is an art, the performances of the common fighting men, on the contrary, whether we look at what they do or what they suffer, comprehending in them nothing, an aptitude for which might not be acquired by means of a gymnastic education, combined with the practice of any other trade, while every citizen must be able to give that security which a firm disposition to preserve the existing order of things supplies, so that the Platonic army, however sufficient the men may be, must ever continue a disproportionate burden upon the productive classes. But, notwithstanding the ease with which he might have avoided this vicious state of things, if he had taken the common soldiers from the working classes, and only made the leaders a separate order, he did not do so, because then the *spirited* principle* in the mind would have had no proper and perfect representation in the state. And thus we see how subordinate an object the representation of the state is in and for itself, and how every thing is only calculated for and regulated by the idea, that it is only to be a magnified form of the mind, in order thus to recognise justice more easily in it.

This subordination is still more confirmed by what immediately follows. For after it has been determined what kind of disposition they must have, and what natural advantages they must enjoy, who are to defend the state, under the easily admitted pretext that this also will be useful for the investigation of justice, the mode of their education is discussed. And thus, what is here set up as the standard according to which all myths used in education are to be judged, that they do not inculcate a belief that the gods are the authors of evil, is manifestly of great importance for the individual mind. For the spirited principle, if it is to fight with effect against destructive inclinations, will be debilitated by the belief, that the same exist in the gods; and as little will it be able to press powerfully forward to abstract truth, if it can be met by the fact that the gods metamorphose themselves and practice deceit to indulge their passions. But upon the constitution and

* τὸ θυμοειδές.

arrangement of the commonwealth such a fancy has no immediate influence, but only in so far as it corrupts individual minds. The same may be argued of every thing in this part of the work connected with education, that it refers most to the individual, and that in a purely ethical relation, in order to effect in the mind a harmony of government and obedience, and that every essential part in it may perform its own office, and not encroach beyond it. Only, that generally regard is paid from the first to the principle, that the state cannot be better than the bulk of individuals composing it, whence its tranquillity depends upon their constancy of character, and its excellence upon the competency of each individual for his own business. As also in the maxim, that those only of the defenders of the state are to take part in the government of it, who are not in a condition to do anything except what may advance the good of the whole, we have that principle already shadowed forth which is not brought out distinctly until towards the end of the work, namely, that reason alone can judge of what is wholesome for the other parts of the mind, and that the reasonable man alone can estimate the value of other modes of life besides his own. To this purely ethical bearing upon the individual, we have indeed an exception in the discipline appointed for the champions, which belongs exclusively to the peculiar character of the Platonic Republic. But for this very reason it is here only superficially described, as not properly belonging to this place; and this description is only to be understood from what is said at full length upon the subject sometime afterwards. On the contrary, the law, which at the end of this part is made good in opposition to Adimantus, that happiness must exist in the whole of the state and not in a particular division of it, as well as the maxim that riches and poverty must in an equal degree be withheld from the commonwealth, these are perfectly appropriate to this place, and are intended not less for the individual mind than the Republic. But what answer is to be made when a well-meaning though somewhat austere friend of truth asks, what, in a work constructed upon a basis so purely ethical, is to be made of the fact, that Plato thinks to bring about that wholesome stability of character by a false pretence, or, as they say, by a pious fraud, falsifying as far as may be the truth of childish recollection, and jesting with divine commands and prophetic sentences, so that even Socrates himself appears timorous enough with this part of his argument. This timidity, however, is to be taken more in jest; as if Socrates was apprehensive that persons might be inclined to reject with a strong hand, totally and entirely, every thing mythical. For when Socrates previously explained mythical tradition generally upon the principle, that most that is in it is falsehood, but some part truth, he means now to convey the notion that the good is chiefly distinguished from the bad in this kind of tradition according as it is the seat of truth or fiction. Now, in the present instance, the form of representation only is fiction, while the essence of the subject-matter is true, and almost every single point is otherwise brought forward in strict connection with the fundamental views. For the variety of natures does indeed result, under divine Providence, from the most secret operations of planetary life, and an education which is to do nothing else, so long as the pupils are still unable to guide themselves, beyond developing further what has thus come into existence, is fairly referred in the end to the same principle. And it results accordingly on all sides as matter of divine ordinance, that a commonwealth must go to ruin in which unsuitable men, and with no inward call, attain to the government; so that on this account our author may not indeed be without his justification. Neither, again, can it be fairly explained as simply the result of a cautious fear in Plato of the fate which befel his master and others, that he refuses himself to legislate upon the worship of the gods, and consigns that task to the native Apollo. We at least, knowing as we do, how little at any time modern philosophers have ever done, who thought to found a new worship of the Supreme God capriciously and extemporaneously, without historical foundation, should the less expect any thing of the kind from Plato, as he belongs to a period at which no one could have any conception of a god-worship which was not national, and since he is here by no means fabulously compiling actual earthborn matter upon a soil perfectly new and devoid of history, but every thing, however different from all hitherto known, does still proceed in a spirit entirely Hellenic. And, although Plato in the books up to this point, declares with sufficient spirit against all fabling, that has a tendency to degrade the idea of the Supreme Being, he was at the same time too profound to assimilate himself to certain sophists in their rationalizing annihilation of the gods, and not, on the contrary, to hold in honour the strange tissue of natural feeling, and historical legend in the Hellenic theology, and to attempt to turn it to good use for his citizens.

Hence be it not interpreted amiss in him that he most prefers committing the ordination of sacred matters to the native god, whose sentences rise up from the most mysterious depths of the central point of the earth.

And here, when the fundamental outlines of the Republic have been sketched thus far, the *third part* of the work begins. And the commencement of it is marked distinctly enough by Socrates calling upon Adimantus to summon now not only his brother, but also Polemarchus and the rest together. This part, though comprehended within the remainder of the fourth book, not only projects the idea of justice, but gives explanations as well of all other virtues, and first of the manner in which they exhibit themselves in the state. And then, after it has been shewn that this process is to be applied to the individual mind, and how it is to be so applied, the same virtues are also exhibited as existing in that subject.

Now it is here, first of all, remarkable, that the four otherwise well-known cardinal virtues are represented as exhausting the idea of the good, and that without any proof whatever being given, or any such having been communicated in any other piece. And yet it is upon this hypothesis that the correctness of the whole proceeding rests; for it is only by assuming that these four constitute the whole province of virtue, that it can be said that when three of these constituent parts have been demonstrated, the still remaining part must necessarily be justice. And moreover we cannot even suppose that proof to have been known from oral discussions, or to have been communicated in any lost work. For such a proof could not have been given without at the same time the four virtues being thoroughly explained, and accordingly the whole of the work before us would in the last case be superfluous, and in the first, there would be no reason why the proof as well as the explanations should not have been repeated in writing. Plato, therefore, can only be justified upon this point, if the structure, as it is here erected, contains itself in itself, and the whole process by which the explanations of all these virtues are obtained does by immediate palpability claim the conviction of the reader in such a manner that he desiderates nothing further for his satisfaction. Since then the virtues are first investigated in the Republic, the completeness of this investigation rests entirely upon the proper relation of the three classes into which Socrates divided the inhabitants; and if the four virtues cause by their means each one of these classes to fall into proper relation to the rest and to the whole, then indeed no one can refuse to allow that the state, through their agency, must be good. And strange indeed to every one must the brevity and conciseness appear with which this is shewn; nay, this brevity in the execution does itself appear to be at the same time the fairest justification of the whole ethical preparatory process, as well in the earlier books of this work as in the preceding dialogues. However accurately then in this section also every thing is referred to the Republic, still the individual mind is constantly and prospectively kept in view in a manner not to be mistaken. Thus, in the case of wisdom, the general law that it is not by any particular knowledge of anything in the state, but by that of the state itself, and its manner of existence, that the state is wise, is set up especially on account of its application to the mind. In like manner the observation, somewhat too easily conceded, and which, if its truth were disputed, would perhaps be found untenable as regards the state, that this knowledge can only exist in a very small number of the citizens, seems to have been produced more with reference to the mind. For however strange it may sound that the reason is the smallest component part of the mind, it is, notwithstanding, certain that the principle of desire, spreading as it does into such manifold ramifications, is the largest, and therefore the simple principle, which ever continues consistent with itself, and is never other than the most internal, naturally appears to be the smallest. Also in the case of courage, the remark, that the explanation given is immediately that of civil courage, is to be referred to the fact that the courage of individual minds not only comprises in itself what is developed from civil relations, but that to it every thing belongs which the reason can offer to set in opposition to pleasure and pain. By such indications then the application accordingly of the explanations given to the virtues of the individual mind, is still more abridged. Next, again, it must appear to the reader a somewhat precipitate method, and obscure from beginning to end, that all the other virtues are honoured with an investigation, while justice alone, notwithstanding that it is the precise object of the investigation, not only remains left to the last, but is not even immediately and directly found and described, which would certainly be the clearest method of proceeding, but only comes to light indirectly, as that of the four which remains after the discovery of the other three. The first point then, that this virtue is left untouched to the last,

may indeed be explained upon the ground that there
would otherwise have been less occasion to reduce the
others also to a satisfactory explanation; but this is
not the only one; on the contrary, the discovery of
justice last, and the discovery of it by such a method,
are closely connected together, and the following may
be given as the account of the matter. Virtue in general
had been already explained above, cursorily and in the
more extended sense, to be that quality of a thing by
means of which it is in a condition to perform its
own proper function. Now the four virtues are supposed to have been discovered in this state, and in the
same state we have had shewn to us the three classes
or orders of citizens, of which two do indeed respectively perform their own appropriate functions in the
state, while the third, that of those who work for hire,
comprises a multiplicity of functions, which are not
properly functions in the state, each individual seeking
only his own advantage by the performance of his own.
In this manner, then, the four virtues separate into
two classes, for these two orders have each of them,
by reason of its own peculiar function, a virtue also
peculiar to itself. For be a state ever so wise, it is
so only by the wisdom of its guardians, and be it
ever so brave, it still is so only by the courage of
the youth of that class, namely, its champions, while
to the third class neither wisdom nor courage are ever
even in any degree attributed. Now it is indeed true,
that the state is only wise by virtue of the wisdom of
the wise, when this wisdom can operate in legislation
and guidance, that is, when obedience is rendered to it;
and in like manner only brave by the courage of its
champions, when these, like the governing parties, have

the necessary services done for them; and thus with these two virtues of the more honourable division in the state, since those who love wisdom must ever be but a small selection from the courageous, two other virtues of the inferior order seem to be connected, obedience, namely, and industry. And thus four virtues would be proportionately and homogeneously distributed among the four main divisions in the state; and certainly, as regards the Platonic Republic, nothing could very easily be objected to such a construction. But obedience and industry are not discretion and justice, and the particular virtue to which all that is said refers, would thus not be found at all, neither in the state, nor, by this method, in the mind, the application to which, however, manifests itself as well here as elsewhere to be the main problem. Going back, therefore, to the four virtues first assumed, and considering that discretion and justice are differently circumstanced from wisdom and bravery, at least in so far as that these two latter can only be attributed to some, while the two former can be neglected by none, it follows that discretion and justice are indeed to perform what obedience and industry answer for, but that they must be not exclusive virtues confined to one division, but universal and extending to all. But even thus, inasmuch as they exist in the more honourable division, they can only refer in operation to the particular incapacity and deficiency of the less honourable, and as they exist in the latter, only to the appropriate virtues of the former: hence, therefore, these latter virtues must necessarily precede the others in the exposition. But in what manner discretion and justice are themselves distinct from each other, and why, without regarding the circumstance that justice most properly forms the conclusion, discretion must precede it in and for itself——the absence of any explanation upon these points makes this the weakest part of the exposition, and that not only in so far as these virtues are exhibited in the state, but also in the mind. For the agreement of all divisions as to which is to command, and the conformable activity of each in reference to government and obedience, each of these positions is far more difficult to explain than it is to distinguish these two virtues, discretion and justice, from the other two, or even these from one another, and it therefore appears not inappropriate that after the three first virtues have been discovered, so many particular and laborious preparations are made, in order further to find justice as one separate from the others. For it may be said on the one hand, that that to which justice first gives its appropriate power, is not so much a compound of all three virtues, as discretion alone; inasmuch as the agreement assumed to exist in this passes into action by means of justice, and consequently becomes operative; and then, again, on the other side, that in these two together the whole perfection of the state is exhausted, for that wisdom is only that part of justice which belongs to the first, and courage, that which belongs to the second division; inasmuch as it would be clearly unjust, if the lovers of wisdom were not to develop ideas and appoint laws, and if the courageous would not stimulate others, and repulse dangers themselves. And further on, in like manner, where the explanations given are applied to the individual mind, and, in order to test that of justice, the familiar common topics are brought for-

ward *, it might be said that even the discreet man
would avoid all these merely by a freedom from extravagant and unnatural passions. Meanwhile, let no
one take this to be a critical censure upon the matter
itself, which lies so near the centre point of the whole
work. This censure falls at the most upon the description of these four connected virtues, which Plato,
manifestly enough, only took up in a true practical
sense from regard for an existing theory, as they had
already passed in a similar manner from common usage
into the philosophy of Socrates. But instead of these
four virtues Plato was perfectly at liberty, on the
one hand, to set up wisdom as the only virtue, if he
only saw in the reasoning part the power of putting
the whole mind in a state of activity by means of
courage, or, on the other hand, justice, as the only one.
He might either say, that the state and the mind are
virtuous by means of the efficiency and power of that
single part, or that they are so from a right and
proper state of activity in all the parts. That Plato,
as is sufficiently clear from the position which he assigns to justice in this work, preferred the last, is,
with reference to the state, an agreeable extenuation
of an otherwise almost intolerable aristocratism. For, if
wisdom is regarded as the only virtue, then the par-
takers in the government, who also supply their vacancies
from the collective mass of the people, have alone a
share in the civil virtue, and even the next more distant
circle, the champions, no less than the great hireling
multitude, are excluded from all participation in it,
and reduced to a state of obedience so strict that
they can display no activity otherwise than the govern-

* Book iv. c. 16.

ing party has ordained, and if one of the two rebels from ambition or self interest, the parties do not bear the guilt themselves, but only the weakness of the governors. But since Plato defines justice as that virtue which does in fact include all others within itself, all the essential elements of the state bear a proportionate part in the morality of it. In this point of view, therefore, the choice made must appear meritorious. But with reference to the individual mind, we should, according to our mode of thinking, unhesitatingly prefer the opposite course, and, defining wisdom to be the only virtue, however immoderate a height the sensuous desires might reach, we should rather look for the cause of guilt in the weakness of the reasoning principle, than attribute to that subordinate faculty any peculiar share in the morality of the whole. And upon the same ground we should at once take an exception to the premised explanation of discretion, inasmuch as the expression of a free agreement among all the parts of the mind with reference to the government of it, is more in accordance with an æsthetic than a strictly scientific treatment of the moral element. And yet this Pythagorising view, which conceives virtue as a harmony, which first appears in full perfection when discretion, considered as a free agreement of the inferior powers with the superior, is placed upon a higher ground than temperance, which consists only in a commanding position being usurped by reason above all presumptive claims of the inferior powers,—this view, which we cannot avoid designating as heathenish in an especial sense, is yet but too much the key of the whole work, and is most closely connected with every thing in it which most shocks us, nay, which appears to us utterly objectionable and vicious. For this is the immediate ground of the theory, that the moralization of a society must be the result of a right system in the procreation of the members of it; as also, that the morality of the individual chiefly depends upon his being born under a lucky star. Now, if it would indeed have been too aristocratical in the state, especially as a Hellene could not easily conceive such a society to be a mixture of two perfectly heterogeneous masses, totally to deny the possession of the social virtue to the great bulk of the people, and yet, in the application of this theory to the mind, an equalization cannot fail to arise destructive of the most essential distinctions; we then see how the process of making the state, as the larger body, the basis in the consideration of virtue, however, ingeniously it is fenced round, and however artfully executed, is still not without danger, and we see how even the greatest genius, in a scientific construction, may not with impunity violate the law of simplicity. But now if so much is conceded to the inferior powers of the mind, as that they have of themselves a share in virtue, still, when these three subdivisions, the governing, the defending, and the preserving, are to be pointed out as existing in the mind, and as separate from one another, it appears somewhat capriciously assumed as a general experimental rule, that the courageous principle, though it is not always found in alliance with the reason, does never at all events connect itself with the passions. On the contrary, this corruption is found to exist in the sense of honour as well as that of shame, when they follow a false opinion which praises the excited passions and degrades the rules of reason to the denomination of prejudices; and

even the very principle which Plato attacks with such
righteous zeal in the Gorgias, and in the introduction
to this work, in opposition to Thrasymachus, could not,
without such a league, have spread so far and gained
such ground. But criticism upon these subjects is
almost disarmed by the very important declaration,
which we must not overlook, that a really accurate
and thorough knowledge of the mind is not to be
gained by this process. Otherwise, however, the indication of these three functions existing in the mind,
particularly by the application of the method of exhibiting them in the gross in the prominent and characteristic traits of different nations, is very fine, and
shows enlarged views of the subject; although many
a noble Hellene may have been very ill pleased to
learn that the much extolled *spirit* is still only to be
the Thracian or the Scythian in his mind, and generally
indeed it is only by an over partiality that the often
destructive barbarism of these nations can be preferred
to a cultivation, narrow-minded indeed, and mechanical
only, but still of use to the whole of mankind, such
as that of the Phœnicians and Egyptians was. But
since the problem, properly speaking, was, not only to
define the idea of justice, but rather to decide between
the just and the unjust mode of life, which of the
two is the more desirable, after the investigation of
justice, injustice also is described as pragmaticism, and
rebellion of one part against the rest; and Socrates,
although obliged to grant to his interlocutor that the
matter is already dispatched, and that it is unnecessary
further to follow out the rest, announces notwithstanding that he will, for completeness sake, likewise trace
in the gross the various vicious modes of life throughout

their whole career, under the corrupt forms of government. As then he announces this at the end of our fourth and the beginning of our fifth book, he does accordingly execute his intention in the fifth main division of the work as contained in the eighth and ninth books. But at present he is drawn away into other investigations by Polemarchus and Adimantus, backed also by Thrasymachus, and these, occupying the fifth, sixth and seventh books, form the fourth main division of the work; but notwithstanding their important compass and still more important subject-matter, they are yet, both here, and still more at the beginning of the eighth book where the original thread is again taken up, most distinctly marked as an occasional and almost extorted episode.

The whole of this, the *fourth grand division,* stands in immediate connection with the request of Adimantus, that Socrates, before proceeding further upon the course prescribed, will first describe, with a view to the completion of the model state, the particular education of those in it who are destined for its government and defence, and at the same time explain himself more accurately than has hitherto been done with regard to the connection of the sexes; and he does indeed request this as a thing of very great importance, not at all with reference to the question of justice, but to the right constitution of the state; so that every fine-drawn application in any way of the matter .discussed in these books to that main question respecting justice in the individual mind, and the relation between a just life and happiness, is at once by this expressly protested against. Now, the first investigation with regard to the state, refers almost exclusively to that original state peculiar to Plato, while the second, which treats of the cultivation of these men and women to that which they are to unite in themselves, has naturally a far more general tendency, and is, considered as a continuation of what was said in the first book respecting the general means of education for early youth, as it were a universal Platonic encyclopædia and methodical synopsis for all knowledge, drawn up indeed from a pædagogic point of view, but still in the most extended sense, as a systematic regulation of life was generally, in the Hellenic mind, the highest problem of philosophy.

Now as regards the first division of this part, that which treats of the connection of the sexes, it does not appear to me that the way in which it is introduced, Socrates' reluctance to enter upon it, and his wish to avoid the subject, refers to the circumstance that he was here about to introduce into the language of the people a thing contrary to all current opinion, and as yet unheard-of. I rather discover in this the clearest traces of the fact that this doctrine was already known, as it naturally might be from the oral lectures and the communications of his pupils, and had experienced some satirical treatment: consequently, if we suppose this to be the case, the allusions of the comic poets to the Platonic community of women could prove nothing for the period of the composition of the work before us. But this is so completely a matter of critical feeling lying without the limits of argument, that I can do nothing but invite those readers who are interested in such questions of historical criticism to an attentive consideration of the passage. The regulations then here made for Plato's state with reference to the connection of the sexes, are founded upon the doctrine

of the similarity of both sexes; where, though it is
certainly allowed that the female sex is the weaker,
this is done with the reservation that no powers are
wanting to that sex to qualify women for every kind
of human activity; in this respect, consequently, this
doctrine stands in decisive opposition to the predominant views and practice of Plato's time. Now though
Christianity has upon the whole struck into the same
road, in so far as it has, generally, brought the condition of the female sex nearer to a similarity with the
male, still it can by no means be said that this doctrine
does in any way belong to or partake in those approximations to the Christian mode of thinking which will
be found in Plato. On the contrary, the grounds upon
which he starts, as well as the consequences which he
developes, are such that, from the standing point of
Christianity, we must enter the most lively protestations
against them. For instead of going back to the identity
of reason in the two sexes, which must, therefore, be
in the main developed by the same means in both,
and thus brought to supremacy, from which indeed no
possibility of a correspondence in gymnastic exercises
would be deducible, he refers, in order to prove his
position, to brutes, without its occurring to him, however profoundly he endeavours to penetrate into the
depths of nature, that the organic opposition between
the two sexes becomes more widely strained correspondingly with the gradations in organic life, and, consequently, in the human race, must be at its maximum.
And he seems quite as little to reflect what a wide
distinction, in reference to common occupations, arises
from the fact that recipiency and pregnancy is not
periodical in man, but free from all influence of the

seasons. Meanwhile this treatment of the subject, so manifestly and pre-eminently physical, sufficiently shews that Plato took it not in a Socratic but a Pythagorean point of view. And as, again, Christian morality, proceeding upon the greater similarity of the sexes, introduced into the world the purest idea of marriage, and the most perfect form of domesticity, Plato's view on the contrary misled him on the ground of this similarity to an utter destruction of both; and this is what every individual of sound mind among our contemporaries would gladly erase out of this work, even to the very last trace. But these traces lead very far; nay, I might almost say, that here is concentrated all that was mistaken in the development of the Hellenic mind; and we have a clear proof of the incapacity of that nature to form a satisfactory system of ethical relations. Even Plato, to whom in this respect utterly false honour has been ignorantly awarded, is so confined within the merely sensuous view of the sexual relation, that he recognises no motive for the determination of the sexual passion to a particular personal inclination other than the feeling of beauty, which the contemplation of beautiful forms in manifold and animated attitudes produces; so that a spiritual element in sexual love remained utterly unknown to him. Now in the Platonic state a passionate inclination of this kind cannot itself attain its object, but it is only a motive co-operating to assist those persons who bring the couples together. And they, in order to make it yield the greatest possible advantage for the commonwealth, and yet prevent any discord arising about much wished-for beauties, have recourse to a fraud, not publicly indeed, but privately authorised, and consequently, with truth and honesty, sacrifice to the public good the most essential element of personal morality. But from the same sense of beauty inclinations also in men towards youths might be developed; and Plato by no means regarded even the right of the plastic power of nature sufficiently high to wish to overcome such a direction of passion by shame, but these inclinations were to be favoured as the reward of courage, so that the ambition in the citizens to distinguish themselves in that character might be nourished by the prospect of obtaining the most beautiful out of the two sexes as a reward; and the susceptibility of being thus stimulated to forward the common weal and the common good is numbered among the characteristic traits of more noble natures; a thing at which our more moral austerity is with justice shocked and dismayed.

Nay, we see not only that sensual passion is sanctioned even in the noblest natures as an important motive, but it is difficult to see how, in such a system of life any other source of free personal inclination remains. On the other hand we must certainly allow, if the principle is once granted that the guards, in order to prevent any self-interest arising in them in opposition to the spirit of community, are to be excluded from all private property, that it follows only much too easily that they can have no home and no marriage, and then a state of community in the procreation and education of their offspring appears to be the most natural result. When an extended fraternization is extolled as the most splendid fruit of this regulation, best calculated to prevent all discord, we reply, that this cannot extend further than the limits of that common school-house, resembling in its dimness the place of the subterraneous pre-education of the earth-born inhabitants of the state ; and therefore under this law none but a very small community could exist and continue, such as the Platonic one is to be, and as also in America lately, upon the very similar principle of common profits, and a common education from the tenderest period of childhood upwards, it has only been found possible to bring about the establishment of a small society. And in such subordinate forms the destinies of the human race cannot be fulfilled, but only by great civil unions, based throughout upon the system of united families in separate homes, as organic unity in its most finished form. The sacrifices, therefore, that are made upon the principles of falsehood and passion to such a subtly compounded commonwealth, cannot, all of them together, contribute any great advantage. Otherwise there are interwoven with the exposition of this theory maxims of national law, especially with regard to relation of war, containing strong censure of Hellenic immorality, although in this also Plato is not free from the contracted views arising from the opposition between Hellenes and barbarians.

This first section of our fourth main division concludes with the concession, that the state as described is only designed as a model, with a view to defining under what conditions perfect justice, and an individual of such a character, is possible, but that we must in reality be satisfied with what can be attained by the greatest possible approximation to that model. And this approximation is projected by a strict separation of those who, as possessed of subordinate natures, are only appointed to be conversant with material things, as well in their industry and employment as their ocular pleasure, from those who, as possessing the more honourable natures, are qualified for the cultivation of the faculty of pure knowledge, and can raise themselves out of the confused multiplicity of material things to the contemplation of the pure unity of ideas, and, consequently, to that of which the Platonic Socrates in the earlier dialogues so often shows those to be incapable, who are partly themselves engaged with the conduct of public affairs, partly with the education of those who are to govern. But this requisition is intended also to have the effect of excluding, in the actual commonwealth, that class entirely from the government, that the power of the state may be always in the hands of those men alone who also philosophise. Here an elucidation of what is to be understood by philosophising, naturally comes under consideration, and this is given by Plato in a somewhat forced discussion, in which, referring back to his principles as far as he could without directly quoting himself, he palpably presumes all that we know from those dialogues of which the Sophist is to be regarded as the germ. And now, while he explains, keeping close to his subject, that a nature which is in a condition to follow this object, must also possess all the qualities appropriate for governing, he suddenly transplants his reader out of the fantastic world of his Republic, though but for a short time, into the existing circumstances of that period, in order to gain a small space for self-justification against an accusation, which has been often, and even a short time since, again renewed, charging him with desertion of the interests of his native city, and even with endeavouring to make the youths distinguished for natural qualifications disinclined for public life. When

Socrates has enunciated that principle, Adimantus takes the side of the opponents, who appeal to experience in confirmation of the fact, that they who employ themselves seriously upon philosophy have ever been useless to the state; while Socrates, in order to defend his position, entrenches himself behind the assertion, that the subject cannot be judged of upon the utterly corrupted state of things of that period, and expounds how in such universal confusion the true philosophical natures sink from foul treatment, and then base individuals of the hireling class possess themselves in a plausible manner of philosophy. These descriptions, in one of which it is impossible to mistake Alcibiades and those resembling him, while the other is especially pointed at the rhetorizing sophists, continually suggest to the mind the subjects of the earlier Platonic polemics, in order to justify his conduct. And at the same time, also, to conclude the subject by a tacit declaration, that until other principles can be made current in the state, and a more correct condition of morals and modes of living come to the assistance of theory, men of this description will always continue to come forward. And thus, this forms the transition to the second section of this part, in which the education of those who are destined for the government is to be more accurately described. Here then the idea of the good is represented to be the highest object to which the faculty of knowledge in man can apply itself. But it is to be regretted that not even that master-genius, rarely to be met with in speculative demonstration, but here displayed, is thought capable of coping with this subject; but the satisfactory discussion of it is referred to I know not what place still more grand than this, while here the good is only most nobly extolled in images, and by a further extension of imaginative language, in such a manner, however, that undeniable reference is made to what in the Philebus is partly sketched and partly worked up upon this subject. And the style of execution is far more gratifying here than there; nay, even the image that the idea of the good stands in the same relation to the region of the intelligible, as the sun created by the good as its typical emblem does to the region of the visible, affords, by an excellent application of all the resulting relations, a clear and unimpeded survey of the whole subject, how that reason bears the same relation to the intelligible as the eye does to the visible, and that as light and the eye——and here we may recollect what spontaneous activity in reference to light has been already attributed to the eye in the exposition of earlier theories——are not themselves indeed the sun, but more connected with it than anything else, so also human reason, requiring as it does such an effluence from the good in the exertion of its power of knowing, is not the good itself, but that which is most of all connected with it. And it affords us a deep glance into a subject, not improperly treated of in our author with much mystery, in what manner Plato conceived the identity of objective being and consciousness; that it is namely the same effluence of the good——the spiritual light so to speak——which imparts truth to the intelligible essence of material things and to ideas, and to reason the power of knowing, which is likewise the truth of their being. And this means to say that the reason cannot know anything otherwise than with reference to the idea of the good, and by means of it, and that to the whole

range of the visible, or we might indeed say, the perceptible generally, no *being* whatever corresponds, and
that there would indeed be nothing but the eternally
inconstant flux of the non-existent, if flux were not
stayed by the living operative influence of the idea of
the good, and thus something at length produced, which
although still participating in the inconstant and rest-
less, may yet be referred to real existence. To all
this, indeed, the reader only meets with slight allusions,
but they carry the attentive mind, in conjunction with
what is brought forward above in the general explanation of philosophy, back to the earlier dialectic dialogues,
which now develope themselves to such results. But
if, on the one hand, the two provinces of the visible
and intelligible are placed parallel and compared with
one another, neither is that subordination of the one
to the other, with which we have already been m e
acquainted, here wanting. The sun, it is said, is only
a type of the essential absolute good—the corpore light
bears a precisely similar relation to the spiritual, and
when contemplated from the spiritual region is nothing
but darkness, in which every mind gropes about which
is enchanted by the charm of the terrestrial sun, and,
without endeavouring to rise higher, lingers among the
material things illuminated by it. And as the whole
range of the visible world stands in the relation of a
type to the intelligible, so is there in each of the two
again a similar distinction; one thing real in its kind
and the typical form of it. Now here it may surprise
us that the subjects of mathematical thought, number
and figure, are described as types of the ideas; meanwhile we should continue to be well satisfied that this
branch of intellectual activity here attains a fixed posi-

tion, and we possess at the same time a key to the Platonic use of number and figure in the region of philosophy, and to the relation in which Plato stood to the Pythagorean school in this respect. Very remarkable also are the elucidations given with regard to the relation between the mathematical method and the dialectic, although they stand in no connection whatever with the former theory, unless by the introduction of a middle term, here not even alluded to, in so far, that is, as mathematical hypotheses can be considered also as types of real premises or first principles. Thus, at least, upon these arguments it would be quite consistent in Plato to distinguish himself from those who think themselves able to define the essence of things by means of number and figure, and fancy that they know, in the philosophical sense of the word, while they are only forming mathematical connections. But if already at an earlier period material things have been described as constituting the true in the sphere of the visible, and called also types of the ideas, still mathematical processes, as belonging to the province of the intelligible, have justly the precedence of them, and thus the four gradations that follow obtain among the objects of intellectual activity: corporeal vision has for its object the types; belief, real things; abstract intuition, mathematical subjects; and real knowledge, ideas. To this gradation, then, the whole series of studies of those intended for the government is to correspond; and that we may the better survey this, and learn to estimate the reciprocation between studies and practice, Socrates suddenly transports us out of the midst of these investigations into that cave, in which the tenor of life and condition of those who, because it is impossible for them to turn themselves with their eyes to the spiritual sun, take external appearance, and the types, that is, visible objects, for reality and being, is represented in such vivid colours, that one scarcely sees, even though the illuminated were to give up their own happiness which they enjoy above, and to bestow it there, why it should be even worth while to lead such a destitute life, in which there is nothing to improve and nothing to lose; so that he is indeed no common patriot who, as is here demanded, applies to this point also that magnanimous sentiment, that it is not an object that any one part of the whole should be prosperous above the rest*. But if, notwithstanding all guidance, the great mass of the people ever continues what it was before—and Plato does not appear to conceive the existence of society upon any other principle, or to have an idea of a progressive improvement comprehending the *people*—then even the most magnanimous self-devotion can only receive any compensation in so far as it is by this means alone possible, in the case of every rising generation, to discover the more honourable natures, and bring them to a better lot. And if to this we add the further consideration that the population in Plato's state, to which we are now again introduced, is not even to multiply itself, and that the relation between the producers and the consumers must appear to him confined within very narrow limits, we may say that the problem of the Platonic state, and consequently of collective human activity considered in the gross, is no other than to preserve human nature without deterioration in its once given relations. So that our philosopher appears in the character of the strictest and

* VI. c. 5.

most consistent champion of stability. In what manner, then, the small selection of more noble natures is to be tried, and by degrees practised in and accustomed to their better lot, is immediately developed by Plato by an elegant reference of this image of the cave to the original one of the sun, in which it is at once self-evident that the capability of gazing at the sun itself can only be acquired by manifold preparatory exercises. As then the common corporeal and mental exercises of the children were unavoidably much conversant with typical images, by reason of the mythical matter involved in them, and the world of real material things, and consequently of faith, is the scene of the whole development of infantine life, so also the preparatory exercises of the grown-up boys of distinguished powers are conversant exclusively with the world of intuition, subjective thought, which is constituted by the mathematical sciences in their natural order. Yet even here Plato draws a distinction between two different processes, separated by a couple of strictly gymnastic years. The first is the delivery of those sciences, according to his notions improperly so called, each for itself, though always—setting aside all merely experimental proceeding, and all practical reference to material things—exclusively bearing upon number in the abstract, figure in the abstract, and in like manner motions and relations in the abstract. The next is the setting up of these sciences in their connection with, and their relation to, the nature of absolute existence; and those only who can follow up to this point, and join in the contemplation of this, are recognised as dialectic and consequently regal natures. But it is not until a late period, and after they have been compelled to divide their time very unequally between that enviable scientific life and the joyless service in the cave, that even these men attain to the pure contemplation of the idea of the good, and to government; to which last, however, they have only to devote intermittingly the smaller part of their time, dedicating the greater to contemplation, until at length in due time, and extolled by all, they close their mortal career.

And with this, Socrates, after having first given a cursory hint as to the manner in which, provided only first of all that true philosophers but once had the power in their hands, such a state might actually exist, has fully acquitted himself of the whole task which Adimantus had set him, and returns back at the beginning of the eighth book to the point at which this great digression was imposed upon him, and we now take our leave of this singular Republic. And if I may be allowed to say a few words upon the same, I would first call attention to the point, how little Plato deserves the accusation not unfrequently brought against him, of contempt for his own nation; how highly, on the contrary, he thought of the Hellenic nature, as he not only ascribes to it a pre-eminent development of the knowledge-seeking element in the human mind, but even in so contracted a population as we have to conceive his Republic capable of containing, he calculates upon finding that rare union of qualities, and these in sufficient strength, to engage successfully in all these exercises and trials, in so many individuals, including even the female sex, that he will never want rulers, although no one attains to the highest power before his fiftieth year, and then several are to relieve one another by turns. Perhaps even in our own populous states we would not undertake to effect this, though with the total difference in our method of education it can never be possible that the attempt should be made. Meanwhile, however, we have gone so far as to require from all those who would exercise great influence upon society, a combination of scientific accomplishments with those requisite for war, and vice versâ. And if we cannot desire that they who have to exercise the highest power should possess the most dialectic genius, with us the supreme power does not comprehend so much as in Plato; and we count moreover much upon the fact that they who live most in the kingdom of ideas, by exercising a manifold influence upon education, will also have a predominant influence in the formation of public opinion, which always, though unconsciously, regulates the exercise of the supreme power. Nay, even though temporary mischief might not always be avoidable in so doing, we might pretty confidently leave it to the emulous principle in our nature, in the development of which we are so far in advance of the ancients, to decide where self-seeking and counterfeit sophistry is endeavouring to play the part of the philosopher, and falsify the description of the good.

Now this perfect Republic being only constructed for the particular purpose of exhibiting justice in the gross, after those general outlines also have been sketched which do not stand in immediate connection with this object, a nearer approximation is now made to what was to have been done at the end of the fourth book, we mean, to answering the question as to what mode of life is the most desirable. And here the same method of proceeding is adopted as that by which we were conducted to a definition of the idea of justice. For imperfect characters also must exhibit themselves under more express and better developed forms in the imperfect constitutions, that deviate from that archetypal model, and it is desirable with this view to describe these, and to consider them in a continually retrograde process, until at last the most perfect injustice is brought to light in the most corrupted state. This *Fifth grand division* of the whole work, which now brings the original question to a decision, comprises the eighth and ninth books. The whole process appears to stand in a sort of contradiction with what Plato frequently and distinctly enough gives us to understand, I mean, that his Republic never has in reality existed, and that there is not even any necessity that it ever should exist. For if this is the case, how can he, notwithstanding, represent the forms of government which have actually and historically existed among the Hellenes, for scarcely any mention of others is made, as a graduated series of revolutions, which he developes, historically, from that ideal conception? What, therefore, is here historical is, undoubtedly, mere form, but which lay very ready at hand, because, in fact, the different constitutions have, not rarely, succeeded one another in the same series, and by this method only the various degrees of distance from perfection are to be made manifest, and that only with a view to a better understanding of this gradual degradation of moral worth in individual minds; and this retrograde career which the individual mind runs appears always as the principal subject. Starting, therefore, from the perfect Republic, which exhibits the union of all virtues in the gross, Plato's next problem is to show how imperfection arises from perfection ; for it appears less difficult to see how what is imperfect continually deteriorates after the initial change has once taken place. Now, since his perfect state can only exist for any length of time by means of the intermixture of the sexes being conducted by the philosophers upon correct principles, it is evident that the commencement of the deterioration must be grounded upon a flaw in this process; and Plato, therefore, has recourse to an unavoidable fatality by means of which, at some time or other, the same wisdom in this department is not observed. If an important deviation is ever made from this there immediately ensues a deficiency of properly tempered natures: and then the consequence of that must be a diminution of public spirit, and an excitement of self-interest. This then tends to a dissolution of the mutual relation hitherto kept by the men and youths destined for the government, as also of their general relation to the people, and in this is at once contained the germ of the utter ruin of the constitution, and consequently of all in which virtue can be seen in its enlarged and general form. In the same manner, upon the principle that the constitution of a state is at all times in accordance with the prevalent morality, it is shown further below, how individual minds, under certain conditions of descent from one state, become such as to carry within themselves the type of the next worse, and how they then by degrees summon into existence the constitution which is in conformity with them.

Now, it must be allowed that the images here given of different moral characters are not only drawn with striking truth, considered in and for themselves, but also with reference to the main principles of the Platonic philosophy, constitute definite gradations. The first point is that at which after the small part has been once suppressed by virtue of which the mind is wise, the *spirited* principle (το θυμοειδές) then gets the upper hand, and is attended only by the principle of desire, whether appearing under the form of love of money or love of enjoyment. Or, secondly, if the former principle sinks to the bottom, then the various passions exist upon friendly terms with one another in the mind, or some single one usurps universal monarchy. But, on the other hand, the manner in which one of these characters arises out of the other, is not quite intelligible by and for itself, but only as it is effected by the presence of those different civil constitutions; and the transitions of those into one another are indeed described with great truth, and in a manner immediately intelligible, but properly they should, according to the principle stated above, have only been intelligible from the predominance of the analogous disposition in the great majority of individuals. So that it looks as if the political representation, which, if accurately considered is only here as an apparatus, obtains a prominent independence, and unconditional importance, contrary as it were to the inclination of the writer. This is particularly shown in the instance of the tyrannical constitution of mind, in which Eros indeed and Dionysus are intelligible as sole monarchs in the mind and without any political relation, while the melancholic temper on the contrary, although it is self-evident that this might in like manner assume a despotic character, is left without the psychological foundation in this connection, as indeed it did not usually appear in the case of private individuals in the same way and to the same degree with the Erotic and Bacchic excess; only tyrants, properly so called, especially such as Plato had himself become acquainted with, not rarely exhibiting this form in all its extravagance. The reader, however, very easily passes onward over all these little obstacles, since the striking description of the principal features carries him away with it. Among them a mysterious psychological factor is especially prominent, at the opening of the ninth book, an idea which is seldom quoted when the preindications of christianity in Plato are mentioned, but which to me appears to be the most profound sentiment he ever uttered in this feeling. It is, that the germs even of the most perverted extravagances lie concealed in the noblest and purest minds, but only stir in them during the suspension of the will in dreams, as they on the contrary, may break out into the most horrible actions when reason no longer maintains its supremacy in the mind. It is indeed undeniable generally, that the image of the tyrannical mind is not only the most important part with reference to the whole tendency of this section, inasmuch as it is that which exhibits injustice in perfection, but also in all its features in detail the most successful, and gives us at the same time a decisive impression of the boding anxiety with which Plato saw in general in the degenerate democracy of his native country such tyrannical dispositions developing themselves. Upon this description of the tyrannical mind there now follows quite close, and without any intermission, that threefold proof, properly completing the whole work, of the proposition that the just life alone is the truly desirable, and the unjust the contrary. A multiplicity of proofs for one and the same proposition, if they are not merely different forms of one and

the same proof, and consequently the multiplicity only
apparent, do certainly excite our suspicion, because a
want of confidence in each particular proof appears to
lie at the bottom of that proof: and here it might be
further said in particular, that upon any reader whom
the previous description of a well regulated supremacy
of reason does not convince as well as charm, all further proof must certainly be lost. And yet we should
have been left without an important and striking explanation with regard to the relation of reason to the
other two parts of the mind, if Plato had not subjoined
these proofs. Now, even if it is not quite the case
with these that, accurately taken, they are but one and
the same, they are yet connected with one another in
very natural gradation. The first, strictly understood,
concerns only that state of perfect injustice. For if
the desires become multiplied, and, forming the largest
part of the mind, agree about a change of the government, because they cannot all be satisfied alike, it
cannot then indeed be said that what the whole mind
wills takes place, nor yet what the greatest part of
it does not will, but this largest part remains free
and is in unity with itself. Hence then, there follow
further upon this particular proof two general ones,
each implying the tripartite division of the mind, and
supposing that each of the three parts has its own particular pleasure, and that the supremacy of each gives
rise to a particular mode of life. Now if these modes
are to be compared together, this may be done by a
more subjective method, if, says Plato, since there is
no umpire to decide between them, there being nothing
more existing in the mind, it is asked which of them
can be qualified to pass a correct judgement upon the
others as well as upon itself.

And then again it may be sought, more objectively, whether the solid content of pleasure which they afford cannot, purely as pleasure, be measured and estimated. And in this last proof much is presumed which was said upon the distinctions of pleasure in the Phædo, but above all in the Philebus, which, viewed from this point, appears as the true and immediate introduction to our work. And Socrates crowns this perfect proof for the good cause of justice by a new image of the mind. I say new, because no true reader will be able to avoid, on occasion of the present image, recurring to that description in the Phædrus of the chariot and its driver. Now if we compare the two, we shall find that that would yield an excellent work of art, if a sculptor or painter executed as Plato designed it; and even in words it developes a much-admired, and we may add, a truly admirable brilliancy of description and elegance of application. That at present under consideration, on the contrary, seems coarsely and almost negligently treated in the execution, and the application, extremely prosaically, is step by step in correspondence with the preceding didactic exposition. And should an attempt be made to express it as an image, it would, as Plato makes us feel distinctly enough, turn out a random performance, and acquit itself but little better than those well-known ascetic counterfeits of the human heart, in which the evil principle dwells, and from which all evil thoughts proceed. It is, however, excellently conceived for the purpose of clenching all the doctrines set up in this work with regard to the mind, and exhibiting in detail the different relations among them, and is perhaps only all the more effective as it will not bear the pencil or chisel, but can only be expressed in words. But if we consider how, if otherwise our

arrangement is to be of any value, Plato's entire doctrine of the mind, in so far as he treats of it in a
preponderantly ethical view, is confined as it were between these two images, we are then drawn deeper
into the comparison. Neither of the two indeed represents the human mind as a perfect unity, or makes the
distinct elements which may be discovered in it intelligible from a common centre-point; but still the
strangely-compounded monster must ever be more a
living unity than that chariot. The subdivision is in
the main the same, but in the instance of which we
are now speaking it comes out in much better relief,
as the complexity of the principle of desire is here
expressed, which in the other case is utterly wanting.
And thus we come by degrees indulgently to attribute
the luxurious abundance in the earlier picture, which
has something of a coquettish character, partly to the
rhetorical form of that work, and partly to the youthfulness of the composer, while in the one now before
us we praise as meritorious the absence of all pretence
to imitative *virtuosity*, which, standing as it does in
strong contrast with the former, is at the same time
perfectly in character with the philosophy of the work
itself. And as this image recapitulates all that is properly ethical in the collective subject-matter of the work
itself, it certainly appears to be a perfectly fit conclusion to the books themselves. For such it really is;
the problem is solved, inasmuch as the superiority of
the moral life is proved; nay, even the conditions under
which such a life is possible are laid down. And if
questions, not falling within the limits of the problem,
and referring only to the great image of the perfect
Republic, interwoven with the whole work, are digres-

sively answered, this noble image itself has as it were the spunge passed over it; for as when, after the completion of the structure, the scaffolding is again broken away, Socrates expressly declares that this republic exists only in imagination, and nowhere upon earth, and he leaves it standing only as a heavenly model, according to which every man is to regulate himself, and can then perform the duties of this constitution only, and of no other.

At the end, then, of the ninth book every reader would go away satisfied, and miss nothing connected with the subject. But it can in no way be intended to be only an exhibition of the Socratic gluttony in conversation, when, as if he were yet far from the end, Socrates subjoins immediately something new, and that without even taking breath; as if he were afraid that otherwise interlocutors and hearers would not let themselves be again brought to the task.

On the contrary, we must be the more curious with respect to the subject-matter of this *sixth grand division,* which occupies the tenth book, forming the only real concluding piece, because it is clear that Plato must have felt himself imperiously called upon to make this addition before quitting his work, or he would not have done so. The composition of this part is as follows. The first section recurs once more to the subject of poetry, a subject out of whose province some matter is discussed in the third book, and being renewed in this, is to be here dispatched. It is, what the prevailing character should be in the descriptions given of men in order to be employed with advantage in the education of youth. And, as was said also in that book, this matter cannot be dispatched until the grand question is decided which these descriptions always involve in their ultimate result, whether unjust men can be happy or just men miserable.

This subject accordingly could not have been taken up earlier than in this place, though it must be allowed that no one would have felt the want of it, if it had remained where it was. For it is now clear at once that Plato, according to all appearance, would have had strict poetical justice in this department of the fine arts treated in a manner completely contrary to the rules that have become valid among us. Meanwhile he does indeed profess himself satisfied provided only the just man proves himself a happy one amid tortures and insults, to which even our own critics would have no objection to make. But instead of here explaining this point, he again takes up the general accusation against the art of imitative composition generally, which had already made its appearance in the third book; only as he had there shown more that the guards themselves should not practise the mimic arts, he here enlarges more upon the disadvantage which must ensue only from hearing and seeing mimic exhibitions. Now there may indeed be truth in what Plato says, that poets would be bad poets if they were only to represent perfectly just men, but it is not on that account necessary that men of contrary characters should be so represented and extolled, as to seduce others to follow their example. And quite as little can it be overlooked that Plato proceeds upon a very narrow hypothesis, when he thinks that every one is inclined, at least, in solitude to indulge those effeminate emotions which in company he attempts to restrain, as well as when he wagers his head with even

the best of men, that they would always relax something of their strictness towards themselves in relation
to what, if publicly exhibited, is not only overlooked but
praised and admired. So that the censure cannot properly apply to the dramatic and dramatising art of
poetry in and for itself, but only relatively to a certain
inferior order of moral cultivation, and moreover, not
to the art in general, but only to the Hellenic form
and method of it, in which, however, Plato does not
seem to have regarded even in the slightest degree its
historical value. And it must surprise us all the more,
that Socrates maintains with perfect confidence that this
art will never be able to defend itself, and that the
feud between philosophy and it, as it existed from the
very earliest times, is likewise to endure for ever for
life and death. There does not however appear, utterly
unworthy indeed as such an ingredient would have been
of such a work, the slightest trace that Plato wrote
this in a humour excited by the comic poets, notwithstanding the very great probability there exists of their
having already satirized his Republic from hearsay,
before this work was publicly put forth. But it is
because the dramatic art is only conversant with the
mind in its present scarcely understood, though multifariously deformed state, and although so far removed
from truth, affects nevertheless to be considered as something true, this it is which, to Plato, represents the
state of antagonism with it as unintermitting. And if
in the corresponding passage of the third book he seeks
more to expose himself to the censure than in any
degree to excuse himself from it, because, as he says,
the perfect writer is as little as possible, and only in a
case of the most extreme necessity, to make use of

mimic representation, a rule which he himself trans-
gressed so far, he now seems on the one hand to
wish entirely to renounce this method for the future,
and on the other tacitly to justify himself upon the
ground, that, though he may indeed have introduced
sophists, rhetoricians, and statesmen speaking in characters the reverse of praiseworthy, still, so far from
bestowing upon them any commendation calculated to
seduce others to imitate them, his only object was to
expose their real worth and to exhibit them as warning
examples. And as Plato spoke at last of his Republic
only as a model to which approximations are to be made,
so he comes in the present instance also to a very
mitigated conclusion, implying that if this art is not to
be entirely banished, yet still men must be always on
their guard against its seductions, and hear them as
if they heard them not. As then for Virtue's sake,
and from interest in her this matter may not be otherwise ordered, the second section is now subjoined to this,
embracing a subject which must indeed form a match-
less conclusion, as it returns to the rewards of Virtue,
and thus refers us rather to the second book. For,
it is argued, the desire there expressed, that the whole
question should be decided without introducing anything
relating to rewards, is now satisfied, and now perfect
truth requires a return to that point. Since then at this
point, as has already been hinted at the commencement
of the work, the discussion is to be about rewards in
the present and future life, the immortality of the soul
is first of all treated of, a doctrine which, independently
of all other considerations, every reader acquainted
with Plato's method and art would have been almost
pained to miss out of this work. And nearly as

surprising does it appear that this important subject is quite cursorily dispatched in a space not occupying above a couple of pages. So that one might almost think that Socrates would rather have referred to it as already made out elsewhere, and have made his friends concede it as a thing known. And he has indeed more to do with the subsequent description of the condition in the other world, than with the proof that there is such a condition, and we should only regard this as a supplement as it were to the more copious discussions in the Phædo. Now the proof which is here given is such that if it is granted—an hypothesis which in the two earlier dialogues is always assumed, and in the Phædo is to a certain degree illustrated by the refutation of the position that the soul is nothing but organic *disposition*—that the soul is to be conceived as a self-existent being, only united to the body but quite distinct from it, it is in fact perfectly sufficient, and therefore we are not here referred at all to the earlier proofs. Moreover, since in the description that follows, the immortality is to appear most strictly in the form of the transmigration of souls; after the proof of immortality is general, it is further proved that the number of souls always remains the same. In the Phædo also this doctrine has been already indirectly laid down, as a circular career is so placed intervening between life and death, that no other way remains in which animation by the introduction of souls can arise; a point which in the Phædrus is not brought forward at all in the same way, and consequently that dialogue, relatively to this subject, is more remote from the work before us than the Phædo. In this last too the argument from which that constancy in the number of souls is proved, was already sketched. But when in the Phædo the immortality is also demonstrated upon the assumption that only what is compound can be dissolved, and that the soul is not compound, it might be objected that in these very books Plato composes it of three essential parts. On this account, therefore, Socrates now takes up the same point conversely, and proves that what is immortal cannot easily have in it much that is dissimilar and different, and lets it be understood that the soul is far from appearing here as it originally is, but comes partly encumbered with foreign additions, partly also deprived of much that was originally in it. What else then can be here meant, but that that sea-weed and shell-work with which Glaucus is overgrown by his long sojourn in the depths of the sea, in the same way as the soul, as we already know from other sources, is here immersed in a dim abyss, are to represent the various forms under which the principle of desire appears, so that only the reason, either alone or in connection with the *spirited* principle, constitutes the original essence of the soul, as moreover, that unwieldly encumbrance is but little suited for the peregrination through heavenly spaces. Only it is difficult for us, according to our mode of thinking, to unite with this the hypothesis that the souls of brutes are in kind so perfectly the same with those of men, that the latter can also become brutes, and the former men; and it is moreover, hard to conceive how Plato should have adopted this only in compliance with the Pythagorean tradition without assimilating it to his own theory. The souls of brutes must therefore, according to him, have originally contemplated the ideas, only that they, and that, as we are taught in the Timæus, in consequence of their first human life, banished as they are to such an organism, can attain to no recollection whatever. They are accordingly those souls which appear deprived for the most part of their original nature. But against this it may be again objected, that as every species of brutes developes but few and simple desires, they are less burdened with those foreign encumbrances than the human souls, in which the whole army of desires displays itself, furnishing indeed one ground for placing the two in comparison with one another. This theory also agrees, therefore, with that, which in the right ·conduct of the plastic powers of nature contained in the human race, discovers the only true principle upon which all efforts to form mankind to wisdom and justice are to be founded. And in like manner it may be said that the pædagogic regulations of the Platonic state receive a new light from what is here said about the influence of the present life upon the future. For in that passage above which places the choice of a new life between unavoidable destiny and free-will ingeniously combined, every thing depends upon the soul being in a proper condition to choose, and not too strongly possessed by the impressions of what it may have encountered in its former earthly existence, to be able to seize that which is in conformity with its inward essence, and calculated to promote its improvement. Only it does indeed seem as if that art of superintending the connection of the sexes might come into some difficulty, if, notwithstanding, upon this method a soul quite foreign and unsuitable, in no way connected with this state, can insinuate itself into it; and it is not very easy to see, under what particular divine protection this circumstance must be placed, that such a misfortune may not occur before it is significantly felt in the exercise of the art itself; unless it is to be said that this is a far more worthy and important object, than all those trifling concerns of an individual life, for that beautiful feeling of confidence which suggests that for him who is dear to the Godhead every thing must work for the best. In this description, finally, that interchange between the happy wandering through heavenly space and the return to the region of imperfect existence bears a manifest similarity to the interchange to which the lives of the guardians of the state are to be subject, between the longer period which they are to devote to philosophical contemplation, thus surrendering its right to the wish of the philosopher for death, or rather for being dead, and the return for one day only to the burdensome employment of government in the cave. So that even in this point of view Plato will not be denied the merit of having regarded the eternal arrangement of the universe in the regulation of his Republic. But he has left almost all this for the reader only to discover, and the whole section, indeed, most manifestly bears the impress of having been intended to awaken and stimulate the mind of the hearer in every way to bestow the most diligent pains upon the subject of justice, and never to consider anything as more profitable. Such is the tenor of its commencement, such of its conclusion; hence what does not contribute to that object might be only alluded to, and what is further enlarged upon is only to be regarded as digressive. But we have also here in close connection with that grand object the aversion expressed to the art of imitative poetry, and especially towards Homer, whose heroes quite pointedly furnish most examples of souls that make

a bad choice; Odysseus only, the passionless, was made
wise by the experiences of his travel, and Plato honours
him by setting him up as a model for the choice of
a life withdrawn from public affairs.

And now that we have arrived with our analysis
at the end of the work, a question very naturally
arises, if the case is as our results have represented
to us while we pursued the dissection in the most
accurate manner, that the question originally raised
regarding the advantage of a just and moral life does
in fact predominate throughout, so that every thing
not relating to this is only to be regarded as digression—the question, I say, arises, whence the work comes
to bear the title of the Republic, in comparison with
which the other, of the Just, has in no way been able
to make good its claim? How happens it that the
work, we may indeed say since it has been in existence,
has always been quoted under this name, and under
no other, so that it at least goes back to the immediate disciples of Plato? Nay, can we not say that
Plato himself was, mediately at least, the author of
it, since in the opening of the Timæus Socrates himself manifestly appears to be speaking of these dialogues
when he says that they have discussed the main question of the constitution of the state? And so far is this
from being an incidental or subordinate notice, that on
the contrary, the whole idea of the Timæus and Critias,
as well as of that which Hermocrates was to adduce,
is immediately developed from this. Must not, therefore, most confidence be placed in this Platonic Socrates
himself? and would he not smile at the analysis of the
whole here given, the upshot of which is that justice
is the grand subject? Is not an argument in favour

of the supposition that he did by no means here construct his Republic as a mere scaffolding, afforded by the elaborate execution with which matters in it are discussed, which will bear no immediate application to justice? And if there is some ground for the supposition that this ideal state, even before Plato described it in the books we have, had been a subject of satirical allusion as sketched in his oral instruction, are we to believe that those oral sketches were in all respects so similar to the written works, that Plato in them also introduced the ideal of a Republic only as a scaffolding for his theory of virtue? These are, indeed, important and weighty grounds; but our view also of the work in its whole connection rests upon no authority but the same Platonic Socrates, whose own advices we have most accurately followed. Are we, therefore, to believe that in the work itself he has only played with its proper subject, and that he begins all at once in the Timæus, and not before, to take a serious view of the question? But to attend to this latter dialogue exclusively would be at least quite as partial as not to pay any regard to it whatever. But if we are to start upon the supposition that the representation of the state is the proper grand object, it would be hardly possible to conceive why the appearance of the contrary is pointedly produced. And even if it could be explained why Plato combined the investigation concerning justice with this grand object, still the form and the manner in which this is done would then be perfectly unmeaning and absurd. It would have been much more natural to introduce the main subject at once, and then, after the internal existence of the state had been described, to say in what the justice and discretion of such a whole consist; and then the application to the individual mind, and the ethical problems, still unresolved in this point of view, would have resulted most naturally; consequently, a perfectly converse relation between these two grand objects and the essential parts of the work referring to them must then have obtained. And if, indeed, upon this supposition it would be more easily conceivable that the regulations about the commerce of the sexes should be treated of with the copiousness which now appears, then too, on the other hand, all that is in connection with the rewards of virtue would have to fall much farther back as mere subordinate matter; and it is impossible that this subject could be so prominent as it is here made, partly by the style and method of the execution, partly by the fact that the exposition, constituting as it does a return of the end to the beginning, very properly concludes the whole. Other discussions, such as that upon the nature of dialectics, upon the conditions of this intellectual activity and its relation to the others, and in like manner those upon the art of imitative poetry bear, indeed, a similar relation to both suppositions, and the question how they are necessarily connected with the grand Thema is in both cases equally difficult to answer. Accordingly it does not appear that by the method actually pursued even the slightest step is gained for affording a clear insight into the connection, if the whole work is only to be regarded as a representation of a normal constitution; although, on the other hand, if it is to be merely a defence of justice, a disproportionality remains, and an excess of unnecessary and subordinate matter, which the preceding attempt to explain the connection has in no way endeavoured to conceal. What remains then but to confess that the Platonic Socrates is here a double-faced Janus? In the work itself the backwards looking face speaks, and to that we have until now listened; in the Timæus the front one lets itself be heard. And with the supposition the fact agrees, that in the work itself so many problems previously set are again taken up, and so many previously isolated investigations combined, and that this whole tissue into which are worked many particulars which are as keys and talismans to what has gone before, affords extreme satisfaction; while in the Timæus the same work appears as a new member of a new series of theoretical expositions, in which Timæus, Critias, and Hermocrates are to follow Socrates; and this two-fold relation seems to be the key to all that may yet have continued obscure in the connection of the work. The idea of virtue in general, and of the four virtues in particular, is defined, and in this we have the key-stone to all the earlier and preparatory labours upon ethical points, and the doctrine of the Republic has no other concern with this task, but that which Socrates professes from the beginning onwards. But as the idea of virtue is on the one side so essentially connected with the idea of the good, which in Plato's view is the grand object of dialectic science, and, on the other side, would not come under discussion at all unless there was an interest in the right regulation of life, it is equally natural, first, that this interest, as it here appears as an apologetic ground of morality, should also conduct and predominate through the whole work, and then that the elements of dialectics in it, as well as of ethics, should be again taken up, combined with one another, and as it were fixed by a key-stone. Now, we observe that Plato discovers the idea of virtue without having even a conception of an absolute freedom of will, such that by means of it man may at any moment, and independently of all previous conduct and existences, be any thing that he likes; but according to him this free will is so connected with that state of conditional existence in which man is here plunged, that a combination of the elements of the soul may arise in which the existence of a weak principle of virtue is all that is possible, and that there is but one style and mode of education which can enable virtue to develope itself to its full extent. And thus the constitution of the state attains a high degree of importance, and it is natural that this theory in particular should be expounded at the same time, as well as that the process in it of the continuation of the species from which, it is argued, the various tempers in different minds arise, should be placed under the dominion of common reason, and quite as natural that the theory of dialectics, and with it at the same time, the polemics against that imitative poetry which, according to Plato's conviction, most effectively crushes the endeavour after truth—should be interwoven with the theory of political education. Every step is professedly only laid down as it is necessarily evolved from the idea of human nature, without any historical conditions, which is tantamount to a declaration that the state cannot exist in actual practice, but only with a reality such that the further an actual state is removed from this standard the less virtue can appear in it. And thus, the Republic in our work attains a more important prominency than at first appears, but yet never such as to become the proper and main subject. The relation, however, of the work before us to the following dialogues is distinctly marked by Plato himself, as one not to be taken into consideration until we are arrived at a more advanced stage in the development of the philosophy of this series. In the dialogues that succeed, no one but Socrates of the whole company to whom we are here introduced bears any part; Glaucon and Adimantus, and whoever else may have appropriated those Socratic arguments, all go away perfectly satisfied, a sure sign that the work according to its original plan is only the keystone to all that has hitherto appeared. It does not become the commencement of a new series until its repetition. This is indeed a repetition which we now possess, but as a clear confirmation of what has been just said, we do not here learn to whom Socrates again repeats it, but we see first from the opening of the Timæus that the hearers were the aforenamed, and a fourth besides who is not named. These persons then, as is clear from the expressions we there meet with had wished especially to hear Socrates' arguments about the state, and although he was in consequence obliged to repeat the whole discussion, the Republic was to them the main subject. It is therefore to this circumstance that the title, and all who quote the work from Aristotle downwards, particularly refer; it seemed however all the more necessary to establish first of all the first and original relation of the work.

Now, when Socrates on the following day requests as a repayment from those who desire him to repeat his arguments, that they, as masters in the province of practical life, will show him, better than he can himself, his own Republic in living motion with reference to internal as well as external circumstances, this wish does in no way contradict the confession previously made, that this Republic exists only in imagination. For, although as near an approximation to it as is possible is the highest point at which all others are to aim, still a standard for every thing that can take place in the life of a state can only be given by such a living representation; and this must be the best means of exposing in their nakedness all immoral, and therefore corrupt, politics. Socrates had already this return in mind when he repeated the work, and had cursorily explained, with a view of establishing a ground whereupon to found his claims to it, in what manner generally such a state might be framed, provided only genuine philosophers had once the power in their hands. But on this second meeting every thing does not come off as he had anticipated; but having once for all committed the subject to the hands of others, he must also be content with what they resolved. Now, they resolve that he must have patience to listen to the romantic history of his state. For Timæus, in order that the subject may commence with the true beginning, is first of all to treat in a historical form, which nearly all more ancient physiologists have adopted, of the origin and formation of the world, down to the beginnings of the human race; and then Critias is to exhibit that state according to its internal and external history, not indeed as Socrates appears to have intended, now for the first time existing and localized, but as the ancient Athens, of which he has received information from foreign legendary lore. Thus, accordingly, our work, under new authority, comes into a still more comprehensive series than that which Socrates, according to his own expressions, had in view. But, although the annexation of that philosophy which concerns the theory of Nature to this work appears to overreach his original plans, still not only is the necessity for it declared in his own words, but even the first outlines drawn according to which they are to set to work upon this subject. For the principle already laid down in the Phædo, that nature must be conceived from the idea of the good, is virtually repeated in the Philebus as well as in these books, where that idea is pronounced to be absolutely the highest: and further, we here find it stated pretty early as a principle to be generally established, that the Deity is not the efficient cause of every thing without distinction, but that he can only be the cause of good, and it is upon this principle especially that the theory in the Timæus of the formation of the world is constructed. The necessity for a science of abstract being in general is clearly declared by the remark, to the principle of which so striking a prominency is given in these books, that an accurate knowledge of the mind is not to be attained by the method hitherto pursued. Now, what is wanted can be nothing but a knowledge of the relation between the mind and objective existence collectively, and of the place which the mind is to occupy in the system accordingly. And thus the manner in which the Timæus connects itself with the books of the Republic is a declaration of the essential identity of ethics and natural philosophy. The same principle also is expressed under another form in the last fable about the migration of the souls. For this myth, in which at the same time the system of the world brought forward in the Timæus is graphically prefigured, is meant also to declare it as a

Socratic view, that every soul, in the intervals between its
appearance on earth is happy in the contemplation especially of these general mundine relations, and strengthens
and recruits itself anew; whence it follows that during
life also that renewed recollection, which is likewise his
leading principle, is most awakened when the mind is
employed in speculations upon nature, and most powerfully enlivened by them, and on that account adepts
in this science are best qualified to apply the all-per-
vading idea of the good to all human relations. It is
clear, accordingly, from the way in which, as we have
shewn, the subject-matter of the former series is interwoven with that of the new, that in the latter also
the ethical element has the preponderance, as natural
philosophy is itself ethicised by the idea of the good
which is placed at the summit of it; and therefore the
formation of the world, as an expression of the divine
mode of acting, furnishes the model which, notwithstanding that creation, deliberation, and government
constitute the proper business of every mind, can yet
be followed but indistinctly in so contracted a sphere.
The establishment, however, and conservation of general
prescriptive regulations, such as the constitution of every
state must include, is in the first degree a plenary and
distinct imitation of the Deity. But what Critias undertook to say, as well as what Hermocrates would
have said, was undoubtedly to have been ethical, only
certainly, if Socrates' wish was to have been complied
with in so doing, directed to a comparative application
to political life. And from this point of view not only
might the whole of the subject-matter contained in this
work be intelligible, but it would also be an easy task
for every one to make it clear to himself, how all pre-

vious works determine to this, and all the threads laid out in them centre in it. But at how early a period Plato designed the plan of this great and splendid structure, and whether or not out of many, especially of his juvenile works, several points were at a later period taken up, and a determinate reference given to them, which they had not before, to the philosophy of this, is a point which now probably it might not be very easy to decide. Only it can scarcely be doubted that when Plato wrote these books he had already resolved to subjoin to them the Timæus and the Critias.

NOTES.

PHÆDRUS.

Page 72. *Several of the conceptions in this Myth.*

I CANNOT help maintaining what is here said, notwith-standing what Boeckh adduces (Heid. Jahrb. i. 1). I can neither discover the coincidence with Philolaus, nor put such firm faith in the genuineness of the fragment ascribed to him. But this is a subject which can only be discussed in another place *.

P. 73. *We are not to look for too much.*

Ast, in his commentary, has construed this passage very literally. It is, however, too profound for my apprehension how the poetic life above is indeed removed from all real representation of the true and beautiful, when below it forms the fourth kind of real life, and thus appears co-ordinate with the poetical and gymnastic life. Again, I know not in what sense a higher conception of the true and beautiful can be said to belong to the χρηματιστικός than to the γεωργικός. And thus I leave it to others to enjoy this philosophy.

LYSIS.

P. 78. *To have had the Lysis in his mind.*

Whoever reads, with a view to comparing the passages with this dialogue, Eth. Nicom. VIII. c. 1. 2. 10. (p. 59. A.D. p. 63. B.) Magn. Mor. II. c. 11. (p. 111. E. and 112. C.) and Eudem. VII. 2. 5. (p. 162. B. C. p. 165. B. Ed. Casaub.

---

* But see the extract from Boeckh's Philolaus, p. 104. at the end of this volume. (Tr.)

NOTES.

1590.) will scarcely continue to doubt of this, although Aristotle neither names Plato nor the dialogue, and one might feel some suprise, if he really had it in view, that this is not done more frequently and thoroughly.

PROTAGORAS.

P. 82. *Perished.*

I learnt this from an investigation regularly instituted into this family by Heindorf out of the fourth speech of Andocides. Athenæus, Deipnosophist. v. p. 218, does not adduce this authority, but only concludes from the comedy of Eupolis, brought forward Ol. 89. 3, and in which the extravagance of Callias is exposed, that Hipponicus must have died not very long before this time.

P. 83. *To justify Plato.*

See Bibl. of anc. Phil. v. 122. Every thing else that this author says about the chronology of the dialogue is very bad, and betrays but little study of the Protagoras, and some ignorance of the history.

P. 84. *Absent abroad.*

When it is said that Protagoras lodges with Callias, this does not make much against the supposition, as Callias was at an age to superintend his father's house. There is perhaps more difficulty in that subsequent passage which says that Hipponicus had formerly used the chamber as a store-room; which is intended certainly to give us to understand that Callias had introduced more liberal manners than his father. But, perhaps this too might be explained by supposing a somewhat long absence, which, at a time when there were always Athenian armies in the field, is not inconceivable.

P. 85. *Banished from Athens.*

This is clear from Diog. Laert. ix. 54. where his accuser Pythodorus is called one of the four hundred, with whom

Menagius over-hastily asserts that he is unacquainted. Meanwhile there is a possibility that this accusation may have taken place at a later period, and Pythodorus may only be designated from his participation in this revolution—a possibility however which can scarcely be supported by any probable fact.

P. 97. *Imitated after Protagoras.*

This has been already remarked, intelligently enough, or copied, by Philostratus, who in the life of Protagoras, Vit. Soph. 494, says : γνοὺς δὲ τὸν Πρωταγόραν ὁ Πλάτων σεμνῶς μὲν ἑρμηνεύοντα, ὑπτιάζοντα δὲ τῇ σεμνότητι καί που καὶ μακρολογώτερον τοῦ συμμέτρου, τὴν ἰδέαν αὐτοῦ μύθῳ μακρῷ ἐχαρακτήρισεν. *Plato, knowing that Protagoras expressed himself with dignity, but was notwithstanding careless withal, and more diffuse than neat, imitated his style by a long speech.* Only it is inconceivable how Olearius came to refer this to the Theætetus, when it manifestly relates to the myth in our present dialogue.

———— *Another poem.*

See Brunckii Anal. I. 122. X.

CHARMIDES.

P. 108. *In his challenges.*

See Plato's Letters, Ep. vii. p. 324. D.

———— *Notorious attempt.*

Xenophon tells this Mem. Soc. i. 2, 33.

P. 109. *As Xenophon represents it.*

Mem. Socr. iii. 7. A dialogue which should be compared generally with this, that the reader may convince himself that there is here no such imitation or connection as to render our dialogue liable to suspicion.

PARMENIDES.

P. 122.   *From a passage in the Charmides.*

See Charmid. p. 169.   Μεγάλου δή τινος, ὦ φίλε, ἀνδρὸς δεῖ, &c.

P. 129.   *Another of that name far younger.*

The greatest difficulty in understanding the father of
Lysias to be the person here meant would be found in
the two accounts, supposing them to be true, that Lysias
was born at Athens, and that his father had already died
before Lysias set out to travel to Thurii. Dionysius agrees
with the first account, while the last is only supported by
the composer of the Lives of the Ten Orators; an author
sufficiently despised by all sound investigators. By it the
supposition made in the Republic would be completely destroyed, for Plato's brothers could in that case never have
been in conversation with Cephalus. By the first account,
Cephalus' immigration would be placed so early that the
dialogue between Socrates and Parmenides could not then
have taken place. But this would indeed be a subordinate
circumstance, which Plato might easily have overlooked. He
represents Cephalus as a person who often came to Athens,
and even his presence at this time does not look like an
immigration, but a visit or a journey on business—whereby
the impossibility of this dialogue having taken place, if Cephalus did really settle altogether at Athens before Ol. LXXX. 2,
becomes still greater. Meanwhile it is difficult to decide in
such matters about Dionysius, how much is accredited information, or when he only follows an opinion generally
adopted. I may take this opportunity of advising the reader
that in the Phædrus likewise, where the question turned upon
the chronology of the life of Lysias, that the accounts of
Dionysius, and not those in the Lives of the Ten Orators, are
universally followed. And upon this point a few words now
remain to be said, only for the reason that F. C. Wolf, in
his translation of the Republic, has taken the opposite course.
Both agree in the date of Lysias' return to Athens, fixing it
at the time of the first archonship of Callias, *i. e.* Ol. XCII. 1.
Dionysius adds, that Lysias was at that time forty-seven years
old, according to which his birth falls in Ol. LXXX. 2. On

the contrary, the "Lives" place it in Ol. LXXXII. 2. According to both accounts he goes at the age of fifteen years to Thurii; which, according to that of Dionysius, falls in quite correctly with Ol. LXXXIV. 1, when the colony was actually being founded; according to the other with Ol. LXXXVI. 1, eight years later, when something important was to be distributed there. The confusion of the last account proceeds also from the circumstance that the author makes Lysias stay at Thurii till his sixty-third year, and consequently contradicts himself; wherefore Taylor's endeavour by means of an emendation to bring the first account to agree with Dionysius is useless. So also the notice of the early death of Cephalus may be only a supposition, because the writers could not explain, what is nevertheless very easy to explain, how Cephalus should have permitted his sons, and one of them so young, to go abroad. And it might be a question whether the assumption, by no means general, or resting upon any sufficient testimony, that Lysias was born at Athens, may not have arisen only from the fact that nothing was known to the contrary. Then, like many others, he may perhaps have travelled to Thurii without coming straight from Athens, and his father may have fixed his residence at Athens after this emigration of Lysias, and not before, being persuaded to do so by Pericles, as indeed Lysias himself so distinctly asserts.

P. 129. *Plutarch and Proclus.*

See Plutarch de frat. am. II. 484. E. "As Plato has given his brothers a celebrity by introducing them into the most beautiful of his writings; Glaucon, namely, and Adimantus into the Republic, and Antiphon, the youngest of them, into the Parmenides." For the rest, Plutarch would hardly have wished that Antiphon to share with this one the celebrity of having transferred his tastes from philosophy to horse-breeding. Proclus also recognises this half-brother, and thence concludes very rightly that the dialogue between Cephalus and Antiphon cannot have been held until after the death of Socrates, without, however, expressly declaring that he considers this Cephalus to be a different person from the father of Lysias.

P. 131. *If any one.*

As Ast has notwithstanding lately done: see his Essay
on Plato's life and writings, p. 250. I may add, that I
should not envy those readers their opinion to whom Ast
has satisfactorily proved that the Parmenides was written
at the earliest after the Theætetus, since in the latter the
solution is at once so decidedly commenced of those problems
which in the Parmenides are but slightly indicated. For,
Ast has by no means distinctly shown in what respect the
Parmenides completes the Theætetus, and even the Sophist
and Statesman. Nor even if we allow that Socrates here,
in the pains he takes and the problems he enunciates,
shows himself to have arrived at the summit of dialectics,
will, therefore, the investigations which Parmenides conducts
and in which Socrates is perfectly passive, constitute the
completion of those in the above-mentioned dialogues. The
notion that from that perfection in the enunciation of the
problems, and the success of Socrates' endeavours, Parmenides may be intended to represent the erring philosopher,
must appear to all persons accurately acquainted with Plato
too ridiculous for anything to be said about it. I agree,
however, with Ast, that in this dialogue the representation
of *virtuosity* in investigation is the principal point, and it is
upon this, as well as upon the circumstance that it contains
only germs, that the arguments rest for the position which
I have assigned to it, so that I find it unnecessary to enter
more accurately into what Ast alleges in favour of his own
opinion.

APOLOGY.

P. 134. *Let not the reader start.*

These words seem now no longer suitable after Ast's
total and uncompromising excommunication of this dialogue.
But I believe there are very many persons to whom even
my opinion will at first sight seem too bold, and hope that
few only will allow themselves to be persuaded by Ast's intricate criticism, that the Socrates here upon the stage is a

conceited sophist, and that the whole of this defence belongs
to the common and counterfeit art of rhetoric.

P. 136. *Which Diogenes.*

See Diog. Laert. Lib. II. s. 41. We are there told that
Plato wished to defend Socrates from the rostrum, but that
at the first word the judges put him down by a sally of
Attic wit. But this tale is too little accredited and too improbable in itself for anything to be built upon it. (Πλάτωνα
ἀναβῆναι ἐπὶ τὸ βῆμα, καὶ εἰπεῖν Νεώτατος ὤν, ὦ ἄνδρες Ἀθη-
ναῖοι, τῶν ἐπὶ τὸ βῆμα ἀναβάντων· τοὺς δικαστὰς ἐκβοῆσαι κατα-
βάντων, τουτέστι, κατάβηθι.)

P. 138. *Much to change.*

These imperfections are, in Ast's opinion, among the
sufficient grounds for excommunicating the piece; but an
imitating sophist, and one who proceeded according to the
rules of rhetoric, must have been far worse than the one here
otherwise is, to commit such faults. But Socrates may commit them, because on every occasion he is hurried onwards
by his higher objects, and the whole defence in particular
looks like an occasion, such as common life might present,
for following his calling.

——— *Of the actual defence.*

For Socrates must have defended himself, and I should
have wished Ast to have given us some slight hint as to
how, in his opinion, Socrates dispensed with this task.

HIPPARCHUS.

P. 157. *Two great Masters.*

Valckenaer on Herod. p. 398. and Wolf. Prol. p. 154.

——— *Striking out.*

Even Ælian mentions his doubts whether the Hipparchus is really a work of Plato; but this, in itself, would be
but of little importance.

P. 159. *For even the Menon.*

Other points of resemblance between our dialogue and the Menon are mentioned by Boeckh. (in Minoem, p. 40.)

_____

MINOS.

P. 163. *Minos was never.*

For an account in Diodorus that an Athenian conqueror at the Olympic games was called so has been already corrected by Boeckh. (See Pref. in Minoem.)

_____

GORGIAS.

P. 175. *In the Protagoras.*

Compare the conversation in the Protagoras beginning p. 358.

P. 180. *From the Lysis.*

It must be left for the reader to decide, whether he can more easily conceive this to have been the case, or, on the contrary, that these hints afforded matter for his composition to the composer of the Lysis. Only, in that case, the composer will still remain entitled to be considered a more ingenious person than Ast will allow him to have been.

P. 185. *No trace appears.*

None, at least, according to my notions. Ast indeed thinks otherwise, and would conclude hence that Plato composed the Gorgias during the Socratic process, when I think it must be allowed he could scarcely have been in the humour for a work so extremely artificial, and, as even Ast will allow upon the whole, so extremely deep. But I refrain from saying more upon this point, and leave the case in the hands of every skilful reader.

_____ *In the Ecclesiazusæ of Aristophanes.*

See the commentators upon different passages of this comedy, and more at length as to the whole of it, *Mor-*

genstern, Commentat. de Platonis Republ. p. 76—78. Should it be objected that this comedy did not perhaps contain so many allusions to Plato as is generally believed, it is still clear enough that philosophers, and especially Socraticians, are comprehended under its satire, and among them Plato was more effectively hit, inasmuch as he was distinguished above the rest by reputation and rank.

P. 187. *The example of Archelaus.*

Athenæus, in the well-known passage, XI. 507, Ed. Bip. IV. p. 384, writes strange things concerning this subject, which authors have copied from him, and hence have dreamed of a relation between Plato and Archelaus which is perfectly impossible. The passage runs as follows: " In the Gorgias he censures not only the person from whom the dialogue takes its title, but also Archelaus, the king of Macedonia, both as a man of low descent, and as one who had killed his lord and king. And this is the same Plato of whom Speusippus says, that by means of his close friendship with Archelaus he was the cause of Philip's coming to the government." Then, after bringing forward the passage of Speusippus referring to this point, Athenæus continues: " But whether or not this was actually the case, God knows." In truth God knows how it could be the case not, that is, what Speusippus says, but what, in Athenæus, is thence inferred. Plato, by means of a confidential relation with Archelaus, who died in the same year with Socrates, is supposed to have been the cause that ten years later Philip came to the government. And how? Listen. Carystias of Pergamus, says Athenæus, writes as follows in his *Memorabilia.* When Speusippus learnt that Philip spoke ill of Plato, he wrote in a letter as follows: " As if it were not known that Philip owes even his kingdom to Plato. For Plato sent Euphræus to Perdiccas, who was influenced by him to assign some province to Philip. And as Philip maintained there an armed force, he had, when Perdiccas died, the means in readiness, and could put himself in possession of the kingdom." Now is there here a single word about Archelaus, or any relation with him. Unless we do the sophist the injustice of accusing him of a monstrous falsification, he has confused, in the strangest and most ignorant manner, the Alcetas whom Archelaus slew, and the Perdiccas whom he succeeded, and the far later Perdiccas who reigned before Philip, all together. Too many words already for the contradiction of such miserable prattle. Only we see hence what bad authorities Athenæus followed in what he says against Plato, or what inconsiderate use he has made of his collectanea, without even taking care not to confound names and times. What Speusippus otherwise says must be true, if he really did say it, and may serve for the correction and completion of other accounts, which make Philip remain in Thebes till the death of Perdiccas.

THEÆTETUS.

P. 192. *A contradiction.*

See the Preface to the Laches (p. 100) and Charmides (p. 108), and the passages in each dialogue referring to what is there said.

P. 203. *So Proclus.*

In the second book of his commentary upon the first book of Euclid.

MENON.

P. 219. *A son of Anthemion.*

Plutarch tells a little story about the love of Anytus for Alcibiades, at one time speaking of Anytus the accuser of Socrates, at another of Anytus the son of Anthemion. But it might not be well to build too much upon this story; for it seems to be almost at variance with what is said in the defence of Socrates by Xenophon, that the son of Anytus at the time of that accusation was still a growing boy, and with the conclusion which we cannot help drawing from this passage in connection with the Menon, that the father of Anytus first attained to riches gradually by an extensive trade; hence it could hardly occur to his son in his younger years to fall in love with Alcibiades.

——— *The same of whom Xenophon.*

But when Gedike thinks that he can be the same as occurs in the first book of Thucydides, and that this Menon, who in the campaign of Cyrus owed his office of commander to his youthful beauty, also led an army at the beginning of the Peloponnesian war, he may, if he can, come to an agreement with dates as to this point.

EUTHYDEMUS.

P. 220. *Though no one.*

Even Ast's rejection, since published, does not take up this ground, but only because Plato so often exposes the sophists occasionally, he does not think that he could have dedicated a particular dialogue to this purpose. As if Plato did not treat of many things in this dialogue *occasionally,* and expressly in the others; and as if his dialogues of this nature had not always a variety of objects, and not one merely. And as to Ast's discovery, that it is but lost labour to look for any other bearing or object in this dialogue, and his accurate method of examining and explaining it in consequence, both are now before the world, together with my introduction, and every reader may try and choose. But any one inclined for a jest might say that he should not be sorry if another author besides Plato were to be found to whom such a dialogue as this could be ascribed.

P. 223. *Xenophon.*

In the third book of the Memorab. of Socrates, chap. i.

P. 224. *In the Cratylus.* Just at the beginning.

——— *Aristotle also.*

De Soph. El. cap. xx. Ed. Bip. iii. p. 599, with which compare Rhet. ii. cap. xxiv. Ed. Bip. Vol. iv. p. 292.

——— *Another passage.*

De Soph. El. cap. xxxiv. Ed. Bip. Vol. iii. p. 639. Tennemann, if I mistake not, has already expressed the supposition that when Plato mentions these ὀψιμαθεῖς, Antisthenes is meant. We see how this does, indeed, refer immediately to his Euthydemus; but there are still some other grounds for the supposition.

PHÆDON.

P. 291. *In the speech of Diotima.* See Symp. p. 205, 206.

P. 294. *To interest itself.* Phædr. p. 246.

ᴾ. 301. *Here in the Phædon.* See p. 72, e. 73, a.

P. 304. *The Protagoras.* P. 68, 69.

P. 305. *As it is said.* Politic. p. 269.

THEAGES.

P. 321. *In the Apology.* P. 33, e.

———— *Two notices.*

The other is in the Republic, B. vi. p. 496, where it is said that his health compelled him to keep to philosophy by withholding him from politics.

———— *A parenthetic digression.* P. 150, 151.

———— *In the Apology.* P. 31, d.

P. 324. *The expressions of Xenophon.*

Particularly in the Memorabilia, i. 1, 2—4. 19.

———— *In the Euthyphron.* P. 3, b. c.

ERASTÆ.

P. 326. *The other professedly.*

There is a passage quoted from Thrasyllus in Diog. ᵀ.aert. ix. 37, which most persons have understood to imply that this critic thought that the nameless μουσικὸς of our dialogue was Democritus. But the passage is probably not free from corruption, and Thrasyllus can scarcely have intended this piece of folly, but only meant to say that Democritus was a philosopher such as the other person alluded to in the passage had described him to be, who resembles an athlete (πένταθλος), something in every thing, good in nothing. Moreover the same passage contains the most ancient doubt on record of the genuineness of our dialogue, in the words, Εἴπερ οἱ Ἀντερασταὶ Πλάτωνός εἰσιν.

MENEXENUS.

P. 337. *Which Thucydides.*

But how does it happen that Plutarch, in his life of Pericles, does not mention this oration? thus tacitly giving us to understand that Thucydides only ascribed it supposititiously to Pericles, while on the other hand he celebrates another oration of the great statesman delivered at an earlier period, during the Samian war. Dionysius also says that in his opinion Plato here imitated Thucydides. But may not Plato, when he makes Socrates say that Aspasia supplied much that was omitted in the speech she made for Pericles, have had in his mind that earlier and more genuine one?

P. 340. *When Socrates.*

If Menexenus, as we must conclude from the beginning of the Phædon, was one of Socrates' more intimate friends, it is scarcely possible that this should only appear so accidentally as it does; if he was not, then this is a stupid and pointless expression of respect.

But we must not overlook the fact, that even Aristotle (Rhet. III. 14, p. 376, Bipont.) quotes from the dialogue which surrounds the speech, under the head of Σωκράτης ἐν Ἐπιταφίῳ, the passage, that it is easy to praise Athenians before Athenians.

EXTRACT from BOECKH's PHILOLAUS, referring to Schleiermacher's note on the PHÆDRUS, p. 72.

" BUT in determining the relation between the doctrine of Philolaus and the works of Plato, I come a second time upon a question, with regard to the solution of which our countryman Schleiermacher and myself have been many years at variance. It is whether traces of the system of Philolaus are or are not contained in the Phædrus of Plato, and I cannot help a second time answering it in the affirmative, and defending my friend's opponent against him in a matter, from which, moreover, not the slightest inference can be drawn for or against Schleiermacher's arrangement or views of the Platonic works, with which I fully coincide. Now that, first of all, the possibility of Plato's acquaintance with the writings of Philolaus cannot be denied, appears from the above investigation; for the accounts as to the sale of the Philolaic books in Sicily have proved incredible, and it is more probable that he published in Thebes, where he taught, something which, considering the short distance of Athens from Thebes, might be early known in that mart of arts and sciences. But even supposing that he wrote nothing during his residence in Thebes, still it is scarcely conceivable, with the lively zeal for philosophizing, which Anaxagoras, Socrates and the Sophists had excited at Athens, that none of the ideas of the neighbouring philosopher should have penetrated to Athens from Bœotia; that the mental feast and the mental light should have remained among the sensual Bœotians, while Copaic eels for the Attic palate, and Bœotian wicks for the Attic lamps, came to Athens. And are we to suppose Simmias and Cebes to have retained nothing whatever of the doctrine of Philolaus, or to have mentioned nothing of it in Athens? The only question, therefore, is, whether in the Phædrus Philolaic echoes can actually be heard; a point which can only be made out by comparison with the fragments and extracts preserved; the spuriousness of which, I am firmly convinced, can never be hereafter proved. Now,

in the Phædrus, the souls, in their circuitous route through
the universe, for the purpose of contemplation, start from the
house of the gods, in which Hestia alone remains behind,
and climb up, upon it, to the highest sub-celestial arch; breaking through this, they come at last to the super-celestial region,
where they contemplate the formless and pure essence of
things, that is, the ideas here mythically represented. Not
intending again to defend all particulars referring to this point,
contained in an earlier essay, I am nevertheless compelled to
recognise it as perfectly Philolaic; not, however, in such a
sense as that Philolaus said exactly the same, but as grounded
upon the Philolaic conception of the form of the universe.
Hestia remains alone in the house of the gods: is not the
Pythagorean Hestia, the house of Zeus, clearly enough indicated here—of that Zeus, I say, who in Plato leads the procession of the gods? Is not, on the other hand, the supra-
celestial region exactly the Olympus of Philolaus? Observe,
moreover, that these conceptions are perfectly unplatonic.
Plato himself considers the earth as the centre-point, as is said
in the Timæus; he knows nothing in his system of such a
dwelling of the gods as we find in the Phædrus; but that
in the Phædrus the earth is not the dwelling of the gods and
the earth of the world he is clear at once from this, that
those souls which cannot follow the gods in that procession,
fall down upon the earth, which must therefore, certainly, be
something different from the dwelling of the gods; and that
this conception also may be explained without obscurity, and
without confusion, out of the Philolaic system of the world, I
have shown in the treatise *de Platonico systemate cœlestium glo-
borum et de verâ indole astronomiæ Philolaicæ*, (p. 27—32). Then
again the assumption of a super-celestial region is quite as
little Platonic; for as Aristotle remarks, (Phys. III. 4.) the
developed Platonic doctrine places nothing *without* the heavens,
not even the ideas, which are not indeed in space at all; some
foreign matter, therefore, predominates in the Phædrus, of
which Plato availed himself for the purposes of a mythical
composition; but, though foreign, not unsuitable. For in the
Pythagorean super-celestial region is the Unlimited, a formless
entity, the pure first origin; and it is precisely the formless,
pure essence of things which, according to the Phædrus, the

souls contemplate there. But enough of this. Moreover, it appears from what has been said, that in the Timæus no coincidence with the Philolaic doctrine is to be found; and the only point they have in common is, that in the Timæus the soul of the world proceeds from the centre, and the whole universe is again enveloped in it, and Philolaus also regards the central fire as the chief seat of the soul, or the divine principle, and represents the *All* as surrounded with the soul. It is not therefore my opinion that Philolaus, as, according to some authors quoted in Simplicius, was the case with certain Pythagoreans, considered the central fire as the formative power, situate in the centre of the earth, and nourishing it from thence, and the counter-earth (ἀντίχθων) as the moon; which, when applied to Philolaus is perfectly unsuitable: but it can scarcely be overlooked, that the central fire has the same relation to the soul of the world, which, according to some physical conceptions, the brain, according to others, the heart, has to the human soul."

PHILOSOPHY
OF
PLATO AND ARISTOTLE

An Arno Press Collection

Aristotle. **Aristotle De Sensu and De Memoria.** Text and Translation with Introduction and Commentary by G[eorge] R[obert] T[hompson] Ross. 1906.

Aristotle. **Aristotle Nicomachean Ethics.** Book Six, with Essays, Notes, and Translation by L. H. G. Greenwood. 1909.

Aristotle. **Aristotle's Constitution of Athens.** A Revised Text with an Introduction, Critical and Explanatory Notes, Testimonia and Indices Revised and Enlarged by John Edwin Sandys. Second Edition. 1912.

Aristotle. **The Ethics of Aristotle.** Edited, with an Introduction and Notes by John Burnet. 1900.

Aristotle. **The Ethics of Aristotle.** Illustrated with Essays and Notes by Alexander Grant. Fourth Edition. 1885.

Aristotle. **The Fifth Book of the Nicomachean Ethics of Aristotle.** Edited for the Syndics of the University Press by Henry Jackson. 1879.

Aristotle. **The Politics of Aristotle.** With an Introduction, Two Prefatory Essays and Notes Critical and Explanatory by W. L. Newman. 1887.

Aristotle. **The Rhetoric of Aristotle.** With a Commentary by Edward Meredith Cope. Revised and Edited for the Syndics of the University Press by Sir John Edwin Sandys. 1877.

Bywater, Ingram. **Contributions to the Textual Criticism of Aristotle's Nicomachean Ethics.** 1892.

Grote, George. **Aristotle.** Edited by Alexander Bain and G. Croom Robertson. Second Edition, with Additions. 1880.

Linforth, Ivan M. **The Arts of Orpheus.** 1941.

Onians, Richard Broxton. **The Origins of European Thought About the Body, the Mind, the Soul, the World, Time, and Fate.** 1951.

Pearson, A. C., editor. **The Fragments of Zeno and Cleanthes.** With Introduction and Explanatory Notes. 1891.

Plato. **The Apology of Plato.** With a Revised Text and English Notes, and a Digest of Platonic Idioms by James Riddell. 1877.

Plato. **The Euthydemus of Plato.** With Revised Text, Introduction, Notes, and Indices by Edwin Hamilton Gifford. 1905.

Plato. **The Gorgias of Plato.** With English Notes, Introduction, and Appendix by W. H. Thompson. 1871.

Plato. **The Phaedo of Plato.** Edited with Introduction, Notes and Appendices by R. D. Archer-Hind. Second Edition. 1894.

Plato. **The Phaedrus of Plato.** With English Notes and Dissertations by W. H. Thompson. 1868.

Plato. **The Philebus of Plato.** Edited with Introduction, Notes and Appendices by Robert Gregg Bury. 1897.

Plato. **Plato's Republic:** The Greek Text, Edited with Notes and Essays by B. Jowett and Lewis Campbell. Volume II: Essays. 1894.

Plato. **The Sophistes and Politicus of Plato.** With a Revised Text and English Notes by Lewis Campbell. 1867.

Plato. **The Theaetetus of Plato.** With a Revised Text and English Notes by Lewis Campbell. 1861.

Plato. **The Timaeus of Plato.** Edited with Introduction and Notes by R. D. Archer-Hind. 1888.

Schleiermacher, [Friedrich Ernst Daniel]. **Introductions to the Dialogues of Plato.** Translated from the German by William Dobson. 1836.

Stenzel, Julius. **Plato's Method of Dialectic.** Translated and Edited by D. J. Allan. 1940.

Stewart, J. A. **Notes on the Nicomachean Ethics of Aristotle.** 1892.